AF650233

DIGITAL ECONOMY
STRATEGY AND BEHAVIORS

DIGITAL ECONOMY
STRATEGY AND BEHAVIORS

BY

ARIA BAKER
HARWELL WEBSTER

KNOWLEDGE
BAKERS

KNOWLEDGE BAKERS

© 2024 AUTHORS

ISBN: 9789390013166 (HB)

All rights reserved under International Copyright Conventions. No part of the book or part thereof, including title of the book, be reproduced in any printed form or language without written permission of the author and the publishers.

Published by : **Knowledge Bakers**
Pune, India
Email: knowledgebakers2019@gmail.com

Digitally Printed at : **Replika Press Pvt. Ltd.**

PREFACE

The digital economy has transformed the way we live, work, and interacts with one another. It is an economy that is powered by digital technologies, where digital products and services are the key drivers of growth and innovation. The rise of the digital economy has also led to the emergence of new business models, such as e-commerce, online marketplaces, and digital platforms., We will explore the strategies and behaviors that businesses can adopt to succeed in the digital economy. One of the key strategies for success in the digital economy is to embrace digital transformation. This means adopting new technologies and processes to improve operational efficiency, enhance customer experiences, and create new revenue streams. Businesses that fail to adapt to the digital economy risk being left behind by competitors who are more agile and responsive to market trends. Another important strategy is to leverage the power of data. In the digital economy, data is a valuable resource that can be used to gain insights into customer behavior, market trends, and industry dynamics. Businesses that can harness this data and turn it into actionable insights are better equipped to make informed decisions and stay ahead of the competition. A third strategy is to focus on creating a strong digital brand. In the digital economy, a company's online presence is often the first point of contact with potential customers. It is important for businesses to invest in creating a strong digital brand that reflects their values, mission, and unique selling proposition. This can be achieved through a combination of effective web design, social media marketing, content marketing, and online advertising.

In addition to these strategies, there are several behaviors that businesses can adopt to succeed in the digital economy. One of these is to be customer-centric. In the digital economy, customers have more power than ever before, and businesses that fail to meet their needs and expectations risk losing their loyalty. By focusing on delivering exceptional customer experiences, businesses can build strong relationships with their customers and gain a competitive advantage. Another important behavior is to be agile and adaptable. The digital economy is characterized by rapid change, and businesses that can quickly pivot in response to market trends and emerging technologies are more likely to succeed. This requires a culture of innovation and a willingness to experiment with new ideas and approaches.

Businesses in the digital economy need to be collaborative and open to partnerships. No business can succeed in isolation, and collaboration with other businesses, startups, and industry experts can provide access to new ideas, technologies, and markets. By building strong partnerships, businesses can create a network of support that can help them navigate the complexities of the digital economy. The digital economy presents both challenges and opportunities for businesses. To succeed in this dynamic and fast-changing environment, businesses need to adopt a range of strategies and behaviors that enable them to adapt and thrive. These include embracing digital transformation, leveraging data, creating a strong digital brand, being customer-centric, being agile and adaptable, and being collaborative and open to partnerships. By adopting these approaches, businesses can position themselves for success in the digital economy.

It provides a comprehensive overview of various aspects of the digital economy and highlights the importance of digital transformation, innovation, and collaboration in achieving success in the digital age. It explores various aspects of the digital economy, including digital transformation, intellectual capital management, big data, organizational control, entrepreneurship, and collaborative behavior. Discusses the role of digital leadership in developing business model innovation for telecommunication incumbent firms and also explores the relationship between intellectual capital management and economic development in a quasi-information society. The book also delves into the underlying forces of organizational control on administrative behavior. The ecosystem strategy for startups growth is another key topic explored in the book. The strategic use of zero-rating of mobile data is also discussed in the book. The authors explore how this practice can be used to improve access to digital services and drive economic growth. The book also examines how big data can be used to clarify human information processing in the digital society. The authors provide criteria for analyzing individual traits and behavior in the digital age. The book explores the sharing economy and its potential to create a new economic approach. The transformation of business models in technology-enabled mergers and acquisitions is another topic covered in the book. This is a useful resource for the students, teachers and researchers of business, management and economics.

We are grateful to all those persons as well as various books, manuals, periodicals, magazines, journals etc. that helped in the preparation of this book. In spite of the best efforts, it is possible that some errors may have occurred into the compilation and editing of the book. Further queries, constructive suggestions and criticisms for the improvement of the book are always welcomed and shall be thankfully acknowledged.

Aria Baker
Harwell Webster

CONTENTS

Chapter 1

Digital Transformation: Digital Leadership Role in Developing Business Model Innovation Mediated by Co-Creation Strategy for Telecommunication Incumbent Firms

Abstract

Incumbents have a challenge to sustain their business due to new attractive business model offered by new entrants. Incumbent firms are required to transform their existing business to a new paradigm of business which is digital business through developing new capability in business model. In developing innovation in the business model, there is a challenge for incumbents due to existing legacy business and routine process. The fastest way in developing new capabilities through collaboration is called co-creation strategy. In driving co-creation strong culture and visioning of digital leader is required. The study of the digital leadership role in developing business model innovation and co-creation strategy was limited; hence this study has an objective to assess the role of digital leadership, whether it will direct or indirect through co-creation strategy in developing business model innovation. The study was conducted on 88 senior leader respondents. The statistical data analysis used SmartPLS application. The result explained that digital leadership impacts indirectly through co-creation strategy on developing business model innovation. Co-creation strategy plays a mediating role in the relationship between business model innovation and digital leadership.

Keywords: digital transformation, digital leadership, co-creation strategy, business model innovation

1. Introduction

The impact of digital technology through the Internet and cloud brings the new paradigm in terms of structure in all industries. The Internet creates a borderless economy and new whole mind and results in the information era changes into the conceptual age era [1]. The change is not only in the customer but also in the market; the incumbent has to transform their process to be more fast, simple, and effective and has an ability to personalize their products by digitizing and providing the process learning [2]. Digital technology creates a certain paradox between the opportunity and efficiency. In terms of opportunity, it will generate revenue through innovation in business model and in terms of efficiency will be created through digitization process [3]. In the digital era, there are four factors in the driving of change that are key success factors of the firms which are innovation, collaboration, integration, and interoperability [4, 5].

New entries come into the market with an attractive business model, while the incumbent firms still rely on the existing business model based on their existing assets that may not be able to fulfill customer and market needs. Hence, incumbent firms are required to develop new capabilities within their business model to anticipate the changes in customers and market. Co-creation is defined as joins co-values between the firms and partners in order to produce a mutually valued outcome and fastest way in developing business model capability. Co-creation will also accelerate and enable incumbent firms to transform the business to be able to be more innovative, standardized, modular, interoperable, decentralized, and service oriented [6]. The more innovative the firms are, the more value the co-creation model can bring. The need for co-creation is for the development of business model innovations since the combination of strong capabilities between firms and partners to provide a complete supply chain could create valuable business model innovations [7, 8]. A strong business model innovation would bring sustainability with a combination of focus on customers and could create sustainable competitiveness for incumbent firms in the disruptive era [9]. Telecommunication is the main sector where the incumbent firms are significantly disrupted by new entries [10]. Meanwhile, the telecommunication industry in Indonesia is special, since the digital development is still at an early stage, but the growth of innovation through the creativity industry and startups are growing rapidly. This creates an opportunity and challenge for incumbent firms to build its digital infrastructure [11]. The new entries are able to offer customer solutions through over-the-top (OTT) applications that disrupt the incumbent firms. These startups have developed new products and services through economy sharing and co-creation with communities, which have become a disruption to the existing firms. There have been studies and research on this trend of disruption that are conducted worldwide. International business machines (IBM) has also conducted empirical studies on the role of co-creation. According to their 2015 survey on CEOs, 69% of CEOs strongly believe that the role of the CEO is important in order to earn the highest achievements in innovation through collaboration and co-creation with customers and partners. This supports another study on the significance of the role of company leaders and collaboration especially in digital leadership [12].

Digital leadership is a combination between digital culture and digital competence. The study of digital leadership is the part of the study about leadership based upon the upper echelon theory developed by Hambrick and Mason [13] where organization output can be predicted by manager characters. In terms of digital leadership, Pearl Zhu [14] defines the criteria of digital leadership which consist of five characteristics:

1. Thought leader, the capability to be tough in facing the market and competition change

2. Creative leader, a digital leader that has creativity and innovation mindset to formulate the idea into reality

3. Global visionary leader, a digital leader that has the ability to provide direction and to become an orchestra in transforming the digital business transformation

4. Inquisitive leader, with the complex and dynamic ecosystem due to volatility, uncertainty, complexity, and ambiguity (VUCA) factors, a digital leader that has to have the learning capability

5. Profound Leader, a style of digital leadership capability to lead in complex times with has in depth knowledge and understanding, to use their knowledge in interpretation, assumption and synthesizing the information to take the decision making

This study is important for digital transformation since it will bring the new transformation path model for incumbent firm by developing the digital leader to enhance the culture and digital competence. On the other hand, this study is also supporting the new construct of co-creation strategy before it was constructed from the marketing theory; with this study it will extend the new paradigm of co-creation to become a part of the strategy to grow. It will strengthen in developing of strategic management theory in facing market dynamic due to digital technology; the co-creation and collaboration strategy is the proper strategy to accelerate the transformation. Since the role of digital leadership is important to drive business model and collaboration through co-creation, and also limitation study on the role of digital leadership in relation with business model innovation and co-creation strategy [15], hence this chapter is going to discuss the role of digital leadership in developing co-creation strategy and business model innovation. The analysis path of effectiveness is important whether digital leadership has direct or indirect relationship to business model innovation. Co-creation strategy has played a mediating role in the relationship between business model innovation and digital leadership. The essence of this study to contribute more knowledge and add priority transformation actions for management in managing digital transformation and for scholar could contribute in finding the proper path analysis in transforming into digital service for established company. The chapter will start with introduction, thus exploring the theoretical background of the study by describing past research and construct variables. It will then continue with the methodology used in the study including the research model and hypotheses. The findings section covers the management analysis and opportunities for further research. Last, it will also cover the conclusion, implications, and suggestions for future study.

2. Literature review

2.1 Digital transformation in Indonesia telecommunication industry

Digital transformation is the hot topic in telecommunication industry. The concept of digital transformation has been discussed in the early 2000s called as Telco 2.0 [16]. The concept of Telco 2.0 focuses on customer-centric and innovative organization as the key success factors. Value migration consists of a combination of collaboration and business model innovation that leads to co-creation strategies of digital businesses.

There are a variety of types of digital transformation in the ICT industry. Based on the innovation framework, the transformation can be done through the following innovations [17]. There are four types of digital transformation in ICT industry as follows:

1. Transformation by products and services innovations (named inventors). This model is suitable to fulfill the untapped needs of customers, either partially or

completely, to create innovative digital products and services, that is, Apple, Google, GO-JEK with GO-FOOD, GO-CLEAN, etc.

2. Business models/innovation paradigms (named disruption) rely on customer experience, delivery model, and value propositions through digital technologies. Some examples include Uber, Amazon.com, Tokopedia, and GO-JEK. According to Das et al. [11], this disruptive scheme is believed to be the most successful scheme.

3. Business processes (named lean champion) increase the value by leveraging the value chain through digital technologies to increase efficiency and productivity, such as Walmart and Matahari Mall.

4. All round positioning innovation. Its transformation is done through a combination of products, processes, and business models supported by digital technology to strengthen the position of the products and services, such as Tesla.

According to the value mapping contribution and the nature of ICT firms in general, heavy investment is made in connectivity. The World Economic Forum [18] identifies four models of ICT firms with intensive investment to transform into a digital telecommunications firm, namely:

1. Connectivity provider for the future of the network. It has focused on the development of ICT infrastructure to enable other enterprises and OTTs across the industry, by investing and virtualizing the network. This includes investment on software-defined network, cyber security, and extended connectivity. This model is believed to have the highest contribution in the next 5–8 years based on its relevance with the nature and core competence of ICT firms. It requires an expansion of distinctive capabilities and organization of digital capability.

2. Beyond pipe. It integrates IOT and digital services to fulfill customer needs and businesses, to expand the business into becoming a digital player by adding value-added services. Capability in business model innovations is also required to generate new revenue on top existing infrastructure.

3. Redefining customer engagement. It is done to win customer loyalty and mindshare by providing features and tools to create better customer experience and to improve the service to match other industries. This requires capability on telecommunications to enhance customer relation, loyalty, and experience.

4. Bridging the gap in innovation. It is done by transforming the capability of innovation model and by increasing talent capability to work in digital and collaborate to co-create value with stakeholders. This requires the capability of collaboration and co-creation partnership strategy to accelerate and leverage existing assets.

Khanagha et al. [19] formulates the key evaluation of the succeed in digital transformation:

1. First, aligning internal activities with external rate and direction of change to develop strategy formulation and implementation. When the firm responds to the change, the proper time to do action is required to be exact, not too early or too late.

2. Second, retaining resources and capabilities to create distinctive organization capability to adapt to change. ICT firms have a large extent of capabilities and complementary assets; hence, the transformation should integrate with existing core and resource capability through new technology and business models.

3. Last, generating new revenue for product diversification and minimizing cost of change. It can be done by creating business model innovations and co-creation partnership strategies.

2.2 Business model innovation

Business model innovation describes how an organization could create, deliver, and capture value. The construct and modification of a business model is called business model innovation. Business models are broadly used in the value chain of businesses, including the process and integration with existing business processes [20]. Business models are also part of the implementation strategy in the context of sustainability for the incumbent firms [21]. Business model innovation plays a significant role in digital economy [22]. In the digital ecosystem, business model innovation is emerged as an alternative to process and product innovation [23]. In addition, business model innovation has an objective to create value, and the implementation of business model is dependent on the capability of managers and top leaders [8, 24]. Business model innovation is a part of digital transformation through rearranging business activities with greater value than before through the optimization of new digital technology [25–27]. Business model's innovation is a new holistic, integrated, and systematic way for organizations to provide the operation of innovations in order to create value in a dynamical environment through collaboration with their internal and external stakeholders [28].

In this study, we refer the concept of business from Amit and Zott [24] with the dimension of content innovation, structure innovation, and governance innovation.

2.3 Co-creation strategy

Co-creation is customer value chain collaboration activities start from design activities into promotion called as co-design, co-develop, co-deliver, and co-promotion [29]. In relation with innovation, co-creation strategy will strengthen innovation [30–33] including radical innovation [34]; in addition the concept of co-creation has an objective to develop value creation [35–37]. The new concept of customer has changed. In traditional management view, the consumers or partners are outside the value chain, while in modern company the consumer is an integral part of the system. The new paradigm changes the customers not as an object but a subject involving of value chain business activities. Traditional management views the consumers or partners to be outside of the value chain, while modern companies view consumers as an integral part of the system. The new paradigm also views the customers not as an object but as a subject involved in the value chain of business activities. Co-creation in innovation with external partners including customers has been an intense topic and called as an open innovation ([32]; Romero and Molina, 2009).

In a strategic level, co-creation can be utilized as a strategy to transform value propositions, working closely with customers and related party. In this paper, the extended concept of value creation is driven from marketing the co-creation concept based on the new 7S McKinsey framework [38] and value chain to put co-creation as part of the business strategy. In the new 7S McKinsey framework, the strategy is divided into three categories: strategy, capability, and tactical. Hence, the construction of co-creation strategy is defined as a co-creation vision and direction, co-creation capability, and co-creation tactics. Co-creation vision focuses on the direction from a senior leader. Co-creation capability focuses on the development of people and process and technology to support implementation of vision. Co-creation tactics range from co-design, co-production, co-delivery, to co-promotion.

Based on the literature review, this study assesses co-creation strategy by the dimensions of co-creation strategy, co-creation capability, and co-creation tactical.

2.4 Digital leadership

In digital transformation, the role of leader is central in driving fast decision-making process and propelling the change [39, 40]. Digital leadership is a combination of leadership style of transformation leadership and the uses of digital technology. Digital leadership is defined as the combination of culture and competence of a leader in optimizing the use of digital technology to create value to the firms [41].

There are five characteristics: creative leader, tough leader, global visionary leader, inquisitive leader, and profound leader [14]. Since the competition becomes tight, hyper, and complex dynamic of the ecosystem due to VUCA (volatility, uncertainty, complexity, and ambiguity) factors, hence the leader is required to be creative and innovative through in-build capability or collaboration [42]. The global visionary leader is required to provide direction and to become an orchestra in transforming the digital business transformation. The internet and cloud technology as a main driver for fourth Industrial Revolution is heavily knowledge-based and requires overwhelmingly new competencies and capabilities, hence the leader has to have ability Inquisitive learning and has profound ability in knowledge and understand in depth in learning and change. Hence based on the literature review, the dimension uses for this study are creative, deep knowledge, global vision and collaboration, thinker, inquisitive.

In a disruptive era, the role of digital leadership to innovation has been discussed intensely [12, 43]. The previous study found that there is an impact of digital leadership on innovation including developing a business model; hence we develop the hypothesis as follows:

Hypothesis 1: Digital leadership has a direct impact to business model innovation in the Indonesian telecommunication industry.

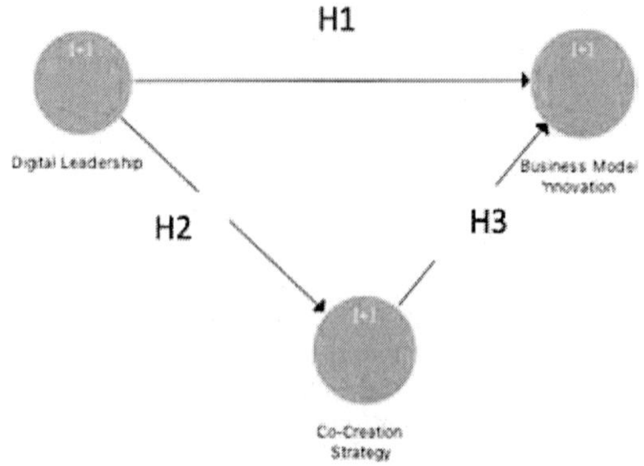

Figure 1.
Research model.

The relation of digital leadership and collaboration including co-creation has been discussed in a previous study [25, 44]. The previous study found that there was positive correlation between leadership in this case digital leadership and collaboration or co-creation study; hence, the hypothesis is formulated as follows:

Hypothesis 2: Digital leadership has a positive impact on co-creation strategy in the Indonesian telecommunication industry.

The strong impact of co-creation on innovation has been discussed in a previous study [31, 45, 46]. It was a strong impact of co-creation strategy on innovation including business model innovation. According to these studies, the hypothesis is formulated as follows:

Hypothesis 3: Co-creation strategy has a significant impact on business model innovation in the telecommunication industry.

Hence, **Figure 1** demonstrates the current research model.

3. Methodology

This study uses a quantitative research design. The units of analysis in this study are telecommunication firms in Indonesia with the management of these firms as the observed unit. The sampling method used is purposive sampling. The sample size is made up of 88 respondents where 75% of them is represented by general manager and manager leaders and 25% by VP and board leader. According to Hair, Hult, Ringle, and Sarstedt [47], the recommended sample size is 52 respondents for the model with an endogenous construct that has two arrows directed, 0.05 significance level, 80% statistical power, and minimum R2 = 0.25. The sample size of this research is 88 respondents. That is more than the recommended sample size. About 88% of the respondents are men and 12% are women. About 83% of the respondents come from the network provider, while 17% from service providers. Data were collected via self-assessment through an online questionnaire and distributed through messenger, WhatsApp, Telegram, and email. Since there is a limitation of the data sample, the statistical tool of analysis is SmartPLS.

4. Result

The result of statistical tool has been tested through outer, inner, and hypothesis testing. The analysis of the outer model specifies the relationship between latent variables and their indicators. Tests performed on outer models include:

1. Convergent validity. The value of convergent validity is the value of loading factor on the latent variable with its indicators. The expected value is above 0.7.

2. Discriminant validity. The value of cross loading factor that is useful to assess whether the constructs have adequate discriminant by comparing the loading value on the intended construct which is greater than the loading value with other constructs.

3. Composite reliability. Data that has a composite reliability over 0.7 which is considered as highly reliable.

4. Average variance extracted (AVE). Expected to be more than 0.5.

5. Cronbach's alpha. Reliability test reinforced with Cronbach's alpha. The result is expected to have a value of more than 0.6 for all constructs.

In testing the construct validity and reliability, the result showed that the result for AVE value is >0.5, Cronbach's alpha is >0.6, and composite reliability is >0.7. It means that research variables have good reliability for all variable and dimension. In discriminant validity, the result showed that the diagonal numbers indicate the square root of AVE is higher compared with the left row number. It means that the dimension has a good discriminant validity. The testing of convergent validity showed that all values of the loading factor of outer path analysis for t value are >1.96 and p-value is <0.05 which means each indicator is a valid measurement tool in measuring latent variables; a similar result for outer path analysis has shown that all constructs have a path coefficient score with t-statistics of more than 1.96 and p-value = 0.000 < 0.05, which means that all constructs have a significant association with their dimensions.

The second testing is inner test or structural model testing. The testing is using a blindfolding score. The result showed that the score of blindfolding, Q2, was obtained for co-creation strategy = 0.277 and business model innovation = 0.486. If Q2 is >0, it indicates that the structural model has adequate predictive

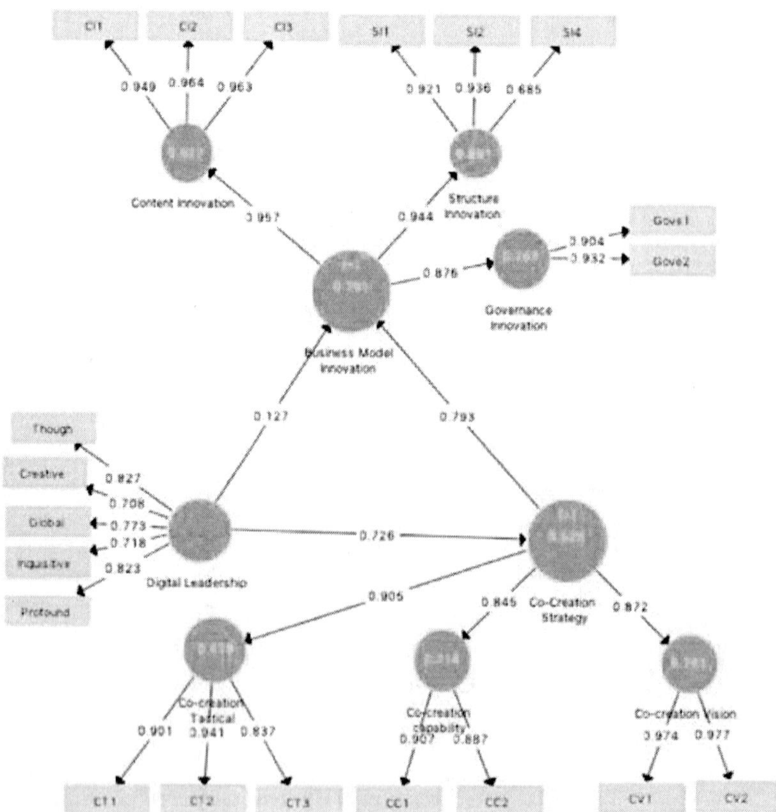

Figure 2.
Path analysis result.

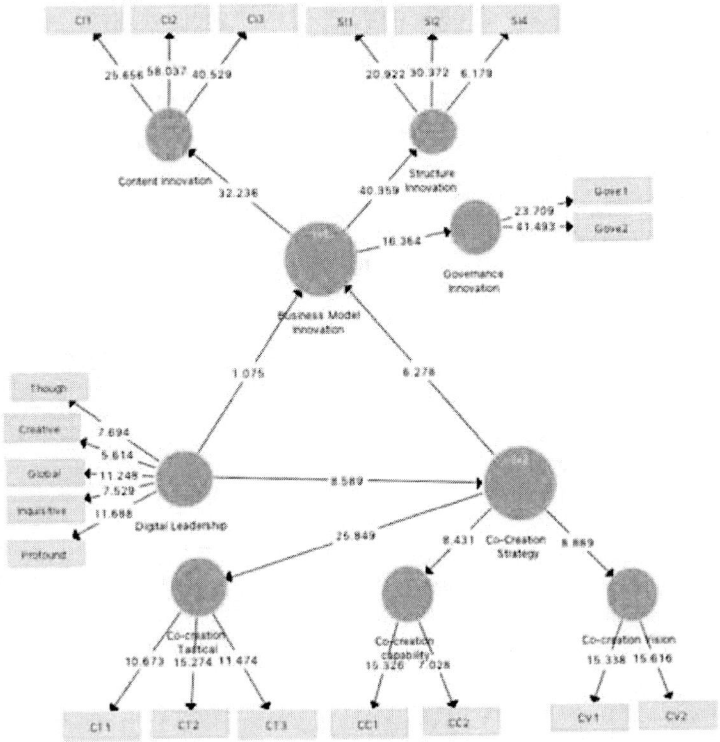

Figure 3.
Research Finding.

Hypothesis	Path analysis	Path	Standard deviation	T statistics	P values	Result
Direct effect test						
H1	Digital leadership > Business model innovation	0.127	0.116	1.075	0.274	Not significant
H2	Digital leadership > co-creation strategy	0.728	0.082	8.589	0.000	Significant
H3	Co-creation strategy > Business model innovation	0.793	0.129	6.278	0.000	Significant
Indirect effect test						
	Digital leadership > co-creation strategy-business model innovation	0.576	0.126	4.569	0.000	Significant

Table 1.
Hypothesis testing result.

relevance. It is seen that the model formed is robust. Hence the next step is to conduct hypothesis testing.

The result is shown in **Figures 2** and **3**. In **Figure 3,** it can be seen that if t value is >1.96, it means that the independent variable has a significant influence on the dependent variable. The result in **Figure 3** shows that digital leadership has a significant influence on co-creation strategy but not a significant influence on the business model innovation; and co-creation strategy has a significant influence on business model innovation.

The direct effect test shows that the relationship between digital leadership and business model innovation has a path coefficient score of 0.127 with t-statistics = 1.075 and p-value = 0.274 > 0.05. This means that H0 is accepted and H1 is rejected. This indicates that digital leadership has no significant impact on business model innovation. The second assessment is the relationship between digital leadership and co-creation strategy has a path coefficient score of 0.728 with t-statistics = 8.589 and p-value = 0.000 < 0.05. This means that H0 is rejected and H1 is accepted. This proves that digital leadership has a significant impact on co-creation strategy, while the relation between co-creation strategy with business model innovation has a path coefficient score of 0.793 with t-statistics = 6.278 and p-value = 0.000 < 0.05. This means that H0 is rejected, while H1 is accepted. The co-creation strategy plays significant role in relationship between digital leadership and business Model innovation (**Table 1**).

The indirect effect test shows that the mediating role of co-creation strategy has a path coefficient score = 0.576 with t-statistics = 4.589 and p-value = 0.000. This means that H0 is rejected, and H1 is accepted. This proves that co-creation has a supportive impact as a mediating role on relationship between business model innovation and digital leadership.

5. Discussion and implication

5.1 Discussion

The results are aligned with the study on disruption technology and innovation conducted by Christensen [9, 48] where the incumbent firm should adapt the changing of market through creating innovation business model by driving digital transformation. The path analysis showed that digital leadership has an indirect path in developing business model innovation. This is aligned with study on agility where the firms have to have agility learning to sustain their business [49]. This also aligns with the transformation stage of digital leadership where the incumbent requires to gradually transform from digital savvy where digital is used for personally and coloration purpose into digital agility where digital is used for business model innovation, and the ultimate of digital leadership is to become a disruptive innovation where the digital is part of radical innovation in exploring the new market [50]. Hence, the collaboration is the fastest way in developing business model innovation due to the gap of incumbent capability. The dimension of digital leadership is derived from Global and profound leader where the leader always thinking global the new way in doing business and they have deep and profound knowledge in taking risk and decision making. This finding supports Rudito and Sinaga (2017) where the digital leadership is becoming a part of culture and competence of the leader in optimizing the use of technology. This finding brings the implication for incumbent firms to use digital leadership to establish business model through co-creation strategy driving for open innovation [32, 51].

Co-creation strategy puts the external parties to be involved in the value chain to develop business model innovations. With a strong reputation, firms can control and attract valuable customers and stakeholders to create more value in a series of activities. From a customer or stakeholder point of view, they will be able to see the benefits of the part of the system for value creation. Customers or other parties can bring influence in the creation of value together with the firm. In this study, we found that in the developing of co-creation strategy, what is important is the factor of implementation which is co-creation tactical. It means that the execution of co-creation concept is important to support the developing of business model innovation. The finding supports the strong influence of co-creation on business model innovation [31, 45, 46].

Business model innovation is mostly supported by context and content innovation due to the relation with co-creation strategy. When the firm has to deal with the collaboration with partners, the structure of collaboration or co-creation and the content of innovation are significant factors to drive and control the co-creation value chain. The finding demonstrated that the governance is still important, but less priority compare with content and structure of innovation.

In an indirect test, it shows that co-creation is a mediating role in the relationship between business model innovation and digital leadership. Co-creation strategy plays a significant role on relationship between business model innovation and digital leadership. Co-creation strategy is developed from vision and direction from digital leadership and combining with external co-creation will impact in strengthen business model innovation. This path is more valuable than using customer experience directly to form business model innovation. This finding supports the findings in previous studies where the leadership through collaboration will strengthen innovation in the business model ([32]; Romero and Molina, 2009).

5.2 Implication

The implication to managerial practice, study has revealed the important of digital leadership in digital transformation to anticipate the digital disruption. The digital transformation is essential started from the vision and mission of the digital company to provide direction of the desired future position of the company. Weill and Woerner [52] define the vision and ambition into four matrices based on the matrix of end customer knowledge and business design. There will be four possibilities of the digital company: (1) when the business design is the value chain and the knowledge of the end customer is partial, the company vision is to become a supplier company such as a manufacture company that part of supply chain business in providing good and commodities without in-depth knowledge of customers. (2) when company has the complete supported ecosystem business but partially recognize knowledge of end customers, the company is characterized as a modular business firm such as payment company, that provide service as plug and play and be likely more innovative due to rapid changing of ecosystem; (3) when the company has the knowledge of end customer completely and business design is based on value chain, the company vision is to become a multichannel business such as a bank company that provides the customer experience over value chain; and (4) the vision company is distinguished as ecosystem drivers when ecosystem business design and the knowledge of end customer are completely accomplished. A digital telco company and Internet service provider are example companies that provide a great customer experience with lean organization and optimize the digital technology to drive ecosystem enabler (**Figure 4**).

The transformation brings the telco company to enabler ecosystem driver. In anticipated the disruption from new entries due to diminishing on innovation and customer experiences, incumbent telco should focus on customer experience and digital innovation while at the same time build the digital ecosystem to support the vision and ambition toward digital company.

The foundation of digital transformation is operational excellence. Incumbent telco shall ocus on developing lean process and organization through digitalization process and developing people capability in digital competence and culture.

Strategic implementation shall be cascaded from vison and mission derived from digital leadership, thus, to build distinctive capability and customer

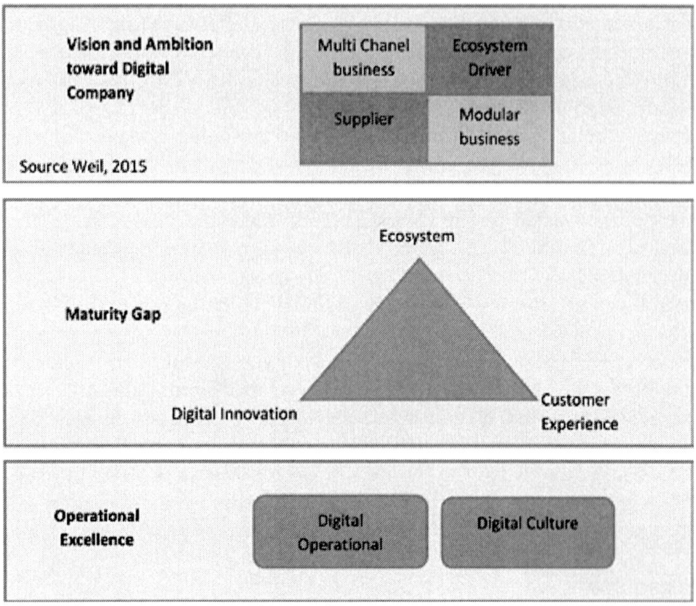

Figure 4.
The framework of telco digital transformation.

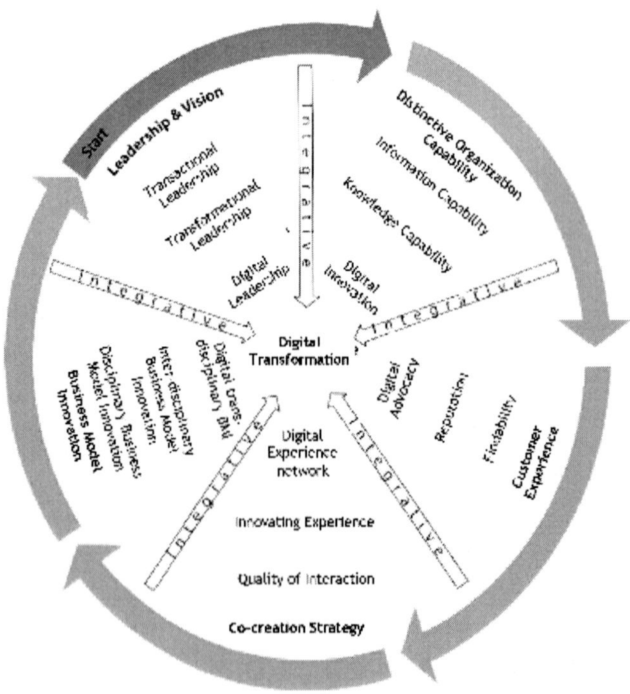

Figure 5.
Digital transformation model based on Mader's framework (2012).

experience orientation, then collaborate with co-creators in developing co-creation value and to build business model innovation. The implementation strategy is a continuous learning as part of developing dynamic capability start from sensing of market, seizing co-design and transform capability. We configure the model of digital transformation for Indonesia incumbent firms based on a framework study conducted by [53] as shown in **Figure 5**.

These findings have practical implications for the management in facing digital transformation. Digital transformation reflects management leadership and vision in transforming leadership from transactional leadership to a more transformational and digital-lead leadership. The leadership and vision will drive the development of distinctive organizational capabilities, from capabilities in the information age to digital innovation capabilities. Co-creation strategy based on distinct organizational capability and customer experience at a customer advocation level could drive the business model innovation up to the level of digital transdisciplinary business model innovation where the business model is developed based on co-creation value across disciplinaries.

5.3 Limitation and future research

This study is an exploratory research that aims to explore but not to confirm the theory. This research just wants to make prediction about the structural model of Business model innovation, and co-creation strategy in relationship with digital leadership. For the future research, this study suggests some recommendation, such as (1) using a larger size of sample for larger telecommunication companies in Indonesia, and it may be better for modeling and statistical analysis to utilize covariance-based better statistical application, (2) using probabilistic sampling methods such as stratified random or cluster sampling so that the result of study could be more relevant to make a generalized conclusion, and (3) longitudinal research should also be done to ensure in assure the role of co-creation strategy in relationship of business model innovation and digital leadership.

6. Conclusion

Based on the results of hypotheses testing, it can be concluded that digital leadership has indirect impact to business model innovation, where co-creation strategy has a mediating role on the relationship between business model innovation and digital leadership.

Further study can be explored using a more extended sampling, with industry, and with consideration of markets outside of Indonesia. A longitudinal research design should also be done to assess a direct and indirect impact of digital leadership into the business model innovation to provide value to the firms.

References

[1] Pink D. A Whole New Mind: Why Right-Brainers Will Rule the Future. USA: Penguin Group Inc; 2005. Retrieved from: http://www.danpink.com/wnm.html

[2] Henfridsson O, Mathiassen L, Svahn F. Managing technological change in the digital age: The role of architectural frames. Journal of Information Technology. 2014;**29**(1): 27-43. DOI: 10.1057/jit.2013.30

[3] Kagermann H. Change through digitization-value creation in the age of industry 4.0. In: Management of Permanent Change. Gabler, Wiesbaden: Springer; 2015. pp. 23-45. DOI: 10.1007/978-3-658-05014-6_2

[4] Bauer W, Hämmerle M, Schlund S, Vocke C. Transforming to a hyper-connected society and economy—Towards an "industry 4.0.". Procedia Manufacturing. 2015;**3**(Ahfe):417-424. DOI: 10.1016/j.promfg.2015.07.200

[5] Kiel D, Müller JM, Arnold C, Voigt K-I. Sustainable industrial value creation: Benefits and challenges of industry 4.0. International Journal of Innovation Management. 2017;**21**(8):1-21. DOI: 10.1142/S1363919617400151

[6] Ibarra D, Ganzarain J, Igartua JI. Business model innovation through industry 4.0: A review. Procedia Manufacturing. 2017;**22**:4-10. DOI: 10.1016/j.promfg.2018.03.002

[7] Amit R, Zott C. Crafting business architecture: The antecedents of business model design. Strategic Entrepreneurship Journal. 2015;**9**(1):331-350. DOI: 10.1002/sej

[8] Zott C, Amit R. Business model innovation: How to create value in a digital world. GfK Marketing Intelligence Review. 2017;**9**(1):18-23. DOI: 10.1515/gfkmir-2017-0003

[9] Christensen CM, Bower JL. Customer power, strategic investment, and the failure of leading firms. Strategic Management Journal. 1996;**17**(3):197-218. DOI: 10.1002/(SICI)1097-0266(199603)17:3<197:AID-SMJ804>3.3.CO;2-L

[10] Bradley J, Loucks J, Macaulay J, Noronha A, Wade M. Digital vortex: How digital disruption is redefining industries. Lausanne, Switzerland: Global Center for Digital Business Transformation; June 2015. pp. 1-43

[11] Das K, Gryseels M, Sudhir P, Tan KT. Unlocking Indonesia's Digital Opportunity. Jakarta, Indonesia: McKinsey and Company; 2016. pp. 1-28

[12] Wasono LW, Furinto A. The effect of digital leadership and innovation management for incumbent telecommunication company in the digital disruptive era. International Journal of Engineering and Technology. 2018;**7**(June):125-130. DOI: 10.14419/ijet.v7i2.29.13142

[13] Hambrick DC, Mason PA. Echelons: The organization as a reflection of its top managers. Academy of Management Review Management. 1984;**9**(2):193-206. DOI: 10.2307/258434

[14] Pearl Z. Digital master: Debunk the Myths of Enterprise Digital Maturity. Lulu Publishing Service; 2015

[15] Coombes PH, Nicholson JD. Business models and their relationship with marketing: A systematic literature review. Industrial Marketing Management. 2013;**42**(5):656-664. DOI: 10.1016/j.indmarman.2013.05.005

[16] Yoon J-L. Telco 2.0: A new role and business model. IEEE Communications Magazine. 2007;**1**(1):10-13. DOI: 10.1016/j.sbspro.2012.05.155

[17] Organisation for Economic Cooperation and Development. Going digital: Making the transformation work for growth and well-being. Meeting of the OECD Council at Ministerial Level. June 2017. pp. 1-33. DOI: 10.1787/9789264276284-en

[18] World Economic Forum. Digital Transformation of Industries. Digital Transformation of Industries, (January), 40:30min; 2016. Retrieved from: http://reports.weforum.org/digital-transformation/wp-content/blogs.dir/94/mp/files/pages/files/digital-enterprise-narrative-final-january-2016.pdf%0Ahttps://www.youtube.com/watch?v=qav1y7G15JQ&t=1678s

[19] Khanagha S, Volberda H, Oshri I. Business model renewal and ambidexterity: Structural alteration and strategy formation process during transition to a cloud business model. R&D Management. 2014;**3**:322-340. DOI: 10.1111/radm.12070

[20] Frankenberger K, Weiblen T, Csik M, Gassmann O. The 4I-framework of business model innovation: An analysis of the process phases and challenges. International Journal of Product Development. 2013;**18**(Numbers 3-4): 1-18. DOI: 10.1504/IJPD.2013.055012

[21] Massa L, Tucci CL. Business Model Innovation. In Oxford Handbooks Online. Oxford, UK: Oxford University Press; 2014. pp. 1-25. DOI: 10.1093/oxfordhb/9780199694945.013.002

[22] Lee CS, Vonortas NS. Business model innovation in the digital economy. In Social and Economic Transformation in the Digital Era. IGI Global; 2004. pp. 163-181. DOI: 10.4018/9781599049472.ch260

[23] Eksell A, Harenstam A. Business model innovation for a digital future: A two-sided single case study of the drivers, opportunities, and barriers of business model innovation in a digitalization context, 2017. p. 158. Retrieved from: http://publications.lib.chalmers.se/records/fulltext/250572/250572.pdf

[24] Amit R, Zott C. Creating value through business model innovation. MIT Management Review. 2012;**53**(3):41-50

[25] Berman SJ. Digital transformation: Opportunities to create new business models. Strategy & Leadership. 2012;**40**(2):16-24. DOI: 10.1108/10878571211209314

[26] Li F. The digital transformation of business models in the creative industries: A holistic framework and emerging trends. Technovation. 2018:1-10. DOI: 10.1016/j.technovation.2017.12.004

[27] Prem E. A digital transformation business model for innovation. The Proceedings of The 2015 ISPIM Innovation Summit in Brisbane, Australia: 6-9 December 2015. Retrieved from http://www.ispim.org/abstracts/theproceedingsofthe2015ISPIMinnovationsummit,brisbane,australia:6-9/december/2015/prem_erich.html

[28] Abdelkafi N, Makhotin S, Posselt T. Business model innovations for electric mobility—What can be learned from existing business model patterns? International Journal of Innovation Management. 2013;**17**(01):1340003. DOI: 10.1142/S1363919613400033

[29] Sawhney O, Verona G, Prandelli E. Collaborating to create: The internet as platform for customer engagement in product innovation. Journal of Interactive Marketing. 2005;**19**(4):1-14. DOI: 10.1002/dir

[30] Frow P, Nenonen S, Payne A, Storbacka K. Managing co-creation design: A strategic approach to innovation. British Journal of

Management. 2015;**26**(3):463-483. DOI: 10.1111/1467-8551.12087

[31] Hamidi F, Shams Gharneh N. Impact of co-creation on innovation capability and firm performance: A structural equation modeling. AD-Minister. 2017:73-90. DOI: 10.17230/ad-minister.30.4

[32] Ramírez-Montoya MS, García-Peñalvo F-J. Co-creation and open innovation: Systematic literature review. Comunicar. 2018;**26**(54):9-18. DOI: 10.3916/C54-2018-01

[33] The Wharton School and Mack Center for Technological Innovation. Innovation through co-creation: Engaging customers and other stakeholders. Mack Center for Tech Nological Innovation; 2011. pp. 1-32

[34] Perks H, Gruber T, Edvardsson B. Co-creation in radical service innovation: A systematic analysis of microlevel processes. Journal of Product Innovation Management. 2012;**29**(6):935-951. DOI: 10.1111/j.1540-5885.2012.00971.x

[35] Galvagno M, Dalli D. Theory of value co-creation: A systematic literature review. Managing Service Quality. 2014;**24**(6):643-683. DOI: 10.1108/MSQ-09-2013-0187

[36] Kambil A, Friesen GB, Sundaram A. Co-creation: A new source of value. Outlook. 1999;**2**:38-43. Retrieved from: http://kambil.com/accenture/cocreation2.pdf

[37] Prahalad CK, Ramaswamy V. Co-creation experiences: The next practice in value creation. Journal of Interactive Marketing. 2004;**18**(3):5-14. DOI: 10.1002/dir.20015

[38] D'Aveni RA, Gunther R. Hyper competition: Managing the Dynamics of Strategic Maneuvering 1st ed. New York: Free Press; 1994

[39] Li W, Liu K, Belitski M, Ghobadian A, O'Regan N. E-leadership through strategic alignment: An empirical study of small- and medium-sized enterprises in the digital age. Journal of Information Technology. 2016;**31**(2):185-206. DOI: 10.1057/jit.2016.10

[40] Kohli R, Johnson S. Digital transformation in latecomer industries: CIO and CEO Leadership Lessons from Encana Oil & Gas (USA) Inc. MIS Quarterly Executive, 2011; **10**(4):141-156

[41] Rudito P, dan Mardi FN, Sinaga MBA. Digital Mastery Membangun Kepemimpinan Digital Untuk Memenangkan Era Disrupsi. Jakarta: PT Gramedia Pustaka; 2017

[42] Sandell S. Digital Leadership how Creativity in Business Can Propel your Brand and Boost your Results. Rochester, UK: Allen House Publishing Company Limited; 2013

[43] Kreutzer RT, Neugebauer T, Pattloch A. Digital Business Leadership. In: Meffert A, editor. Digital Business Ladership Digitale Transformation – Geschäftsmodell-Innovation – agile Organisation – Change-Management. 1st ed. Berlin, Deutchland: Springer Gabler; 2017. DOI:10.1007/978-3-658-11914-0

[44] Doz YL, De Roover B. Responding to digital disruption through alliances (No. 2017/25/STR). France: SSRN Electronic Journal, INSEAD Business School; 2017. DOI: 10.2139/ssrn.2940284

[45] Basceanu L. Business model innovation and value co-creation: Based on a single case study on Liz Claiborne. 2014. Retrieved from: http://studenttheses.cbs.dk/bitstream/handle/10417/4570/lelia_ecaterina_basceanupdf.pdf?sequence=1

[46] Gazaro DA, Santos D, Zen AC, Schmidt VK. Entrepreneurship

ecosystems and the stimulus to the creation of innovative business: A case in the app industry in Brazil. Journal of Research in Business, Economics and Management. 2017;**8**(5):1537-1543. Retrieved from: www.scitecresearch.com/journals/index.php/jrbem/index%0Awww.scitecresearch.com

[47] Hair JF, Ringle CM, Sarstedt M, Vinzi E. Editorial partial least squares structural equation modeling: Rigorous applications, better results and higher acceptance. Long Range Planning. 2013;**46**(1-2):1-12. DOI: 10.1109/MCSE.2008.47

[48] Markides C. Disruptive innovation: In need of better theory † business-model innovation. Harvard Business Review. 2006;**23**:19-25. DOI: 10.1111/j.1540-5885.2005.00177.x

[49] Saputra N, Abdinagoro SB, Kuncoro EA. The mediating role of learning agility on the relationship between work engagement and learning culture. Social Sciences and Humanities. 2018;**26**:117-130

[50] Ernst & Young. Sustaining Digital Leadership! Agile Technology Strategies for Growth, Business Models and Customer Engagement. San Jose, USA; 2015

[51] Romero D, Molina A. Collaborative networked organisations and customer communities: Value co-creation and co-innovation in the networking era. Production Planning and Control. 2011;**22**(5-6):447-472. DOI: 10.1080/09537287.2010.536619

[52] Weill P, Woerner SL. Thriving in an increasingly digital ecosystem. MIT Sloan Management Review. 2015;**56**(4):27-34. DOI: 10.1287/isre.1100.0318

[53] Mader C. How to assess transformative performance towards sustainable development in higher education institutions. Journal of Education for Sustainable Development. 2012;**6**(1):79-89. DOI: 10.1177/097340821100600114

Chapter 2

Implementation of a Digital Workplace Strategy to Drive Behavior Change and Improve Competencies

Abstract

Digital technologies are integrated in many aspects of life and work and present benefits and challenge for organizations, employers, and employees. In order to have advantages from digital transformation, organizations should be creative for new working environments and their culture around digital developments in the workplace in order not to lose clients, productivity, and employees. Some keys of success of digital workplaces are an effective implementation of a digital workplace strategy with a changed learning and culture as an incentive for staff behavior. This should suit to technological solutions and support its adoption and use it for work, communication, and cooperation. Entrepreneurship education should be also adapted to digital transformation in order to prepare employees and employers for digital workplaces.

This chapter presents besides some aspects like a digital European workplace initiative and a framework, which could be the basis of a digital workplace strategy, some proposals for improving entrepreneur's skills. As an important issue of a digital workplace strategy is a suitable learning concept to foster a digital culture and employees' behavior which can be integrated into entrepreneurship education and training programs in order to prepare entrepreneurs for the digital transformation and digital workplaces. The author works in many European projects aimed to improving work and education/training of entrepreneurs in digital era and included in this chapter issues necessary for small- and medium-sized companies (SMEs) resulted from surveys done within some of these projects about SMEs' problems that have in connection with digital transformation and of organized training.

Keywords: digital transformation, digital workplace, digital workplace strategy, culture, behavior, entrepreneurship, SME

1. Introduction

The increasing integration of digital technologies in all aspects of our lives is both a benefit and a challenge for organizations, employers, and employees.

Organizations are benefiting from such digital transformation including also digitization of the workplace, i.e., through increased productivity, cost savings, a more mobile and agile workforce, increased flexibility, and adaptability in marketplace. Enterprises are collaborating more globally and with more diverse and global staff. Employees could work from anywhere and stay connected through smartphones, collaborate with peers, and stay on top of digital trends. Organizations should be proactive in creating new systems and policies and rethinking their culture around digital developments in the workplace in order not to lose clients, productivity, and employees.

The keys of success of digital workplaces are an effective implementation of a digital workplace strategy with a changed learning and culture. Culture is an incentive for behavior; organizations and managers should assure that staff behavior suits to technological solutions, supports its adoption, and uses it for work, communication, and cooperation. Entrepreneurship education should be also adapted to digital transformation in order to prepare employees and employers for digital workplaces.

This chapter presents besides some aspects like a digital European workplace initiative and a framework, which could be the basis of a digital workplace strategy, some proposals for improving entrepreneurship skills. As an important issue of a digital workplace strategy is a suitable learning concept to foster a digital culture and employees' behavior which can be integrated into entrepreneurship education and training programs.

The role of entrepreneurs and of entrepreneurship education and how it will be changed in order to prepare entrepreneurs for the digital transformation and digital workplaces are shortly presented.

The scope of this chapter is on one hand to discuss with academics who work in the field of digital transformation and with students to find new scientific methods for problems like cultural and behavior change; on the other hand, the author has experience in learning methods for entrepreneurs and would like to help organizations and employees particularly in SMEs to achieve skills and competences for a successful digital transformation and digital workplace results.

The author works in many European projects aimed to improving work and education/training of entrepreneurs in digital era and included in this chapter issues necessary for small- and medium-sized companies (SMEs) resulted from surveys done within some of these projects about SMEs' problems that have in connection with digital transformation and of organized training. The author works currently at the planned training modules and will organize training sessions with SMEs from Germany within the current European project Reinnovate.

We think the problems discussed in this chapter will be used also within the German initiative Mittelstand 4.0-Kompetenzzentrum standards which supports companies and staff within digital changes. The author discussed with some companies within this program about changing culture and staff behavior within digital workplaces and how to improve entrepreneurs' digital skills.

2. Digital transformation

It is known that the development and proliferation of information and communication technology changed the ways in which employees connect, collaborate, and communicate.

These changes have been accelerated also due to trends like:

- Aging workforce and the need to capture their knowledge;
- Necessity to meet the varying needs of a multi-generational workforce;
- Information overloaded and technology helping employees to find what they need to work faster.

These trends require a digital transformation and a reshaping of work environment.

Digital transformation can be understood as improved business processes through digital technology. It means better collaboration between staff, efficient collaboration with customers, stronger and more productive relationships with partners, and increased potential by changing work styles.

The main drivers of digital transformation include traditional digital technologies [1, 2], i.e., infrastructures (i.e., networks, computer hardware) and applications (i.e., apps on smartphones, web applications), and the digital exploitation potentials [2], i.e., possible digital business models and digital value creation networks.

In the narrower sense, digital transformation often refers to the change process within a company triggered by digital technologies and customer expectations. However, it is a process of change affecting a variety of aspects of our society and does not end up in companies [3].

Digital transformation in organizations happens in many ways; employees and employers have different hopes [4]:

Managers want:

- that their employees work together more effectively to boost productivity;
- that their clients are content and to gain new ones through better customer service;
- to use digital technologies to minimize costs;
- to improve business processes;
- to be better than their competitors;
- to use digital transformation to remain relevant in the face of the quickening pace of technology advances.

Employees would like:

- to work with digital toolsets according to their tasks, experience, and working style;
- to have workspaces making possible to collaborate more effectively within their jobs and also due demands to increase productivity and cut costs, making it harder for employees;
- to be helped to meet market expectations.

Achieving such goals can be a long and difficult process because digital technology and change management issues influence workplace transformation. Developing and working on a digital workplace strategy can challenge the most forward thinking of business leaders.

There are big differences between organizations referring their digital transformation initiatives:

- Some of them develop some strategy and understand the benefits.
- Others are still in the early stages of developing a plan not knowing valuable ways about how to go about defining their goals for a digital transformation.

3. What is a digital workplace?

The emerging digital workplace, considered the natural evolution of the workplace, can address issues listed above and helping organizations [5, 6].

The digital workplace includes all digital technologies and services people use to get work in today's workplace—both which already exist and ones to be implemented. It ranges from HR applications and core business applications to e-mail, instant messaging, and enterprise social media tools and virtual meeting tools.

Frank Schönefeld defines the digital workplace as the "totality of the required access infrastructure, applications and device platforms of information or knowledge workers who need them to perform their work tasks and engage in collaboration" [7].

Digital workplaces could:

- support changes in working styles enabling employees to work more transparently and better use social networks.
- unify offline and online communications by keeping employees connected through their mobile devices to provide anywhere, anytime access to tools and corporate information.
- focus on employee experience by providing them with user experience they have outside the firewall. They provide choice, flexibility, and personalization.
- support virtual work environments that allow employees to stay connected in distributed and virtualized work locations while balancing customer privacy and operational risk.
- minimize spending and enhance productivity by providing employees with the right tools and right information at the right time.
- win the war on talent by offering the progressive and innovative environments that top candidates now [8].
- Digital workplace as a portal is "a solution for the integration of information and services in a common user interface" [9] because different services and components are combined in one user interface and made available to the user mostly web-based.

Integrated data can be used via interfaces in different applications. Users can combine existing data and create new applications based on it.

The conception and deployment of the workplace are among the key strategic activities for the European Commission in the years to come. The digital workplace initiative is also an important part of the ICT chapter of the 2016 Synergies and Efficiency Review.

The digital workplace initiative will provide staff with the right IT tools, platforms, and services, enabling users to work and collaborate anywhere, anytime with a fit-for-purpose security and optimizing their work experience and productivity. It will be adaptive and flexible to incorporate different types of users, new behaviors, and new technologies [10].

Within the conceptual framework underpinning the digital workplace initiative in the Commission staff is at the center, with a particular focus on the excellence of user experience. A staff member should be able to connect anywhere and at any time, through simple and secure authentication mechanism, on a variety of mobile devices to a number of corporate services. The data will be stored on a hybrid cloud model, ranging from on-premise (European Commission Datacenters) to public clouds depending on the classification of the data [10].

The six strands of the digital workplace initiative are:

- A balanced mix of mobile devices, either corporate or BYOD, allowing connection from anywhere and at any time. There are constraints about using corporate tools on private devices and vice versa, but they may be resolved with a good compromise between usability and security.

- Office automation comprising supported operating systems, word processors, spreadsheets, presentation-authoring tools, access to files, etc. An architecture enabling hybrid services become progressively more important especially when the mobile dimension perspective is incorporated.

- Mail and calendaring, including the central role of e-mail and its tight integration with calendar tools as a way to send messages, share information, and manage time and meetings.

- Unified communication encompasses different sources of real and near-real-time communication, which include videoconferencing and the future of telephony (telephony becomes an app, the classical telephone is replaced by the single mobile device).

- Collaboration and social networking, covering the main aspects of collaboration (from document to tasks), communities, and social networking, with special attention on their right availability, security, and integration in mobile platforms. Fast access to the relevant information is an essential in the digital workplace. Therefore information management and corporate search, as very strong integration elements, will be part of this component.

- Integration and identity and access management. The future digital workplace will be based on a hybrid platform with a combination of on-premise and cloud-based solutions to take the maximum benefit of technology development and to allow mobility.

By implementing the digital workplace initiative in the European Commission, it is intended to realize the following objectives:

- Increase staff engagement. Engage employees and raise motivation through an effective, efficient digital workplace.

- Increase staff productivity. Allow productivity improvements by providing the most suitable and effective digital workplace to each staff member.

- Enable a more modern and efficient office space design.

- Staff from many organizations already use many of digital components, i.e., responding to e-mails from smartphones, checking their paying online, or digitally enter a sales opportunity, so that organizations do not have to build the digital workplace from the ground up.

In the next years, the workplace continues to evolve, and employee expectations shift so that organizations that do not embrace digital workplace risk falling behind [10].

4. Digital workplace strategy

The key of success of digital workplaces lies in an effective implementation of a digital workplace strategy, and the first step in this transformation strategy is a cultural change supported by learning measures.

Digital workplace strategy can be understood as the dynamic alignment of an organization's work patterns within the digital work environment to enable peak performance and reduce costs. As each workplace strategy, a digital one supports to fulfill business objectives such as reducing property costs, improving business performance, merging two or more organizations/cultures, and relocating or consolidating occupied buildings. The workplace strategy and its implementation quite often occur at an opportune moment such as a property lease break or a company merger or acquisition [4, 11].

Some special reasons to build and adopt a digital workplace strategy could be the following [4, 12, 13, 14]:

- Talent attraction: many employees would opt for a lower paying job if they could work out of office, i.e., at home.
- Employee productivity can increase through online social networks.
- Employee satisfaction can be higher by installing and using social media tools internally.
- Employee retention is more stable when employee engagement increases.
- Newer communication tools, particularly instant messaging, are preferred over more traditional ones like e-mail or team workspaces.

Many organizations are convinced about the importance of a digital workplace strategy and invest money in supporting digital workplace strategies that promise ROI. Sure, to support these outcomes, you need to assure for employee's tools they need to collaborate, communicate, and connect with each other. Clear road maps should be created to ensure digital workplace with measurable business, deliverable, and minimal risks.

Business drivers for building a digital workplace strategy are:

- Rapid technology change is enabling a different workplace and work; some examples are artificial intelligence (AI) and big data combined with increasingly available collaboration tools.
- Employees' expectations of a different workplace experience supported by ubiquitous connectivity and rapidly advancing social technologies.
- Citizens demand digital service delivery and a different relationship with the government: There is clear citizen demand for quality online services to match their experiences with other service providers. This requires a digital-first workplace to work effectively.
- Often workplace strategies are developed by specialist workplace consultants, or by an architectural practice. "The successful implementation of a workplace strategy requires an interdisciplinary team, internal and external to the

organization. A workplace consultant may be retained to engage the team, help define success criteria, manage the process, and assess results" [13].

- External workplace consultants are professionals from a number of backgrounds: business management, interior design and architecture, building surveying, real estate and facility management, human resources, and building research.

In the file [8], a proposal for a digital workplace framework is presented with the following layers:

4.1 Collaborate, communicate, and connect

The employees should be able to do their job by using digital technologies for collaborating, communicating, and connecting with others. Productive business relationships can be created within and beyond natural work groups and enable knowledge sharing across the organization. In the next part, we develop this issue.

4.2 Technology: the digital toolbox

Each organization already has a digital workplace toolbox with different tools to support digital workplace in different ways. It is necessary to adopt the right tools for employees to do their jobs. The digital workplace toolbox can be defined in categories to support the ways in which you communicate, collaborate, connect, and deliver day-to-day services. Often the development of digital tools does not follow a digital workplace strategy where the business focus is clearly defined. Organization culture should be also considered.

4.3 Control: governance, risk, and compliance

Some components of digital workplace governance are:

- Guiding principles: identify the business goals to be achieved with the digital workplace, and translate them into guiding principles to drive ongoing development.

- Information governance strategy: determine the focus of digital workplace strategy, and align it with organization's existing information management or information governance strategy.

- Roles and responsibilities: identify key stakeholders, and create a suitable and sustainable interaction model.

- Training and certification: ensure employees have access to training to be prepared to have advantages of digital developments.

- Policy training: in addition to technical training, employees need policy training.

- Orchestrated presence: by organizing channels within the digital workplace.

- Crisis management: if a crisis occurs, react quickly (within the first day).

4.4 Business drivers: measurable business value

To deliver the necessary benefits, an organization should guide the direction of digital workplace development.

Some ways to achieve measurable value:

- Increase revenue.
- Reduce operational costs by introducing more effective ways to meet virtually, cutting travel and telecommunication costs and eliminating wasted time at the airport.
- Accelerate time-to-market by using tools to support research and develop, test, and deliver new products and services more quickly.
- Enhance innovation.
- Improve the customer experience.
- Increase agility and flexibility: provide the tools that mimic organization and business changes and reflect employee behaviors.
- Heighten staff satisfaction, i.e., by implementing easy-to-use tools.
- Strengthen talent recruitment and retention.
- Improve employee experience.

5. Cultural change and behavior supporting digital transformation

One of the first steps in the digital transformation is a cultural change in organizations. Culture is an incentive for behavior; organizations and managers should assure overcoming a culture of learned helplessness and spoon-fed training to encourage ongoing personal learning so that staff behavior suits to technological solutions, supports its adoption, and uses it for work, communication, and cooperation. One important issue of the digital workplace strategy is a clear understanding between organizational culture and technology, and this can be achieved within an adequate learning strategy. It ensures that tools, processes, and systems realize their full potential and will not be a failed initiative.

Organization's culture influences the way employees behave and work within digital transformation and so organizational performance, success, and failure. This means employee's culture ultimately determines how and to what extent employees connect, communicate, and collaborate within digital workplaces.

It is important to develop a change management plan and that the digital workplace strategy aligns to organization working culture. This cultural change and suitable technological components can contribute to improve:

- Collaboration by integrating intuitive, easy-to-use collaboration tools that enhance employees' ability to work together and support their own working style and wishes

- Communication by using digital tools to create their own content, rather than simply consuming existing content, to support that right information reaches the right audience, bilateral communication, and personalization of content

- Connections across the organization and outside

The free flow of information at the digital workplace has a positive impact on agility and innovation of organizations, and it promotes employee engagement and satisfaction by delivering the right information to the right people at the right time. One problem is how managers/leaders in organization can influence employee's behaviors and practice changes, conducting to innovative products and services that will enable the transition from old business models to ones successful in a digital world.

Isaac Sacolick presents three ways to enable employees to participate more in digital programs [15].

5.1 Encourage people to ask questions

Determining possible employees to ask questions enables them to move away from "the way we always do" to discussions what is better to do in digital working places.

That is, operations team wants to explore using automation to eliminate repetitive discussions. Someone asks, "How can we learn to be product owners in its agile development process?"

Sure, there are some people in the organization wishing to do things in the old way. Asking questions is an approach, which can open a dialog about new solutions.

5.2 Get out of the office and meet customers and prospects

Customers expect to select products and services intelligent and valuable. Start-ups and market leaders in other categories can steal market share from slow competitors not being in contact with customers but have also opportunities to develop new services into new areas by identifying optimal customer segments to deliver services digitally.

Leaders/representatives from organization should go out of the office, learn from customers, take into consideration their needs, and develop a perspective on how to deliver new experiences. Marketing specialists should learn how to best message and target prospects. Sales should be learning whom their new competitors are and how to defend against sales objections. Technologists should learn about the underlying technical capabilities required to fulfill value propositions.

5.3 Ask for data, then insights, then opinions

A data-driven organization offers practices and tools for people to present a thesis—first presenting data that backs it, then insights they have inferred, and lastly their opinions and conclusions. Behaviors drive organizational change.

Employees' roles in the organization, their jobs, and how they deliver business value are all subject to be changed in digital transformation, in order to convince more employees to support the digital strategy by challenging the status quo, to learn what customers need today, and to use data efficiently to drive bottom-up and top-down decisions.

5.4 Adaptation of employees to digital transformation and digital workplaces

When an organization suffers changes in everyday functioning like digital transformation, both employers and employees must face challenges; if employees do not keep up, chances that transformation to be successful are very low.

In the following experts, make some proposals to help employees to adapt to digital transformation [16].

5.5 Open dialogue

It is known that employees are sometimes resistant to change when the transformation comes only from up, so it is important to create a dialog with employees to discuss which and how they see improvements in digital transformation. If it is possible, the open dialog should start from the top and involve all employee's transformation. One leader in organizing digital transformation should bridge the gap between the actual implementation of technology and the workplace culture and demands.

5.6 Invest in training

"Let people understand the reasons for the change, and make sure they have a clear picture of what will improve when they get there," says Dr. Daniel Cable, professor and chair of organizational behavior, at London Business School. It is important to foster a culture of change and make sure employees develop the skills to keep up with a fast paced and dynamic environment. All employees should be encouraged to go through the company-training program to drive adoption.

5.7 Foster a culture where experimentation is allowed and encouraged

First employees can freely experiment without fearing the consequences of mistakes. Often, they discover new and faster ways of doing everyday tasks, increasing efficiency and productivity.

5.8 Support collaboration

Online and offline communication can easily be unified keeping employees connected through their own devices. Digital connections often reach down generational gaps and bring employees of different ages together. New digital communication fosters collaboration in departments and across the organization. The digital transformation should not be felt only as technology change but more like intuitive ways to complete tasks.

5.9 Involve employees

Embracing digital transformation is more easily achieved through increased employee engagement. Using digital technologies employees can reach consumers easily and directly.

Often, older employees are not enthusiastic about digital transformations, but their insight, wisdom, and experience are invaluable. By improving internal employee engagement, employees can feel more valued and are more open to change. Engagement drives adoption, but digital transformation too can drive engagement. Flexible work has positive effects on employee engagement. In the digital age, flexibility is easier than ever to implement. Employees can work remotely, use their own devices, and utilize digital tools to interact impactful with consumers and each other. Tangible benefits of digital transformations are easier to be evaluated.

6. Learning, training, and entrepreneurship education

A key success factor in digital transformation of an organization is a training and learning concept with three areas of focus [17]:

- how an organization bridges its digital skills and confidence gaps
- how an organization encourages people to take responsibility for their own continuous learning
- how an organization challenges and supports its senior people to become digital leaders

Some years ago, learning was focused on training people to fulfill their tasks (job training) and occasional additional skills, and there was little need for most workers to be always learning. Now, when all organizations must cope with the uncertainty, complexity, and ambiguity of the digital economy, they have to try to become more agile and adaptive. Intelligence and small-scale decision-making must be distributed to the edges of the organization, so that each team and function is free to learn and adapt based on customer and market feedback [17].

The learning process in organizations wishing to be successful within digital transformation should be changed from a process-centric world of job training to a service-oriented world of continuous learning and improvement in the flow of work. Many organizations developed digital workplace platforms and tools; learning around the digital workplace should help employees to understand how these tools can improve their work, achieve digital skills, and help the organization to have more advantages from its existing technology investments.

Some aspects should characterize the learning in the time of digital transformation [17]:

- The digital workplace needs a learning hub/community to accelerate change and adoption of new ways of working.
- A combination of informal, active, social learning + digital guides and a suitable methodology is a good approach to this.
- Minimum digital fluency is required to work in modern organizations.
- Leadership development programs need to change to avoid the behavior of some senior people becoming the biggest barrier to change.
- In the modern technology-augmented organization, learning will not be a separate activity, but a daily part of work with occasional focused learning on new specialist skills.

Referring to necessary skills of entrepreneurs to work within digital workplaces, the European Union team underlines team working, communication, entrepreneurship and innovation, and intercultural skills as as "necessary to drive creativity and innovation and cope with complexity and uncertainty in a fast-evolving workplace" [18, 19] and new skills for success at macrolevel, i.e., digital fluency referring to the ability to use digital tools and resources existing in companies to do a specific task at workplace and be successful. Another skill is the ability to deal with a change which significantly increases. Adaptability and cognitive flexibility help people to change the way when business needs shift.

It is known that information and data are used more frequently to achieve business goals, to make decisions, and to build strategies. The entrepreneurs should be able to asses and analyze data and information.

The EntreComp framework [20] outlined by the EU Commission, 2016, highlights that entrepreneurship should not be limited to those people setting up businesses but in all aspects of life. "Entrepreneurship is when you act upon opportunities and ideas and transform them into value for others. The value that is created can be financial, cultural, or social" [21].

Entrepreneurship requires innovation, knowledge about industry/market, and adaptability to different business. In order to be prepared for a successful career, it is necessary that students understand what means entrepreneurship and use entrepreneurial skills to achieve career goals.

Entrepreneurship education and training refers to the use of a variety of skills to develop a culture of entrepreneurship [21] aimed at the development of behavior, attitudes, and capacities that create value.

Entrepreneurship and entrepreneurship education have an important role in social and economic developments.

Addressing a global challenge such as youth employment requires global actions to prepare them for digital workplaces. It is known that young people are natives of the digital realm, relatively few possess the skills needed in the digital economy, and employers around the world are struggling to find skilled professionals equipped with the technical and soft skills they desire. In context of youth employment crisis and the job opportunities available for people equipped with digital skills, the question of skills training and improvement of entrepreneurship education therefore become central.

Referring learning methods within entrepreneurship education, Chinnoye and Akinlabi [22] affirm that this is most successful through active learning approaches such as experiential, team-based project, and problem-based approaches.

Learning the concept of global citizenship through global collaboration helps students to work cooperatively with people around the world; this is often necessary for their future jobs.

Small- and medium-sized enterprises (SMEs) are very important and numerous in Europe but small, and their resources are constrained. Because, their staffs need to adapt to digital transformation changes and learn new competences and skills relatively quickly; new learning/training opportunities for their staff have to be found, in addition to the daily operations of the company. Most entrepreneurship programs are targeted at new business owners or start-ups. There is, however, less research on the relationship between entrepreneurial skills of employees in existing SMEs, digital transformation, and innovation capacities in this context.

The European ongoing project Reinnovate with participation of the author focusses also on encouraging all employees in SMEs to develop an entrepreneurial mindset, increasing the chances of the small firm's survival within digital transformation. Project partners come from five European countries (www.iat.eu). Within the framework of the project, an intense cooperation with SMEs, research organizations, and representatives of higher education is crucial. The provision of a training program and model accreditation will assist employees in SMEs to find/create the knowledge required to become more competitive, to develop a digital culture of entrepreneurship, and to become more innovative.

Reinnovate uses results of the European project Archimedes and a survey with 150 European SMEs about their existing skills and corresponding training needs suitable also in connection with digital transformation. The methodology of Reinnovate is direct including interviews with guest entrepreneurs, recording videos, counseling, if possible, group discussions, active learning, learning from mistakes, process-oriented teaching, practical-operational teaching methods like starting a business, and role play [23].

The Reinnovate methodology should help to:

- Take into consideration the most common practices in SMEs which are informal learning and workplace learning.
- Take into consideration effective and preferred practices by employees to keep the employees moral at digital workplaces and extend their employability perspectives.
- Support the interorganizational level of workplace learning, i.e., regardless of life-cycle stages.

Four training modules will be developed and offered to SME staff, each module over the course of a 6 week period; if a learner takes all four modules, they will accumulate credits for a level 7 certificate award.

Module 1 about how to use workplace-oriented research to identify opportunities for new business includes also identifying opportunities from national and international perspective referring digital transformation, social, and cultural problems.

Module 2 has the objective to enable learners to gather and analyze the relevant data to allow them to implement a business opportunity or an innovative idea in connection with digital transformation. The module consists of three units, decision-making, gather data, and assess information.

Module 3 helps entrepreneurs to manage an own research project and module 4 to evaluate success and feature opportunities.

7. Conclusions

There is a consensus between researchers, educators, business observers, and entrepreneurs that digital transformation requires many changes, i.e., cultural and behavioral ones, and that entrepreneurship education and training could significantly increase the number and the quality of entrepreneurs working in SMEs or entering the digital economy.

This chapter has involved a review of different articles, the opinion of some practitioners, SMEs, and of the authors about how could be companies helped to solve some problems in connection with digital transformation.

Finally, it has been established that it is not easy to scale up business from a traditional small enterprise to one working successful in digital era; through new educational practices and a cooperation between educators, research, and industry entrepreneurial mindsets can be supported including behavioral changes and achieving competences like described in EntreComp and also new work-oriented research skills.

The program being developed within the Reinnovate project to develop entrepreneurial culture in SMEs through the provision of a suitable training program can contribute in this context.

The author will work further in collaboration with SMEs to make some adjustments toward transformational entrepreneurship and a sustainable socioeconomic development of SMEs in the digital era.

References

[1] Foegen M, Kaczmarek C. Organisation in einer digitalen Zeit: Ein Buch für die Gestaltung von reaktionsfähigen und schlanken Organisationen mit Hilfe von Scales Agile & Lean Mustern. Darmstadt: wibas GmbH; 2016

[2] Gassmann O. Digitale Transformation im Unternehmen gestalten: Geschäftsmodelle Erfolgsfaktoren Fallstudien Handlungsanweisungen. München: Hanser; 2016

[3] Keese C. Silicon Germany: Wie Wir Die Digitale Transformation Schaffen. Albrecht Knaus Verlag: München; 2016. ISBN 978-3-8135-0734-8

[4] Hoffmeister C, Yorck von B. Think New! 22 Erfolgsstrategien im digitalen Business. München: Carl Hanser Verlag; 2015. ISBN 978-3-446-44228-3

[5] Kruse P, Geißler P. Das vernetzte Unternehmen: Wie der Digital Workplace unsere Zusammenarbeit neu gestaltet. Norderstedt: BoD–Books on Demand; 2015. ISBN 978-3-7392-9620-3

[6] Menkens S. Beim Homeoffice ist Deutschland noch Entwicklungsland. Welt Online; 2016. https://www.welt.de/print/die_welt/politik/article155662124/Beim-Homeoffice-ist-Deutschland-noch-Entwicklungsland.html

[7] Schönefeld F. Social intranet—The new role of the intranet for the digital workplace. In: Wolf F, editor. Social Intranet—Promoting Communication—Sharing Knowledge—Working Together Efficiently. Carl Hanser Verlag: München; 2011. pp. 14-40. ISBN 3-446-42791-0

[8] Available from: https://www2.deloitte.com/content/dam/Deloitte/mx/Documents/human-capital/The_digital_workplace.pdf

[9] McConnell J. Trends für Intranet und digitalen Arbeitsplatz. In: Wolf F, editor. Social Intranet—Kommunikation fördern—Wissen teilen—Effizient zusammenarbeiten. Carl Hanser Verlag: München; 2011. ISBN 3-446-42791-0

[10] Available from: https://ec.europa.eu/info/sites/info/files/digitalworkplacestrategy2017.pdf

[11] Kampschroer K, Heerwagen J, Powell K. Creating and testing workplace strategy. California Management Review. 2017;**49**(2):19-137

[12] Springer T. Fundamentals of Workplace Strategy. Illinois: Kimball; 2011

[13] Savage AE. Workplace strategy: What it is and why you should care. Journal of Corporate Real Estate. 2005;7(3)

[14] EU. Skills Challenges in Europe [Internet]. 2016. Available from: http://skillspanorama.cedefop.europa.eu/sites/default/files/2016_Skills_Challenges_AH.pdf [Accessed: April 23, 2018]

[15] Behaviors That Spark Innovation and Drive Digital Transformation. Available from: https://playbook.amanet.org/training-articles-drive-digital-transformation/

[16] Available from: https://fowmedia.com/helping-your-employees-adapt-to-digital-transformation/

[17] Available from: https://postshift.com/bridging-the-digital-skills-gap-in-the-digital-workplace/

[18] David A, Hamburg I. Entrepreneurship and Entrepreneurial Skills in Europe: Examples to Improve Potential Entrepreneurial Spirit. Barbara Budrich: Opladen; 2017. ISBN 978-3-8474-0568-9

[19] Hamburg I, Vladut G, O'Brien E. Fostering skills for digital social innovations in entrepreneurship education. In: 8th Balkan Region Conference on Engineering and Business Education and 10th International Conference on Engineering and Business Education. Sibiu, Romania, October, 2017: Conference proceedings. Warsaw: de Gruyter Open; 2018

[20] Bacigalupo M, Kampylis P, Punie Y, Van den Brande G. EntreComp: The Entrepreneurship Competence Framework. Luxembourg: Publication Office of the European Union; 2016

[21] Available from: http://publications.jrc.ec.europa.eu/repository/bitstream/JRC101581/lfna27939enn.pdf

[22] Chinonye IM, Akinlabi M. Entrepreneurship curriculum and pedagogical challenges in captivating students' interest towards entrepreneurship education. Research Journal of Economics and Business Studies. 2014;**4**(1):1-11

[23] Hamburg I, Vladut G. Developing workplace research skills to bridge the innovation gap between university and industry. Advances in Social Sciences Research Journal. 2019;**6**(1):144-115

Chapter 3

Intellectual Capital Management and Economic Development in a Quasi-Information Society

Abstract

The study investigates intellectual capital management (ICM) and economic development in a quasi-information society such as Nigeria: a macro perspective. The study adopts the correlational research and secondary data were used. From a macro perspective, data used for the human capital development are literacy level, human development index, and Gini coefficient, among others. Structural capital include telecom rate to GDP, mobile cellular subscriptions, mobile cellular subscriptions (per 100 people), and Internet penetration and use rate. Also, economic development as the dependent variable represents the GDP. Data within the periods of 2005 and 2015 were used, and regression analysis and ANOVA were used to explain the relationships between variables of interest of the study. The findings showed that there was no significant increase in the development of the Nigeria economy in the periods of 2005–2015 and the ICM of the nation does not have significant impetus on the economy. The study recommends that for the level of development to increase in Nigeria, governments and policy makers should concentrate and seek strategies to provide policies that would enhance the IC of the nation such as the level of literacy, innovative research, and development, among others.

Keywords: ICM, macro ICM intervention, economic development, quasi-information society, intellectual capital management

1. Introduction

Economic development is an independent research field and of interest to nations and stakeholders of development at local and global levels. It has a long ancient origin and has been since a major point of attraction in the field of research and also in the practicality in developing economies of nations. Economic development could be said to be a multidimensional process that involves major changes in social structures, attitudes, and national institutions, acceleration of economic growth, reducing inequality, and the eradication of poverty [1, 2]. It has to be more concerned with enhancing the lives lived and the freedoms enjoyed. In the past, economic development of economies was captured from traditional perspectives as accumulation of wealth and includes macro variables such as poverty and per capita income levels, change in real GDP, and change in real GDP per capita, among others.

However, the concept has undergone various dynamics, and in the recent knowledge and information society, economic development has received ample transformation. A major transformation is the inclusion of the human development index which is a comprehensive measure of socioeconomic development into the measure of economic development [3, 4]. The development is no longer approached primarily as a process of capital accumulation but rather as a process of organizational change and transformation [5]. According to Todaro and Smith [2], the three major objectives of development include to increase the availability and widen the distribution of basic life-sustaining goods, to raise the levels and standards of living, and to expand the range of economic and social choices.

Recently, due to the dynamics of information and communication technology (ICT) innovations and the knowledge or information economy, economic development as a concept and practice has received tremendous leap and transformation. Jarboe and Alliance [6] noted that dynamics of ICT innovations and knowledge or information economy are revolutionizing the economies of nations. Also, in recent time of the information economy, productive capability is no longer completely dependent on capital and equipment but also has become a function of workers' skills, knowledge, and expertise—hence the intellectual capital of nations. This economy transformation was what made Stewart [7] to affirm that in the new information and knowledge economy, nations' economy stands on three pillars, and they include knowledge becoming what to buy, sell, and do; knowledge-based assets becoming more important to organizations and nations; and lastly, new technologies, innovations, and strategies are needed to explain the knowledge-based assets.

As information and knowledge become more important to development, organizations and nations have been restructured to better utilize human assets and the intellectual capital. Hamzah and Ismail [8] noted that intellectual capital is a major source of competitive advantage and economic development and there is evidence that success and productivity of nations can be partly explained by its intellectual capital. Intellectual capital includes the intellectual material that has been formalized, captured, and leveraged to create wealth by producing a higher-valued asset [9]. In recent modern economic development under globalization and increased competitiveness, intellectual capital is required. It is a major resource on demand, which leads to the generation of new ideas and creative approaches to existing economic processes [4].

Makarov [10] and Lukicheva [11] noted that assessing intellectual capital is a complex process because of its individual, organizational, national and global functioning among economies of nations. Many studies such as Mavridis and Kyrmizoglou [12], Ahmad and Mushraf [13], Fadaei et al. [14], Ogbo et al. [15], Saeed et al. [16], and Rehman et al. [17], among others, have tend to approach intellectual capital from the micro level. However, few studies have given attention to intellectual capital from the macro and economy level. From the micro level which holds the individual and organizational view, intellectual capital management can be grouped into three components; these include human, structural, and customer capital. According to Fadaei et al. [14], human capital is all the abilities that include attitude, skill, knowledge, creativity, existing mental knowledge, and people and managers' experience of an organization. Structural capital includes the events and interactions among people in the organization and what remains in organization when people leave it. Customer capital also known as the relational capital refers to all the formal and informal relations of an organization with external beneficiaries and their understandings about organization and also exchange of information between them and the organization.

At the macro level, human development index which is a major development in intellectual capital measurement has an ultra-integral character. Konovalova et al.

[4] noted that there are three indicators of national population life quality that are summed up in human development index and include welfare level, expressed in figures per capita income; health level, expressed in life expectancy rate; and education level, measured by the literacy level and the share of young people that are getting higher education in higher education institutions. In summary, measuring human development index cuts across the economic, environmental, and cultural factors of people life.

From the studies of Levashov and Rutkevieh [18] and Konovalova et al. [4], the macro level of intellectual capital management was broken down into its micro constituents. The human capital covers the educational and social well-being potential indicators. Structural capital caters for the indicators of scientific potential and the indicators of information and communication components. Consumer capital captures the indicators of relationship capital. Due to lack of data access at the macro level on the relational capital components, only the components of the human and structural capital would be considered for this study. Adapting the work of Konovalova et al. [4], literacy level, human development index, Gini coefficient, unemployment rate, poverty rate, and growth rate would be used to capture the human capital development indices. For the structural capital, telecom rate to GDP, mobile cellular subscriptions, mobile cellular subscriptions (per 100 people), and Internet penetration and use rate would be used. The GDP would stand as the dependent variable of the study which signifies economy development of the nation. These variables used to capture intellectual capital management at the macro level are based on the work of Konovalova et al. [4] that intellectual capital is developed in two ways: education which is the skilled personnel training and involvement of foreign specialists.

The need to focus on quasi-information society is hinged on the fact that development of economy changes with transformation of the society and this differs across nations. According to the Lewis model of development [19], at the lowest level of development, traditional or unskilled labor is surplus while skilled labor is few. According to Rostow's model of development [20], different countries are at different stages of development. The need to close the wide gap and development dividing between developed and developing countries made the General Assembly of the United Nations in September 2015 to adopt the 2030 Agenda for Sustainable Development and developed a 17 Sustainable Development Goals (SDGs) agenda to drive equal development. Built upon the principle of "leaving no nation behind," the SDGs include reducing poverty, reducing hunger, ensuring good health and well-being, quality education, gender equality, providing clean water and sanitation, affordable and clean energy, ensuring a decent work and economic growth, industry, innovation and infrastructure, reduced inequality, providing sustainable cities and communities, responsible consumption and production, climate action, enhancing life below water, life on land, peace and justice strong institutions, and partnerships to achieve the goal. From broader and global perspectives, education is the pivot on which other SDGs' attainment rests. It operates twofold aspects in the development of nation toward attaining SDGs: first, it is seen as a goal in itself, and second, it is also a means for attaining all the other SDGs [21–23]. Thus, it is an integral part of sustainable development of nations as well as a major enabler for the attainment of other SDGs. A better and improved education system could have positive impact on the development and hence on the attainment of SDGs in Africa such as Nigeria. Shettima [24] noted that Africa which includes Nigeria plays important aspect in SDGs' attainment. This is because success in attainment of the SDGs can be achieved if and only if the SDGs succeed in Africa due to the wide gap and development divide that occur between developed and developing countries such as Africa which Nigeria is part.

Meanwhile juxtaposing the Lewis and Rostow models, the reason for the disparities between the developed and developing economies is not farfetched. In the developed economies such as the UK, the USA, Canada, Japan, and China, among others, the development has elastically reached every nook and cranny of their economies, and development activities are controlled by the information economy. However, in developing countries such as Nigeria, there may still be a high level of underdevelopment, and if at all the nation is developed, it is skewed: while some areas experienced the development syndrome, other areas are lagging behind development. This fact is supported by the studies of Blanchfield and Lawson [25], Easterly [26], and Global Monitoring Report by the International Bank for Reconstruction and Development, the World Bank [45], that African countries which include Nigeria experienced setback and failure in the attainment of major development strategies such as the Millennium Development Goals (MDGs).

This is because most developing economies are experiencing a quasi-information society. A quasi-information society refers to a false information society that has the likeliness and the form of information society but does not fully rely on information for their growth and development due to lack of skills and infrastructural challenges. According to Becla [27], quasi-information society occurs because of lack of accessibility, availability and use of ICTs, high transaction costs, low skill and literacy level, and lack of mechanism for quick diffusion and dissemination and use of information. A clear observation of the major problems experienced in Nigeria with respect to the information and knowledge economy shows that Nigeria operates a quasi-information society. In such information society, intellectual capital management could be hampered, thereby affecting the economic activities and development of the nation. In some economies such as the developed economies, where the society is a pure information economy, the intellectual capital management could be high and higher than those of the quasi-information society. This could also create an impetus on the economic activities and development of the nations.

According to Harrod-Domar growth model, output which in this study is economic development is a function of capital. The concept of capital has received a new approach in the information and knowledge economy. In the past and traditional era and in managerial economics, capital was referred to as credit or money and is known to be a factor of production alongside labor and land. However, in recent times, the elasticity of capital has extended beyond this and has included intellectual capital. Therefore, complexity could be noticed with the concept of "capital" especially in the present information and knowledge economy. This made Nitzan [28] to affirm that the concept of capital remains ambiguous and controversial. However Barman [29] noted that a distinction needs to be drawn between the traditional and information- or knowledge-related capital. Hence, going by Harrod-Domar growth model, economic development is a function of nations' intellectual capital management. This is the basis of this study. Hence, the main objective of this study is to investigate the relationship between intellectual capital management and economic development of Nigeria: a quasi-information society.

2. Previous studies

Economic development has received great attention from scholars, governments, policy makers, and other stakeholders of the development of nations. According to Robbins [30], the essence of economic development is conceived as the rupture of existing patterns of economic relationships—which could emanate from the normal circular flow of statistical analysis. Feldman et al. [31] noted that economic development is often confused with the more easily measured economic growth. Kwong [3] defined economic growth as simply a rise in GDP or GDP per capital, while economic development is encompassing and is a broad concept which economic growth is just a part. Other important developmental dimensions or indices are included in the definition of economic development. Schafer [1] defined economic development as a dynamic process over time, and it makes good sense to employ tools of dynamic macroeconomics.

In a more generalized form, Todaro and Smith [2] defined economic development as a multidimensional process which encompassed major transformations in social structure, popular and important attitudes, and national institutions, as well as the acceleration of economic growth, the reduction of inequality, and the eradication of poverty. From this, it could be observed that economy can be growing but it is not developing. Other economic development indices are human development index, poverty, and literacy level, among others. To this end, Mackintosh et al. [32] argued that it is very possible for the HDI of nations to decline while the measure of GDP increases. They further noted that this scenario is common among developing economies which Nigeria is a part.

This is because, according to Brown [33], in Keynesian economics, individuals, organizations, and institutions at the micro level cannot increase their productivity but need government interventions. These government interventions may include adopting discretionary economic policy which requires that governments make policy changes on the basis of its judgment of the current and future economic circumstances of the nation. Hence, the government is seen as a major agent for economic development and transformation. Also, such policies should address and be targeted toward the interest of the public at the micro level which could create impetus at the macro level. This is because according to Keynesian economics, the aggregate of the micro level determines the economic development indices at the macro level. However, Jarboe and Alliance [6] stated that economic development strategies and practice must adapt to new economic landscape such as intellectual capital management of the nation.

The importance of intellectual capital (IC) has greatly increased in recent times due to the major shift of economies toward the knowledge- or information-driven society [17]. Previous studies on the relationship between intellectual capital management and performance such as Boedker et al. [34], Subramaniam and Youndt [35], Bramhandkar et al. [36], Asiaei and Jusoh [37], and [17], among others, have approached it from the micro level using the individual and organizational acquired data to explain their relationships. However, in recent information economy and society era, attention needs to be drawn to the macro importance of intellectual capital management to nation's economy. Very few studies have addressed this and such study is lacking in developing nations study.

In recent information and knowledge economy, the value of any country is a function of their knowledge and intellectual capital [38]. Marcin [39] and Rusu-Tanasa [40] noted that intellectual capital is a major key factor of socioeconomic development of regions and countries. Mercier-Laurent [41] in trying to investigate intellectual capital management and the economy revealed that the focus on intellectual capital in any economy is due to the fact that it is the root of all organizations' activities which are directly contributors to the nation's economy or GDP. Pachura [42] noted that it aids structural and economic transformation in any nation. Hence, Makarov [43] has opined that intellectual capital is a major indicator of sustainable development of any country.

However, due to intangible nature, its effect on the economy has not been given much attention in developing countries. Intellectual capital forms the basis of the success of the development of countries which calls for the right way of managing the intangible wealth and assets such as the intellectual capital in connection with the tangible ones [41]. Earlier scholars such as Schultz [44] and Becker [45] have noted the effect of education, training, and literacy level which are important intellectual capital indices on economic development of any nation. Drucker [46] pointed out that knowledge which is a constituent of intellectual capital is a primary resource and capital for overall economic development having higher value than the traditional land, capital, and labor in the development of economies. Hence, there have been global attention especially among the developed nations on the role of intellectual capital productivity growth and competitiveness and consequently in its contribution to the sustainable long-term economic development of nation [41]. Also, Mercier-Laurent [41] has also noted that communication technology and innovations are also major intellectual capital that could influence economic development of nations.

Despite the significant value of intellectual capital on the development at the macro level, measuring IC could lead to confusion. This is because most of the studies have addressed it as and at a micro level and at the macro level; its measurement becomes a challenge. According to Makarov [43] and Konovalova et al. [4], at the macro level, national population life quality variables such as the human development index which is captured by welfare level, expressed in figures per capita income, health level expressed in life expectancy rate, and education level, measured by the literacy level and the share of young people that are getting higher education in higher education institutions, among others, are major macro indices for measuring intellectual capital of any nation. Hence, this present study adapts these variables to capture the intellectual capital management at macro level and its effect on the Nigeria economy using the gross domestic product of the nation.

In addition, a major novelty in this study is its link with the failure in the attainment of the past MDGs and with the likelihood of success or failure of the attainment of the recent SDGs in Nigeria. It has been proven beyond measure that Africa has experienced a perfect elastic setbacks and failures in the attainment of global development strategies, the Millennium Development Goals (MDGs), not excluded ([25, 26, 47]). However, recently, the General Assembly of the United Nations in September 2015 adopted the 2030 Agenda for Sustainable Development and developed a 17 Sustainable Development Goals (SDGs) agenda to drive equal development. From the SDGs, education is the pivot on which sustainable development rests, and it is also the pivot of the ICM of the country. To this end, if Nigeria must have success in the attainment of the SDGs, there is need to draw attention and reposition its ICM system within the center of quality education. Hence, this study focuses and tends to establish the relationship between ICM and economic development toward driving the attainment of SDGs in Nigeria.

3. Methodology

The study adopts the correlational research and secondary data were used. Adapting and juxtaposing the Lewis model of development [19] and Rostow's model of development [20], different countries are at different stages of development, and the lowest level of development is the traditional level where there is a high elasticity of unskilled labor. At the lowest level of development, factors of importance seem to fit into the traditional system, while above the lowest levels, considerations of factors are used as major developmental indices change. According to Harrod-Domar growth model, output which in this study is economic development is a function of capital [48]. The concept "capital has been said to be subjective especially in recent times of information economy [28, 29]. In the past, emphasis was drawn to agrarian development, population increase, available of credit, agricultural labor, poverty level, etc. However, in recent times, there has been transformation and extension of this variables of interest. Transformation in the sense that some may remain unchanged while others undergo transformation. With regards to extension, other important variables were added to suit the developmental stages of nations. In recent global development, Makarov [43] and Konovalova et al. [4], among others, have argued the place of intellectual capital management on the development and include variables such as human development index which is captured by welfare level, expressed in figures per capita income, and education level, measured by the literacy level and the share of young people that are getting higher education in higher education institutions, among others. However, there is need to see this in the Nigerian economy, hence, the need for this study.

Due to the lack of access to important data, the data employed in this study include the literacy level, human development index, Gini coefficient, unemployment rate, poverty rate, and growth rate which capture the human capital development indices. For the structural capital, telecom rate to GDP, mobile cellular subscriptions, mobile cellular subscriptions (per 100 people), and Internet penetration and use rate would be used. Also, the GDP stands as the dependent variable of the study which signifies economy development of the nation. Data within the periods of 2005 and 2015 were used so as to obtain an equal number of substantial information to use for the study and were provided in **Table 1**. The study used the regression analysis and ANOVA as its data analysis method to explain the relationships between variables of interest of the study.

The model specification is provided below:

$$Y = \beta_0 + X_1\beta_1 + X_2\beta_2 + X_3\beta_3 + X_n\beta_n + e_i \quad (1)$$

where X_s are the independent variables of the study which is used to capture intellectual capital management in Nigeria, B_s represents the coefficients of X_s and represents the significant changes of Y (dependent variable) with increase in one unit of X_s, and e_i represents the error term.

4. Results

A keen observation on the information on **Table 1** shows that there is no substantial increase in the human development index (HDI) of Nigeria. There is however an increase in mobile subscription from 13.4 and steadily grows to 83.2% in 2015 in Nigeria economy. The same was applicable in the mobile phone subscription per 100 people data. The result shows that there was no significant growth in the nations' Gini coefficient but there was a stochastic and haphazard movement of the development. Also, there was no substantial growth rate in the Nigeria economy. There was also no significant reduction in the nations' poverty rate, and there was a stochastic and haphazard movement of poverty rate. The increase level of unemployment rate in Nigeria economy is a major concern on **Table 1**; it could be evident that unemployment rate increases drastically from one digit to two digits from 2005 to 2015. Also, literacy level reduced from 2005 to 2015, and this also constitutes a major concern on **Table 1**. Also, there was a substantial increase of Internet use rate in the Nigeria economy from 2005 to 2015. In addition, the rate of telecommunication contribution to the Nigeria economy is very infinitesimal, and no increase is felt in this sector. Furthermore, Nigeria economy also recorded a substantial growth

Year	X1	X2	X3	X4	X5	X6	X7	X8	X9	X10	Y (in billion naira)
2005	0.466	13.4	13.38	0.4882	6.51	58.2	2.9	67.7	3.5	0.05	22,269.98
2006	0.477	22.7	22.66	0.457	6.03	58.5	5.8	78.6	5.5	0.06	28,662.47
2007	0.481	27.6	27.59	0.429	6.50	59.3	4.9	64.9	6.8	0.07	32,995.38
2008	0.487	41.9	41.90	0.513	6.41	62.4	5.8	51.1	15.9	0.08	39,157.88
2009	0.492	48.3	48.26	0.43	7.0	65.2	11.8	51.1	20.0	0.10	44,285.56
2010	0.500	55.1	55.05	0.447	6.7	69.0	22.0	56.9	24.0	0.11	54,612.26
2011	0.507	58.4	58.43	0.405	6.9	60.0	24.0	51.1	28.4	0.10	62,980.40
2012	0.514	67.4	67.41	0.362	7.2	35.2	27.0	51.1	32.8	0.10	71,713.94
2013	0.521	74.1	74.05	0.41	6.4	33.1	25.0	55.2	38.0	0.10	80,092.56
2014	0.526	78.7	78.75	0.399	6.3	60.0	24.0	59.2	42.7	0.11	89,043.62
2015	0.527	83.2	83.25	0.387	2.8	60.0	29.0	59.6	45.1	0.12	94,144.96

Source: Sourced and compiled by the author from various secondary sources such as the CBN, World Bank, National Bureau of Statistics, Internet World Stats, and Internet Live Stats, among others.
Note: X1 represents human development index; X2 represents mobile cellular subscriptions; X3 represents mobile cellular subscriptions per 100 people; X4 represents Gini coefficient; X5 represents growth rate; X6 represents poverty rate; X7 represents unemployment rate; X8 represents literacy level; X9 represents Internet use rate; X10 represents telecom rate to GDP; Y represents the GDP.
Also, some of these data sets at one period or the other were found to be missing, and in order to cater for these missing value, the author used a mean strategy between the lower and upper period to obtain the middle data. At some other time, the author simply used the previous year data where applicable.

Table 1.
Selected macro intellectual capital indices and national GDP of Nigeria.

in its GDP. Despite the growth in the GDP of Nigeria, the information in **Table 1** shows that there was no significant development in major intellectual capital indices of the Nigeria economy in the periods of 2005 to 2015.

The result of the regression analysis was provided in **Table 2**. From the result, the adjusted R square for the regression analysis was 0.99, which shows a better goodness of fit of the model.

From **Table 2**, the results shows that, of all the variables of interest in this study used to represent intellectual capital at the macro level, none was found to be significant ($p > 0.05$). Also, from the beta coefficients of the independent variables, most of the coefficients were negative (mobile subscription per 100 people, Gini coefficient, growth rate, poverty rate, unemployment rate, and literacy rate). Only few had negative coefficients such as human development index (HDI), Internet use rate, and telecom rate to GDP. Also, the model deleted the mobile subscription data because of high level of collinearity between mobile subscription and mobile subscription per 100 people. A keen observation on this result shows the low standard of these indices in Nigeria. Even though Nigeria is developing and recorded substantial increase in some of these indices, its effect on the economy is not felt. Also, the result also shows the quasi-information society level of the nation as the rate of telecom increases and other intellectual capital developments have not create a substantial impetus on the economy. The result of the study depicts that though the nation is big, it has little or no internal economic indices that would create impetus to the nation development. The joint effect of the intellectual capital management on the nation's GDP is provided in **Table 3**.

Coefficients					
Model	Unstandardized coefficients		Standardized coefficients	t	Sig.
	B	Std. error	Beta		
Constant	−460044.760	473238.599		−0.972	0.509
HDI	1075564.924	1023024.189	0.899	1.051	0.484
Mobile subscription per 100 people	−831.564	1616.293	−0.782	−0.514	0.697
Gini coefficient	−8766.881	54633.128	−0.016	−0.160	0.899
Growth rate	−1324.654	1204.995	−0.063	−1.099	0.470
Poverty rate	−33.921	275.659	−0.016	−0.123	0.922
Unemployment rate	−56.848	450.897	−0.023	−0.126	0.920
Literacy rate	−13.369	235.757	−0.005	−0.057	0.964
Internet use rate	1357.304	920.721	0.810	1.474	0.379
Telecom rate to GDP	57605.621	513440.948	0.052	0.112	0.929

Dependent variable: GDP.
Source: Secondary data analysis, 2018.

Table 2.
Regression analysis result.

ANOVA[b]						
Model		Sum of squares	df	Mean square	F	Sig.
1	Regression	6.252E9	9	6.946E8	99.325	0.078[a]
	Residual	6993498.081	1	6993498.081		
	Total	6.259E9	10			

[a]*Predictors: (constant), telecom rate to GDP, poverty rate, growth rate, literacy rate, Gini coefficient, unemployment rate, Internet use rate, HDI, mobile phone subscription per 100 people.*
[b]*Dependent variable: GDP.*

Table 3.
Joint effect of the intellectual capital management on the nation's GDP.

The result in **Table 3** shows that the impetus of intellectual capital management is not felt on the nation's GDP. This provides a challenging situation in the nation which needs to be given attention when development at the global level is put into consideration. In the recent global information economy or society, intellectual capital should have tremendous effect on the economy; however, the case of Nigeria is different.

5. Discussions of findings

The findings of this study support the work of Mackintosh et al. [32] that it is very possible for the HDI of nations to decline while the measure of GDP increases, which is a most common phenomenon of developing countries such as Nigeria. Also, if according to Hoff and Stiglitz [5], Jarboe and Alliance [6], Stewart [7],

Hamzah and Ismail [8], and Konovalova et al. [4] that the development of nations has moved from the traditional economic indices such as population growth, GDP, etc. to the intellectual capital and the information economy contribution to GDP, it is evident that Nigeria is not developing. Also, going by the well-known Lewis model of development, if literacy level has not had impetus on the economic growth of Nigeria, it is then a fact that most of the population of Nigeria still operate at the lowest level of development where there is a high unskilled labor and low skilled labor. Hence, going by the work of Becla [27], and the result of this study, Nigeria is a quasi-information society due to the fact that the major intellectual capital indices used in the study have not transformed into economic growth and development. This could also transcend to major sectors of the economy hence affecting their development and economic activities in the nation. This could further lead to threaten the development and sustainable development of the sectors and in extension of the economy in the long run.

Also, going by the work of Edvinsson and Bounfour [38], Nigeria would be said to have a lower value at the global development levels because of the fact that its intellectual capital has not create an impetus on the economic development. Hence, the development in Nigeria is questionable as confirmed by the work of Mercier-Laurent [41], and there may be no structural and economic development as affirmed by Pachura [42], and hence, the sustainability of the economy would be a major problem as attested by Makarov [43]. Consequently, one could say that the future of the nation is questionable and needs urgent attention if it must develop and survive in the recent global information economy and society and transformation.

6. Conclusion and recommendations

In conclusion, in Nigeria economy, intellectual capital management has not created an impetus on the economy of the nation; hence, it is operating in a quasi-information economy (false information economy). In addition, this could constitute a major challenge against the development of the nation and also the development of major sectors of the economy. This could be one of the major reasons for the setbacks and failures in the attainment of major development strategies such as the Millennium Development Goals (MDGs). Also, the practical relevance of this study is to show that, if the ICM of the nation is not given wide recognition and repositioned and developed toward enhancing quality education in Nigeria, there is a high propensity that Nigeria will eventually experience failure and setbacks in the attainment of recent SDGs, hence, lagging behind neighboring developing countries and developed countries who put into recognition and positioned their ICM for development. To this end, the study recommends that:

i. If Nigeria must rise above the present level of development and meet up with global development indices, there is need for the governments and policy makers to concentrate and seek strategies to provide policies that would enhance the intellectual capital of the nation such as the human development index, level of educational development, and level of literacy and unemployment, among others.

ii. Also, attention should be drawn to the need to increase budget allocation to intellectual capital development of the nation and also to its major actors such as skilled workers in the primary, secondary, and tertiary education system, research and development institutes, and other organizations committed to research and education activities in the nation.

iii. The governments and other providers of development programs should deem it fit to see to it that major programs provided to the nation have significant impact on the nation and its development. To this end, there should be need for periodical review and assessments of such major programs to see how effective they are to the economy.

iv. Also, innovative policies addressing users' needs that could create substantial impetus of the telecom industry on the Nigeria economy should be introduced and provided so that the nation could enjoy the benefits of this sector with respect to development.

v. There should also be the need to increase employment in the nation, and the governments should encourage and provide access to business development and a better environment for both local and foreign investors in the Nigeria economy.

vi. To this end, special consideration should be given to the intellectual capital management of nations at macro level and hence should attract future research which could capture more variables of the ICM to observe how it has affected the attainment of SDGs in Nigeria. Also, other African countries can also embark on such research focus; hence, this could help Africa such as Nigeria to reposition their ICM for attainment of development strategies such as future SDGs.

References

[1] Schafer A. Economic Development: Theory and Policy, Course Work; University of Leipzig, Institute of Theoretical Economics. 2013. Available from: https://www.wifa.uni-leipzig.de/fileadmin/user_upload/itvwl-vwl/makro/Lehre/ws/de/DE_T&P_1.pdf

[2] Todaro MP, Smith SC. Economic Development. Harlow: Addison Wesley; 2009. pp. 49-56, 485, 486

[3] Kwong C. Macroeconomics Series (3): Economic Growth and Development, Knowledge Enrichment Seminar for NSS Economics Curriculum. School of Arts and Social Sciences: The Open University of Hong Kong; 2011. Available from: https://www.edb.gov.hk/attachment/tc/curriculum-development/kla/pshe/references-and-resources/economics/Economic%20Growth%20and%20Development(File%205.2).pdf

[4] Konovalova M, Kuzmina O, Mikhailov A, Hansevyarov R, Persteneva N. Intellectual capital as a key factor in the economic development of the region. Global Media Journal. 2016;**14**:27. Available from: http://www.globalmediajournal.com/open-access/intellectual-capital-as-a-key-factor-in-the-economic-development-of-the-region.php?aid=82614

[5] Hoff K. Stiglitz JE. Modern Economic Theory and Development, The World Bank. 2000. Available from: http://www8.gsb.columbia.edu/faculty/jstiglitz/sites/jstiglitz/files/2000_Modern_Economic_Theory_and_Development.pdf

[6] Jarboe KP, Alliance A. Knowledge Management As an Economic Development Strategy, Reviews of Economic Development Literature and Practice: No. 7, U.S. Economic Development Administration. 2001. Available from: http://citeseerx.ist.psu.edu/viewdoc/download?doi=10.1.1.460.3136&rep=rep1&type=pdf

[7] Stewart T. The Wealth of Knowledge: Intellectual Capital and Twenty-First Century Organization. London: Nicholas Brealey Publishing Limited; 2002

[8] Hamzah N, Ismail MN. The importance of intellectual capital management in the knowledge-based economy. Contemporary Management Research. 2008;**4**(3):237-262

[9] Stewart TA. Intellectual Capital: The New Wealth of Organizations. New York: Bantam Doubleday Dell Publishing Group; 1997

[10] Makarov AM. Assessment of Intellectual Capital. Management. Theory and Practice. Izhevsk: Bravado Print; 2003

[11] Lukicheva LA. Management of Intellectual Capital (Tutorial). Moscow: Omega-L; 2007

[12] Mavridis D, Kyrmizoglou GP. Intellectual capital performance drivers in the Greek banking sector. Management Research News. 2005;**28**(5):43-62

[13] Ahmad S, Mushraf AM. The Relationship Between Intellectual Capital and Business Performance: An Empirical Study in Iraqi Industry, International Conference on Management and Artificial Intelligence IPEDR. Vol. 6. Bali, Indonesia: IACSIT Press; 2011. Available from: http://www.ipedr.com/vol6/20-A10012.pdf

[14] Fadaei M, Taleghani M, Noghlebari ES. The effect of intellectual capital on organization's financial performance. Interdisciplinary Journal of Contemporary Research in Business. 2013;5(6):275-286

[15] Ogbo A, Ezeobi J, Ituma A. Impact of intellectual capital on organisational performance: Evidence from Nigeria banking sector. Journal of Research in National Development. 2013;**11**(2):249-254. Available from: www.ajol.info/journals/jorind

[16] Saeed R, Sami A, Lodhi RN, Iqbal A. Intellectual capital and organizational performance: An empirical study in telecom sector of Pakistan. Middle-East Journal of Scientific Research. 2013;**18**(4):517-523. DOI: 10.5829/idosi.mejsr.2013.18.4.11716

[17] Rehman W, Rehman CA, Ilyas M. Linking intellectual capital and knowledge management with organizational performance: A meta-review analysis. Arabian Journal of Business and Management Review. 2015;**5**(2):63-73. Available from: http://www.arabianjbmr.com/pdfs/KD_VOL_5_2/6.pdf

[18] Levashov VK, Rutkevich MS. About the concept of intellectual capacity and its assessment methods. Science Studies. 2000;**1**:49-65

[19] Lewis WA. Economic development with unlimited supplies of labour. The Manchester School. 1954;**22**(2):139-191

[20] Rostow WW. The Stages of Economic Growth: A Non-communist Manifesto. Cambridge: Cambridge University Press; 1960

[21] Bokova I. Why Education is the Key to Sustainable Development, Project Syndicate, World Economic Forum. 2015. Available from: https://www.weforum.org/agenda/2015/05/why-education-is-the-key-to-sustainable-development/

[22] United Nations Educational, Scientific and Cultural Organization (UNESCO). Education for Sustainable Development Goals: Learning Objectives. 2017. Available from: http://unesdoc.unesco.org/images/0024/002474/247444e.pdf

[23] United Nations Educational, Scientific and Cultural Organization (UNESCO). Education for Sustainable Development. 2018. Available from: https://en.unesco.org/themes/education-sustainable-development

[24] Shettima K. Achieving the sustainable development goals in Africa: Call for a paradigm shift. African Journal of Reproductive Health. 2016;**20**(3):19. Available from: http://www.bioline.org.br/pdf?rh16030

[25] Blanchfield L, Lawson ML. The Millennium Development Goals: The September 2010 U.N. High-level Meeting, Congressional Research Service, Prepared for Members and Committees of Congress. 2010. Available from: https://fas.org/sgp/crs/row/R41410.pdf

[26] Easterly W. Was Africa set up to fail on the Millennium Development Goals? 2010. Available from: http://www.nyudri.org/aidwatcharchive/2010/06/was-africa-set-up-to-fail-on-the-millennium-development-goals

[27] Becla A. Information society and knowledge-based economy—Development level and the main barriers—Some remarks. Economics & Sociology. 2012;**5**(1):125-132

[28] Nitzan J. Differential accumulation: Toward a new political economy of capital. Review of International Political Economy. 1998;**5**(2):169-217

[29] Barman S. The micro and macroeconomics of information. In: Annual Review of Information Sciences and Technology. USA: Information Today, Inc; 2006. p. 40

[30] Robbins L. The Theory of Economic Development in the History of Economic Thought Being the

Chichele Lectures for 1966, Revised and Extended. 1966. Available from: https://mises.org/sites/default/files/The%20Theory%20of%20Economic%20Development_2.pdf

[31] Feldman M, Hadjimichael T, Kemeny T, Lanahan L. Economic Development: A Definition and Model for Investment. 2014. Available from: https://www.eda.gov/files/tools/research-reports/investment-definition-model.pdf

[32] Mackintosh M, Brown V, Cortello N, Dawson G, Thompson G, Trgg A. Economics of Changing Economies. Milton Keynes: International Thompson Business Press, The Open University; 1996

[33] Brown V. Chapter 16: Changing economies and economic theory. In: Mackintosh M, Brown V, Cortello N, Dawson G, Thompson G, Trgg A, editors. Economics of Changing Economies. Milton Keynes: International Thompson Business Press, The Open University; 1996

[34] Boedker C, Guthrie J, Cuganesan S. The strategic significance of human capital information in annual reporting. Journal of Human Resource Costing and Accounting. 2005;**8**(2):722

[35] Subramaniam M, Youndt MA. The influence of intellectual capital on the types of innovative capabilities. Academy of Management Journal. 2005;**48**(3):450-463

[36] Bramhandkar A, Erickson S, Applebee I. Intellectual capital and organizational performance: An empirical study of the pharmaceutical industry. Electronic Journal of Knowledge Management. 2007;**5**(4):357-362

[37] Asiaei K, Jusoh R. A multidimensional view of intellectual capital: The impact on organizational performance. Management Decision. 2015;**53**(3):668-697. DOI: 10.1108/MD-05-2014-0300

[38] Edvinsson L, Bounfour A. Assessing national and regional value creation. Measuring Business Excellence. 2004;**8**(1):55-61. DOI: 10.1108/13683040410524748

[39] Marcin K. Intellectual capital as a key factor of socio-economic development of regions and countries, international economic conference of Sibiu 2013 post crisis economy: Challenges and opportunities, IECS 2013. Procedia Economics and Finance. 2013;**6**:288-295

[40] Rusu-Tanasa M. Intellectual capital a strategic factor of socio-economic development of regions and countries, 22nd International Economic Conference-IECS 2015 "Economic Prospects in the Context of Growing Global and Regional Interdependencies", IECS 2015. Procedia Economics and Finance. 2015;**27**:369-374

[41] Mercier-Laurent E. Managing Intellectual Capital in Knowledge Economy, Position Papers of the 2014 Federated Conference on Computer Science and Information Systems. Vol. 3. ACSIS; 2014. pp. 253-257. DOI: 10.15439/2014F476

[42] Pachura P. Regional Cohesion. Effectiveness of Network Structures. Berlin, Heidelberg: Physica-Verlag Springer Company; 2010

[43] Makarov P. Intellectual capital as an indicator of a sustainable development. Journal of Sustainable Development. 2010;**3**(3):85-90. Available from: https://pdfs.semanticscholar.org/6cfa/b57b70b94ec3587866b749dfdc94ab91dbb1.pdf

[44] Schultz T. Investment in Human Capital. The American Economic Review. 1961;**51**(1):1-17

[45] Becker GS. Human Capital: A Theoretical and Empirical Analysis, with Special Reference to Education. Chicago: University of Chicago Press; 1964

[46] Drucker P. The New Society of Organization, Harvard Business Review; September-October 1992; 1992

[47] The International Bank for Reconstruction and Development. The MDGs after the Crisis, The World Bank. 2010. Available from: http://siteresources.worldbank.org/INTGLOMONREP2010/Resources/6911301-1271698910928/GMR2010WEB.pdf

[48] Harrod RF. Towards a Dynamic Economics, Some Recent Developments of Economic Theory and their Application to Policy. London: Macmillan; 1948

Chapter 4

Big Data and Strategy: Theoretical Foundations and New Opportunities

Abstract

The digitization of products, processes, and business models—and the corresponding explosion of big data—has led to an evolution within business organizations. Reaching far beyond information technology's traditional role in business strategy, the implications of this big data phenomenon are considered through an exploration into what big data is, how it is currently being used by existing firms, and how it factors into strategic thinking. As different organizational approaches have developed toward big data, we use resource-based theory and organizational learning as anchoring perspectives to link this phenomenon with traditional strategic management. We also identify four avenues for future scholarship as the nature of business moves increasingly digital.

Keywords: big data, strategy, theory, resource-based view, organizational learning

1. Introduction

The global digitization of products, processes, and business models is reshaping the very nature of business. Entire industries are rapidly evolving as more firms take advantage of increases in clicks, sensors, and technological innovation. Due to advancing technological infrastructure and the advent of the so-called "Internet of Things," companies continue to innovate, finding new ways to capture and leverage ever-expanding amounts of data. With storage costs becoming increasingly affordable and the lure of new (or fear of missed) opportunities, more and more firms are integrating information technology (IT) planning into their strategic thinking.

Given these advances, firms are increasingly aware that every person (or device) is a potential *data generator*. Consumers leave an extensive digital trail as they go about their daily lives. Whether shopping for groceries or fashion, traveling on a daily commute, or mulling around in their own home, individuals' activities are generating consumable data. Connected devices are also doing more to communicate with one another, including the tracking and transfer of data to value chain partners.

In a similar manner, organizations have become *information processors*. They are making considerable investments into analytic capabilities and data science talent to exploit opportunities presented by digitization, seeking to create or capture value and develop competitive advantage. In secrecy or in plain sight, organizations are working diligently to obtain consumer data and attempting to interpret and apply it to their strategic decision making [1].

The concept of "big data"—large data volumes generated and made available on the internet and through current digital media ecosystems [2]—has heralded increasing attention as having important implications for growth, profitability, and survival. Strategy theorists and practitioners alike are currently struggling to understand big data's role in the digitization of business models and how big data initiatives influence functional decisions within organizations, shape entirely new markets, and establish unique new strategies for organizations that break down traditional barriers of existing industries [3].

Executives across a multitude of industries are plunging resources into big data projects with aims to better monitor, measure, and manage their businesses. These strategic leaders are leveraging information to exploit current markets with incremental innovations that influence marketing efforts, product selection, and operational processes. Yet a small number of organizations employ a different role for data within their strategic approach. These firms recognize that information is at the core of most modern radical innovations [4]; their approach is resulting in the unforeseen entry into existing market spaces using innovative business models, the creation of new markets, and the invalidation of long-standing assumptions in traditional strategic thinking.

Scholars in the field of strategic management have an opportunity to play a major role in developing an understanding of how the emergence of big data is changing the nature of competition. Though the conversation has begun, management scholars have yet to build theory around the role of big data in the world of modern day corporate- and business-level strategy. As noted in recent research, big data has the promise of bringing new theories and practices to the organizational sciences, and is likely to play a central role in the development of new strategic approaches to firm governance and leadership [5]. We add to this promising literature through an integrative perspective of familiar organizational theories while triggering broader discussions for management research.

We identify theoretical foundations necessary for an examination of the emergence of big data in strategic decision making through the lenses of resource-based theory (RBT) and organizational learning. Informed by common characteristics used to conceptualize big data, this framework focuses on different applications of big data depending upon management's aspirations as well as the development and maturity of their organization's infrastructure and capabilities (authenticity). The result of such an approach is the realization that the field of strategy needs to be flexible enough to accommodate a new understanding of the interplay among data, technology, and strategy. As the economy turns increasingly digital, scholarship must adapt to better explain new and unique phenomena of interest.

The primary objective for this work is to stimulate the research agenda surrounding the integration of big data and corporate strategy. We aim to engage a broad variety of management scholars via our contributions, spurring on new theories and models to describe the disruption of value chains, supporting the development and reconceptualization of successful outcomes in business, and orchestrating linkages between business analytics methodologies and strategy scholarship methods. While setting forth a theoretically grounded framework that will allow strategy researchers to begin tackling important questions in the field, we introduce components of the discussion that are heretofore absent in the management literature and offer numerous avenues for future scholarship.

2. Background

The term "big data" is used to describe large, diverse, complex, and/or longitudinal datasets generated from a variety of instruments, sensors, and/or computer-based transactions [6]. Big data applies to huge troves of raw data (structured, semi-structured, and unstructured) that cannot be processed or analyzed using traditional methods or tools, leading to increasing challenges in how value is to be extracted [7]. Though the origination of the term is still muddled and under debate, the concept of big data has become a topic of great interest, often under the assumption that it serves as a potential source for competitive advantage in many industries [8].

To understand the evolution leading to the current era of big data, the foundation lies in the development of database management and warehousing [9]. Collecting and storing mostly structured data in relational database management systems was increasingly employed by organizations in the 1990s, with data mining techniques and basic statistical analyses applied as a means to gain insight into growing volumes of information. As the Internet gained prominence and widespread use, more data collection and analytical research and development opportunities were created, with new challenges of text and web analytics for unstructured web content moving to the forefront [3, 9]. Social media forums, web logs, social networking sites, and clickstream data logs created the means for businesses to treat the market as a "conversation" between businesses and customers instead of the traditional business-to-customer, one-way "marketing" [10]. The increasing number of mobile connected devices and other sensor-based, Internet-enabled gadgets are pushing analytical capabilities even further, trapping organizations in a race to adapt to the challenges in collecting, processing, analyzing, and visualizing such large-scale and fluid mobile and sensor data [9]. The compilation and advancement of these technological innovations are increasing organizational competencies, defining new sources of competitive advantage, transforming business models, and opening new windows of entrepreneurial opportunity.

Under the promise of innovation and operational efficiency, big data investments have exploded at major corporations. With McKinsey Global Institute [11] predicting significant benefits to individual industries (e.g., a $300 billion annual impact to the U.S. healthcare industry alone, 60 percent increases in operating margin for U.S. retailers), a considerable and consistent flow of resources into big data projects is expected to continue in the coming decade. Despite noted challenges facing firms with regard to technological advances [12]—or perhaps because of them—a thriving industry has emerged that specializes in the capture, storage, analysis, and interpretation of big data. Niche firms are building platforms and proprietary software to serve clients in both public and private sectors, offering analytic tools and capabilities unable to be matched in-house. Also of note, data-related research centers are springing up at universities across the globe. Nine figure investments in data science programs are becoming commonplace as universities seek new knowledge and aim to produce students with skills sought by an increasing number of organizations. To date, much of the knowledge of the big data phenomenon has been derived by data scientists in both corporate and academic environments through an exploration of essential big data attributes, which have come to be known as the "Vs" of big data.

2.1 The "Vs" of big data

Early conceptualizations of big data were built around three central characteristics: volume, velocity, and variety [13]. *Volume* represents the "big" in big data. The sheer volume of data is exploding, with some organizations collecting as much as a terabyte of data each and every hour, every single day [7]. With societal trends toward social media and remarkable advancements in technology, partnered with decreasing storage costs that have made it more economically feasible to manage, data volume is likely to continue rising. The second core element, *velocity*, deals with the rate at which the data arrives, is stored, and retrieved for processing. With more sensors available, the growing introduction of connected devices, and an ever-rising number of codified transactions occurring globally, we are seeing increasing speed in data flow [14]. With technological advancements allowing for the tracking of data in a multitude of mediums, we are also seeing changes in the *variety* of the data. Beyond traditional numeric data, we are now seeing raw, semi-structured, and unstructured data sourced from web pages, web log files, search indexes, social media forums, email, documents, sensor data, images, video footage, GPS signals, and many other outlets [7, 15].

As the big data phenomenon has evolved to include the identification of additional characteristics of consequence, researchers have suggested several more "Vs" as fundamental to the discussion. There is growing consensus to include the *veracity* of data as a relevant characteristic. Veracity relates to data quality [6, 8], with some segregating data quality into separate dimensions for timeliness, accuracy, consistency, and completeness [16]. Others have distinguished consistency as its own characteristic, choosing to deal with the changing nature of data as an issue of *variability* [17]. In this light, the definition or meaning of data is changing, as evolving forms of media (e.g., blogs, social media, and video) have created new challenges in collecting, codifying, and storing unstructured data.

In a similar notion, some have argued that the relevance of data is another important factor. Such relevance, or *viability*, concerns the possibility of the data to be analyzed in a manner to make it decision-relevant for the firm, i.e., that data selected for analysis is likely to predict outcomes of consequence to the organization [18, 19]. Similarly, *visualization* also has been brought forth and defined as a potentially significant characteristic. Visualization refers to making data comprehensible in a manner that is easily understandable [17].

A final element that is receiving increasing attention, and proves most interesting from a strategic perspective, is the *value* of big data [6, 17, 20]. In essence, this factor is about how data can be leveraged for benefit in the form of financial gain or some other outcome of organizational import, such as operational efficiency or knowledge creation. The propensity of certain data to be used in solving operational challenges and increasing effectiveness of an organization significantly impacts its value to the focal firm. Though, while proprietary data may in and of itself provide value (for consumption or to be sold), the interaction with analytical tools and capabilities allows data to become increasingly useful and valuable [21]. **Table 1** summarizes these eight common Vs described in the big data literature.

Though these individual elements are still being disputed as to their specific validity, there is little debate as to the growing influence big data is having on and

Attribute	*Description*
Volume	Massive amount of data collected
Velocity	Rate at which data arrives, is stored, and retrieved for processing
Variety	Diverse structure and forms of data
Veracity	Trustworthiness of data
Variability	Changing nature of data
Viability	Relevance of the data
Visualization	Comprehensibility of data
Value	Data translated into learning, knowledge creation, and/or economic gain

Table 1.
Eight common Vs of big data.

within organizations today. Ubiquitous conversation and escalating investments signal the current and future importance of big data in shaping strategic thought and direction in organizations [22].

2.2 The evolving influence of big data on corporate strategy

Nearly every industry has made or is making substantial investments in big data. Despite this increasing emphasis, corporate decision makers are often left disconnected from the exact value proposition from big data investments in their strategic decision making. As such, the role of technology, data, information, and knowledge officers in corporate strategic decisions continues to evolve [23, 24]. Standards and best practices have not yet been formed, leading decision-makers to seek guidance wherever possible.

Though data-driven business models are still evolving and somewhat unproven, research suggests that IT capabilities positively influence firm performance [25]. More specific to our line of inquiry, a recent study found that organizations that claim to have achieved a competitive advantage through their data analytic capabilities are over two times more likely to substantially outperform their industry peers [26]. This same study determined that top performing firms were twice as likely to use insights gleaned from big data analytics to guide day-to-day operations and twice as likely to use analytics to guide future strategies.

Such findings would suggest that firms might take different approaches to their big data strategies and seek value through different means and ends [27]. Many, likely most, firms in the new digital economy are currently focused on solving traditional problems in traditional markets with new and creative solutions using big data analytics. These firms are seeking innovations to improve day-to-day decision-making, drawing technology resources out of a centralized IT department and distributing them throughout other value chain functions [28]. Marketing, procurement, inventory management, operations, and customer service operate more efficiently and effectively through various product and process innovations, all driven by information generated by big data investments. As an example, retail companies are utilizing digitized marketing analytics to deliver more effective advertising, incremental product improvements, and increasing rates of customer acquisition and retention. Similar improvements are being made in nearly every industry.

Scholarly works, practitioner manuscripts, and private sector whitepapers describe an evolving competitive landscape and would also suggest that another subset of firms has emerged [11, 27, 29, 30]. These organizations have adopted a data-driven, information-centric focus that subsumes all aspects and decisions for their firm, including measuring how successful certain projects are beyond profitability. Such emphasis has allowed these firms to build extraordinary data stocks and data flows. Access to inordinate amounts of data increases opportunities for learning, transforming new knowledge and ideas into fresh opportunities for exploration, often outside traditional markets. These learning organizations build ecosystems with constantly increasing data flows, developing advanced technical and analytic capabilities and tools along the way, which can be leveraged as they compete with traditional competitors and diversify into new markets.

3. Theoretical foundations

As major corporations, hedge funds, and entrepreneurs are struggling with the emergence of big data, academicians continue working to understand its role in business, the inputs and outputs of big data, and how big data projects are best executed. While active research streams have developed in the information systems (e.g., [31]) and supply chain (e.g., [16]) literatures, there has been a paucity of contributions from the management field [5], and more specifically the field of strategic management. Most contributions to date have been through consulting white papers (e.g., McKinsey, Oracle, and EY) and practitioner-oriented outlets (e.g., [15, 30]). Hence, there is a need for strategy scholars to develop theoretical approaches to better comprehend how big data is shaping strategic decision making and at the core of novel business models that challenge traditional strategic conceptualizations.

Drawing upon the influential Vs of big data vernacular, we move to ground the big data phenomenon in accepted strategic management theory. Recognizing current practices by a wide variety of firms, we arrive at two long-standing theoretical lenses: RBT and organizational learning. Witnessing a vast majority of organizations employing analytics within functional areas of their firm in an effort to achieve sustainable competitive advantage, we draw upon RBT. Noting the organizational philosophies adopted by the minority of firms with truly advanced analytic capabilities, we also recognize the contributions of the organizational learning perspective.

3.1 Resource-based theory and the big data phenomenon

Much of the practitioner-based literature focuses on increasing efficiency and effectiveness in existing markets, and is therefore best viewed through the lens of RBT. Following traditional RBT principles—and with an assumption of resource heterogeneity across competitors—a firm's data stocks (in particular, their proprietary data stocks) are conceptualized as being valuable, rare, difficult to imitate, and nonsubstitutable (i.e., VRIN), and therefore a potential source of advantage relative to competitors [8, 32, 33]. More compelling to RBT arguments are the ability of firms to bundle data resources with analytic capabilities and strategic decision making. The significance of data increases immensely when combined with the dynamic capabilities of a firm that maximize its ability to extract and apply knowledge and insight from the data to the exploitation of business models [34].

Consistent with traditional tenets of RBT, mounting research into opportunities presented through big data initiatives in most every sector would seem to imply considerable value potential [11]. Market conditions exist for the buying and selling of data as well as analytical services, signaling a more definitive value [35]. Further, the proprietary nature of any data stocks or capabilities would suggest a level of rareness. Firms without similar capabilities or infrastructure might also find it extremely costly and difficult to imitate. Finally, empirical research into the linkage between big data, IT capabilities, and firm performance (e.g., [26]) would seem to infer that a reliance on instinctual decision making is no longer substitutable for data-driven strategic and operational planning.

Given the above characteristics, big data and the complementary capabilities associated with handling, analyzing, and applying massive amounts of data can serve as a means for achieving and sustaining competitive advantage. Managers at a significant number of firms are making investments in capabilities that allow them to use big data to generate deeper business insights and optimize existing processes. These firms are typically focused on creating and exploiting advantages in current markets, seeking resolution to traditional problems that have plagued their operations in the quest for profitability. For example, Capital One has used big data to better evaluate consumer spending patterns and connect with individualized consumer needs. Their efforts have led to new customized programming, while also helping to manage repayment risk [36]. Similarly, Progressive Insurance has improved its ability to identify hazardous driving behavior through the use of real-time analytics derived from in-vehicle telecommunications devices [37]. Seeking similar knowledge advances, Coca-Cola has used big data to improve supply chain and innovation. Using Freestyle fountain platforms, the company captures data on geographic and time-related consumption, innovative new flavor mixtures, and inventory replenishment [38].

Through these examples, big data can be viewed as an extension of business intelligence and analytics, enhancing the efficiency and effectiveness of existing functional competencies and fitting with established practices in the use of technology [31]. Such a vision is not using data or advanced analytics to alter strategy, but rather to better execute a chosen strategy. Inasmuch, the relevant data is selected based on a strategy, particular measurements are defined and driven by the strategy, and results allow for organizational leaders to better monitor and control on the basis of the strategy.

Nevertheless, increases in technology, online activity, and mobile computing have led more firms to engage in efforts to secure proprietary data through big data initiatives. These mimetic responses would seem to suggest that firm-specific advantages related to data stocks are, over time, decreasingly sustainable (i.e., diminishing in value and scarcity) [3]. However, a subset of firms with leading analytic capabilities have shifted focus beyond existing capabilities, adopting a more dynamic approach that is changing the nature of business, with impacts evident across multiple types of innovation (e.g., product, process, business model), supply chain management, and diversification. The firms have become increasingly focused on data flows rather than data stocks [28], with an aim for continuous learning. These firms are not beyond using data to exploit existing competencies in traditional markets, but are persistently seeking to learn from new data flows and willing to explore new markets [39]. As such, we now look at the influences of organizational learning on the phenomenon of interest.

3.2 Organizational learning and the big data phenomenon

Organizational learning has been applied broadly across management literatures, though definitional consensus remains elusive [40]. Because we are looking at organization-level innovation and strategic renewal within the context of a general movement toward big data, our arguments most closely align with those by Crossan and colleagues [41]. Relying on premises brought forth by March [39], these authors state that renewal requires that organizations explore and learn new ways while concurrently exploiting what they have already learned. From this perspective, they promote a framework of four subprocesses: intuiting, interpreting, integrating, and institutionalizing. In short, intuiting is the recognition of patterns and/or possibilities; interpreting is the explanation of an insight or idea; integrating is the process of developing a shared understanding among individuals and taking coordinated action, and institutionalizing is the process of ensuring that routinized actions occur.

While the work by Crossan and colleagues argues for a multi-level framework—involving individuals, groups, and the organization itself—we see increasing potential for the collapsing of this framework through advances in technology attributable to the big data phenomenon. With artificial intelligence and machine learning, patterns and possibilities are now being recognized through analytics and coding rather than through individuals' personal experiences. Big data allows for this process of intuiting to occur not through one individual's experiences, but rather through mass analysis of tremendous volumes and variety of data. Interpretation is simplified through data visualization tools common in firms with a mature understanding and application of big data analytics. Though the integration of knowledge across organizational lines still requires entrepreneurial thinking, visionary leadership, and organizational buy-in across groups, this is simplified if an analytical mindset is embraced within the firm.

Complementary scholarship within this literature stream focuses on specific elements of organizational learning, such as knowledge creation/acquisition and knowledge transfer/distribution [40]. Organizational knowledge is created through a continuous dialog between tacit and explicit knowledge [42], and amidst a balance between search and experimentation and the contrary activities of refinement and execution [39]. As such, knowledge acquisition occurs through a process of learning from experience and the recording or probing for information about the organization's environment or performance [40]. Learning is leveraged further when knowledge is transferred to more of an organization's components, who are also afforded mechanisms to enhance the ability, motivation, and opportunity to recognize that knowledge as potentially useful [43]. Hence, due to the complexities and difficulty in instituting or imitating, the creation and effective transfer of knowledge internally stand as a potential basis for competitive advantage [44].

With this understanding of knowledge management capabilities, it is easy to infer that RBT is encompassed within an organizational learning framework. While new knowledge is developed by individuals (and, increasingly, through technology), organizations (and their strategic leaders) play a critical role in articulating and amplifying that knowledge [42]. Advanced technical capabilities, ever-expanding data stocks, and excessively large financial coffers serve as resources that allow learning organizations to eschew established competencies and circumvent traditional industry boundaries and barriers to entry [27]. For example, Alphabet (nee Google) continues to explore and diversify into new markets, expanding well beyond web search and advertising as they seek to capture new data and knowledge [45]. Apple and Amazon are other well-recognized companies also focused on advancing ecosystems, new markets, and the development of analytical and learning capabilities [46]. Leaders at these organizations cultivate a growth mindset and entrepreneurial culture, embracing new technologies and tolerating risk in the pursuit of new knowledge that can push the organization forward in new and unforeseen ways. Exploration and exploitation decisions in these organizations are not solely predicated on profitability; instead, these firms are concerned with enhancing data flows, with the intent to develop innovative service modules that can be easily combined with existing platforms to execute increasing levels of service [8].

In essence, the focus on data flows presents opportunities for learning organizations to build dynamic capabilities through the extension of digital ecosystems, finding new ways to digitize and monetize evolving products and services. Strategic decisions on new product and service offerings are made based upon the potential for human capital development, multiplicative and exponential learning, and an expanding ecosystem of consumer influence. Organizations embracing a learning perspective view data not only as an available resource to be exploited for improving existing value chains, but also anticipate the untapped value of data, seeing unique sources from which to collect new data. They envision how that data can be used to gain novel and original knowledge and explore new markets and opportunities for future business endeavors [47]. From this synopsis, we now move on to an exploration for how the characteristics of big data can be interpreted through the theoretical lenses offered by RBT and organizational learning.

4. Viewing the Vs through RBT and organizational learning

Reflecting upon the Vs customarily espoused within the big data literature, volume, variety, and velocity are seen as primary drivers. Access to more (and more diverse) data, generated at ever-increasing speeds, directly effects a firm's ability to make decisions and allows it to increase its competitiveness versus firms without access to similar data stocks. Firms actively employing a data-driven strategy require significant investment in data collection and storage capabilities, as well as the development of improved analytics to handle the large, diverse, and complex datasets. Due to the nature of volume, variety, and velocity aspects, an investment must be made in the development of necessary infrastructure. Such a commitment of resources (e.g., human capital, financial capital, technological capital), properly deployed, leads to a level of efficiency and greater predictive and analytic capabilities in order to exploit advantages relative to firms without similar investments.

Firms focused on the enhancement of existing capabilities (i.e., a resource-based orientation) build such infrastructure and capabilities as to seek improvement in solving existing problems. It is also reasonable that these firms may outsource some or all of the infrastructure or analytic capabilities to strategic partners who have greater strengths and/or efficiencies in big data-related tasks, still working to accomplish the same goals for the focal firm. Regardless, these big data initiatives, whether outsourced or in-house, are typically localized to functional areas, creating successes to definitive and specific challenges but not sharing them across business units or divisions.

In a similar fashion, firms with a learning-based orientation strive for gains in efficiency and traditional value chain improvements. However, this group of firms tend to stretch their commitments into human, financial, and technical (and, increasingly, social) capital to greater heights. Substantial investments in building immense data storage warehouses, intra- and inter-firm networks, computing power, and analytic capabilities are warranted, with a continuous push toward increasing and diversifying data inputs [28]. While there is value in focusing efforts and big data innovations within specific value chain activities, true strategic impact can only happen with management having a holistic view of the digital threats and opportunities as well as associates buying in to an overall vision for how big data can reshape the firm and its competitive landscape [48]. The learning mindset and big data aspirations embraced by these firms allow for increasing abilities to search for new product or market opportunities in non-traditional spaces. Rather than simply looking for greater volume, variety, or velocity with big data investments, decisions by learning organizations are based upon the belief that greater data flows will translate to increased veracity, variability, viability, visualization, and value of data stocks. Accordingly, an expanded view of the Vs becomes increasingly relevant as the resource-based and learning perspectives are contrasted. Because firms with a resource-based orientation are focused on exploiting advantages primarily in current markets, the remaining Vs are viewed in light of this limitation.

Data veracity is important for firms with a resource-based orientation due to the fact of working with traditional metrics and processes. They need to trust the quality of the data in order to follow through and make the gains in productivity and profitability they are seeking, but are limited by their own aspirations and through their ability to monitor, analyze, and control based upon their data collection and analysis. Because their chosen corporate- and business-level strategy predetermines the data and metrics of interest, resource-focused firms proceed without the benefit of viewing the potential of enhanced data stocks and data flows. In much the same way, data variability can often be overlooked by firms with a resource-based orientation, due to discretionary bias and dominant logics confining the firm to rigidities in traditional proprietary thinking. These firms are focused on existing value chain processes and metrics, and are therefore looking for and expecting consistency in their data to be measured and tracked over time to gauge improvements.

Awareness of data quality and data evolution is critically important to learning organizations, as it affords these firms unique perspective on opportunities to engage in ever-expanding data flows. As learning organizations are open to new opportunities and strategic renewal based upon their understanding of the data, it is incredibly important that they develop a level of comfort with the data and its sources because of the time-conscious decisions and indelible investments that follow. Even though these firms are more willing to take data-related risks, because of the sheer volume of data amassed through their ever-increasing data stocks and data flows, they are able to quickly make assessments in data quality. Their quest to increase data flows also comes with an expectation that the data will change over time, both in its source and its meaning, and so the firm develops capabilities around adapting and learning from these changes in order to parlay them into new business opportunities. Heightened alertness and responsiveness to the quality and changing nature of data contribute to the development of better organizational capabilities that identify trends in a broad array of markets, progressively monetizing data resources via entry into new markets as they extend analytic and predictive capabilities often ignored or underdeveloped by traditional firms [8].

The viability and visualization of data is also limited in firms with resource-based orientations due to contextual factors, as situational analyses are hindered by conventional views of the organization and their markets. In reality, this is restricted by the abilities of senior leadership to see its importance [49] and to break down data silos within the firm [48, 50]. The data is discernably relevant for decision-making purposes because prior decisions on strategy dictate what is to be captured, collected, and analyzed. While tools to help visualize trends in the data prove helpful, it is only for the function of addressing previously determined metrics.

Conversely, in learning-oriented firms, leaders direct their resources to collect data from many data flows, making it more challenging to determine relevance. However, capabilities are developed within these firms to help identify, interpret, and predict new opportunities, even those potentially outside traditional markets. Such efforts may require the learning or development of novel or unfamiliar metrics. It should not be construed that these learning organizations are blindly looking for data and opportunities anywhere and everywhere; there are still likely to be well-defined social, industrial, or organizational challenges that are being pursued. It is simply that the learning orientation of these firms allows them to capture and look at far-reaching data to find the most accurate and data-supported solutions, even if it means developing new and diverse perspectives and taking risks in diversifying to new markets that offer the potential for tremendous pay off [51]. It is in this way that deft visualization actually helps management see the viability of certain data, and organizations are not left to stand solely on the instinctual decision-making of organizational leaders.

Beyond all of the other Vs, it is paramount, of course, that firms actively engaged in data-driven decision making are also seeking and receiving value from their investments in big data initiatives. Resource-centric firms create value from big data through better business decisions that improve and exploit traditional capabilities. They learn to increase the efficiency of employees, improve inventory logistics for suppliers and distribution, and better service their customers. To some degree then, the value through a resource-oriented approach is concentrated on the

Attribute	*Influences on firms w/ resource-based orientation*	*Influences on firms w/ learning-based orientation*
Volume *Velocity* *Variety*	Requires proper infrastructure, commitment of resources, and a level of efficiency in organizational processes as well as greater predictive and analytic capabilities (than firms without digital strategies) in order to exploit current advantages	Same as resource-based orientation, but human and financial resource commitment stretches to greater heights amid ever-increasing data flows, allowing for ability to search for new product or market opportunities in non-traditional spaces
Veracity	Immediate high value placed here due to fact of working with traditional metrics and processes	Takes time to analyze and determine; firm must be willing to take risks here to analyze and uncover value in data; capabilities of analysis to determine veracity may be source of competitive advantage as it may influence survivability
Variability	Limited due to extensive attention and focus placed on existing value chain processes and metrics	Expansive due to quest for increasing data flows; valuable due to firm's adaptability and ability to learn as trends change
Viability	Only measure specific predetermined data elements, therefore all are relevant (but potentially limited)	Collect data from many data flows, therefore must cull and codify for analyses and make determination on relevance; unique capabilities to see and predict new opportunities, potentially outside traditional markets (which may require using new and diverse perspectives to view and analyze the data); i.e., may not be relevant to traditional markets, but could be tremendous new opportunity
Visualization	Aids in measurement and interpretation to solve key issues in traditional processes and markets	Analytical techniques that also helps interpret broad data sources to draw attention to trends and new opportunities to enhance survivability
Value	Created through development of better business decisions in traditional value chain functions and with economically quicker means via advanced and predictive analytics that create and exploit existing and new competitive advantages in traditional markets	Created through ability to analyze data in new ways to enhance knowledge and develop dynamic capabilities to learn, recognize, and act upon large economic and sociocultural patterns and trends, often with such scale as to offset traditional competitive forces in order to create, enter, and/or develop new markets and/or industries with profitable business models

Table 2.
How the eight Vs of big data impact digital business strategy based upon firm orientation.

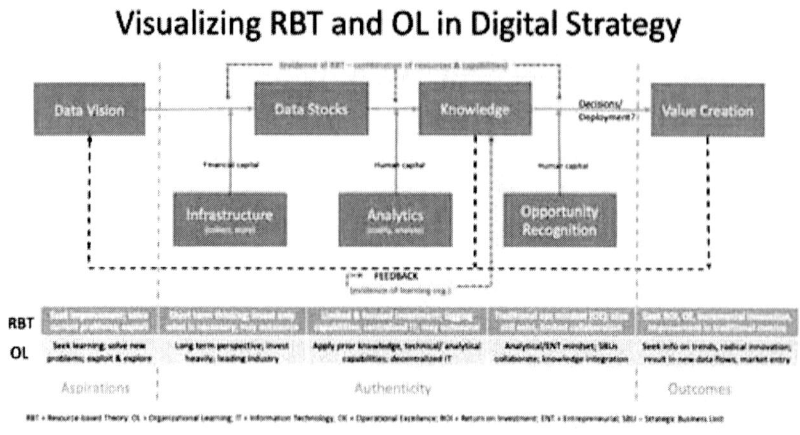

Figure 1.
Visualizing RBT and OL in Digital Strategy.

improved relationships with key stakeholders. Such relationships can be recognized and measured through a variety of financial and operational metrics likely already in service throughout an industry.

For the learning-oriented firm, value is captured through the development of knowledge and dynamic capabilities to recognize, learn from, and act on large socio-cultural patterns, often with such scale as to offset traditional competitive forces in the creation, entrance, and/or development of new markets or industries with innovative business models. They are able to effectively integrate and disseminate new knowledge across organizational silos to drive further innovation and entrepreneurship. Their business models look to expand existing lines of business, building an increasing ecosystem of services that benefit customers and build brand loyalty [30]. Accordingly, these learning organizations follow a pattern that not only builds what they know into their business models, but also incorporates a means to facilitate learning while relentlessly increasing the data gap over competitors. Despite these benefits, it is still evident that most industries still have not even scratched the surface of realizing the potential value of big data and analytics [11, 52].

Table 2 summarizes how the Vs commonly attributed to big data influence firms resource- and learning-based orientations when employing digital business strategies. **Figure 1** offers a visual to further describe how these orientations are staged across organizations.

5. Future management scholarship and the big data phenomenon

Digitization and the increasing value of big data analytics have led to a global disruption of immense proportions, similar to what was experienced during the industrial revolution. Business models and strategic thinking are changing as a result. Communication and computing technologies have developed so radically over the last 20 years that it is easy to forget we are living in an entirely new world. Decades ago, computers sat in rooms and on desktops, not in the palm of one's hand. Inboxes sat on desks, rather than residing in software. Data processing was a long, expensive, and arduous task. Accordingly, the context in which we conduct organizational research—and even *how* such research is conducted [5]—needs to change. What is more, it seems imperative to reflect and examine whether existing frameworks, variables, and measurements are still relevant in today's digitalized business environment. Through such reflection, the evidence of earlier paradigms—specifically the important role that RBT plays—in today's digital era and the relationship with organizational learning is apparent. Yet scholars are now presented with an opportunity to conduct a renewed examination of how technology interacts with strategy. Although leaders of the field have iterated a call for research and theory development in this area, significant movement has lagged. To assist in the advancement toward this end, we present a number of avenues to begin addressing these gaps, not only in strategy, but across the field of management.

5.1 Avenue A: theoretical development across management

Through this paper, we extend theoretical development by looking at how the big data phenomenon is interacting with RBT and organizational learning in new and novel ways. These are overtly and perceptibly not the only theoretical underpinnings found within the big data phenomenon, nor are they the only ones that may be challenged by the changing competitive landscape. As such, scholars have an exceptional opportunity to identify unique applications for existing theories, create new proposed boundary conditions across the field of management, or develop novel theoretical frameworks and extensions, such as in the domains of strategy, entrepreneurship, or human resources.

We make the case to further develop theory around existing streams of research in the extant knowledge creation, knowledge management, and exploration/exploitation literatures. The likelihood that management theories are universally true across all periods of time, contextual situations, and especially after radical innovations have been brought forth to the market is highly unlikely. It is our contention that when the assumptions used in developing theory are challenged by existing realities of the world, the management field should reconsider "what it knows" and look at its theories to drive forward more relevant understandings of the world. This is not to suggest that traditional theories of management will be invalidated. Rather, it is necessary to revisit paradigms, challenge assumptions, and explore alternative explanations. The digitization of business models, fueled by the big data phenomenon, is a massive economic transformation; therefore, a new and concerted effort to look at the underlying theories of our respective fields should be considered at this time.

5.2 Avenue B: investigating antecedents to data- and analytic-related capabilities

Beyond applying theory to better understand the nature of organizational decision making in the era of big data, it is imperative to explore the context and antecedents that allowed these organizations to leverage data and analytics for competitive advantage. What is it that allows for firms to transition into data-savvy organizations? Are there characteristics or nuances that propel firms and allow for the transformation into learning organizations? Externally, are their environmental factors that specifically trigger such adaptation?

Undoubtedly, we see application for traditional explanations such as visionary leadership, organizational culture, strategic resource heterogeneity, and environmental hostility. Yet scholarly examination should better explore the true characteristics and environmental stressors that elicit impactful organizational change that increases data and analytic capabilities. Tracking firms globally and longitudinally—through both qualitative and quantitative investigation—is necessary to properly uncover specifics about firms developing competitive advantage through a combination of big data analytics and strategic thinking. Are CEOs business school educated or do they have STEM (science, technology, engineering, and/or mathematics) backgrounds? Do they have brief or extended tenures in their organization? Were they founders? How was culture characterized before the shift, or was analytics core to the identity of the firm from inception? What was the nature of the industry cycle? Were resources plentiful in the environment? Was the company an industry leader, or falling behind? Were there disruptive innovations occurring (beyond digitization)? There is ample room for discovery of these and many more aspects to better understand the full scope of big data's impact on organizations.

5.3 Avenue C: reconsidering outcomes and consequences

Big data's emergence, in combination with disruptive business model innovations, has created an opportunity to reconceptualize organizational performance. Industry no longer uses a simple measure of profitability or traditional financial ratios, as success now relates to quantities of users on platforms, the richness of data flows, the collection of data stocks, or the knowledge created through the business activity. If we reconceptualize organizational performance more holistically, how does that open the definition of competitive advantage up to include the realities of a new contextual business environment?

Without understanding how senior management at digital-savvy firms perceive performance with regard to certain offerings, our current measurements may not allow us to properly test the hypothetical connections and theories that the big data phenomenon allows us to predict. Deep dive qualitative studies and case analyses surrounding digital transformations, as well as companies that have been founded digital, should be conducted to examine how these firms measure success. Additionally, companies that are founded and run by technological or analytical leaders should be more intimately compared and contrasted with companies founded and run by traditional operational management to better understand the underlying differences and subsequent impact on performance.

5.4 Avenue D: refining and specifying the measurement of variables

The uses and application of big data have so thoroughly transformed methods and processes in the business environment that it is now necessary to not only reconceptualize theory, but also transform how we measure and model behavior, whether at the firm, meso-, or microlevel [5]. In the previous section, the change in how firms define desirable business outcomes was discussed, but future research will derive additional value when firm-level performance is measured in a manner that brings together the divergent ways that firm performance is now viewed by learning-oriented firms.

The same novel tools and data stocks that have digitized businesses can also be used for the qualitative testing of management theories. Therefore, macro level constructs that relied on poor proxies (or simply were unable to be measured) could come within scholars' range as they begin to open their perspectives to how business is conducted, what data stocks and flows are generated, and how they could capture them anonymously. Relying on changes in strategic human resource analytics capabilities in firms to create and predict behaviors will significantly impact our ability to understand organizational phenomenon beyond current methodologies. Learning-organizations have large scale human resource analytics capabilities developed through the recruitment of Ph.D.-level employees and research fellows. For insight into this, we need not look further than the great interest of managers, scholars, and students in Google's people analytics, where HR professionals work hand-in-hand with organizational scientists to identify the most effective fact-based solutions, rather than relying on individual experience and debate.

More precise measurements in management are not only important from the perspective of the scholar hoping to create new knowledge, but also as a means to better understand both the phenomena of big data and, more generally, organizational entities. This translates into better research, teaching, and practice of business strategy and management. As scholars are able to more precisely measure what it is they are defining, the insight gained from research increases by magnitudes in its translation into teaching and practice, resulting in an important reconnection to the community, where business scholarship has strayed over the last several of decades. We believe that the big data being collected en masse by today's firms will be the scholar's playground tomorrow if the field positions itself to advance the practice as well as the theory of organizations. The big data phenomenon has the potential to bring organizational science back to life in a way that should be exciting to a diverse group of individuals, including future scholars.

6. Conclusion

The link between the firm's IT and competitive advantage has long been discussed in the literature (e.g., [53–55]), but we proffer that technological resources and capabilities are now dictating which strategic approach a firm can and will take to the market [27]. How firms choose to explore new markets is not done through traditional strategic planning, but instead evolves through opportunity recognition based largely upon information gleaned from consistently analyzing more and richer data flows and stocks. The emphasis on data and data analytics as strategically important to a firm's success has the potential to contribute to important developments in understanding organizations in a world where digital is rapidly overtaking traditional business models. While there is the possibility for considerable debate over whether big data practices can provide a sustainable competitive advantage, arguments can be made that continued advancements and innovation in infrastructure, analytical capabilities, and organizational processes will leave plenty of opportunity for proactive firms. What is more, while individual data stocks may be imitable, bundles that include proprietary data, dynamic data analytic capabilities, effective strategic decision making, and an entrepreneurial spirit will likely remain unique to a particular firm and translate into the creation of new knowledge and ambidextrous execution (i.e., both exploiting existing markets and exploring new opportunities).

Reinvestigating the interplay between technology and organizational strategy is needed, as big data is likely to play a role in changing the landscape of social and economic policy and research [5]. As such, the importance of beginning this line of study within the strategy literature is imperative. Closing the gap between traditional strategic thinking and how strategy is currently employed in superior performing firms will test the ability of the field to match management theory with reality. In doing so, scholars can erase the perceived naiveté surrounding management theories and demonstrate the complexity witnessed in the real world through contemporary and meaningful scholarship [56].

References

[1] McElheran K, Brynjolfsson E. The rise of data-driven decision making is real but uneven. Harvard Business Review [Internet]. 2016. Available from: https://hbr.org/2016/02/the-rise-of-data-driven-decision-making-is-real-but-uneven

[2] Constantiou ID, Kallinikos J. New games, new rules: Big data and the changing context of strategy. Journal of Information Technology. 2015;**30**(1): 44-57

[3] Lee I. Big data: Dimensions, evolution, impacts, and challenges. Business Horizons. 2017;**60**(3):293-303

[4] Wessel M. How big data is changing disruptive innovation. Harvard Business Review [Internet]. 2016. Available from: https://hbr.org/2016/01/how-big-data-is-changing-disruptive-innovation

[5] George G, Haas MR, Pentland A. Big data and management. Academy of Management Journal. 2014;**57**(2): 321-326

[6] Megahed FM, Jones-Farmer LA. A statistical process monitoring perspective on "big data". In: Frontiers in Statistical Quality Control. 11th ed. New York, NY: Springer; 2013

[7] Zikopoulos P, Eaton C, de Roos D, Deutsch T, Lapis G. Understanding Big Data: Analytics for Enterprise Class Hadoop and Streaming Data. New York, NY: McGraw-Hill; 2012

[8] Morabito V. Big Data and Analytics: Strategic and Organizational Impacts. Switzerland: Springer; 2015

[9] Chen H, Chiang RH, Storey VC. Business intelligence and analytics: From big data to big impact. MIS Quarterly. 2012;**36**(4):1165-1188

[10] Lusch RF, Liu Y, Chen Y. The phase transition of markets and organizations: The new intelligence and entrepreneurial frontier. IEEE Intelligent Systems. 2010;**25**(1):71-75

[11] McKinsey Global Institute. Big Data: The Next Frontier for Innovation, Competition, and Productivity. Lexington, KY: McKinsey & Company; 2011

[12] SAS Institute Inc. Five big data challenges sas.com: SAS Institute Inc. 2013. Available from: https://www.sas.com/resources/asset/five-big-data-challenges-article.pdf

[13] Laney D. 3D Data Management: Controlling Data Volume, Velocity And Variety. 2001. Available from: http://blogs.gartner.com/doug-laney/files/2012/01/ad949-3D-Data-Management-Controlling-Data-Volume-Velocity-and-Variety.pdf

[14] Porter ME, Heppelmann JE. How smart, connected products are transforming competition. Harvard Business Review. 2014;**92**(11):64-88

[15] McAfee A, Brynjolfsson E. Big data: The management revolution. Harvard Business Review. 2012;**90**(10):60-68

[16] Hazen BT, Boone CA, Ezell JD, Jones-Farmer LA. Data quality for data science, predictive analytics, and big data in supply chain management: An introduction to the problem and suggestions for research and applications. International Journal of Production Economics. 2014;**154**(1):72-80

[17] van Rijmenam M. Think Bigger: Developing a Successful Big Data Strategy for Your Business. New York, NY: Amacom; 2014

[18] Biehn N. The missing V's in big data: Viability and value. Wired [Internet]. 2013. Available from: http://www.wired.

com/insights/2013/05/the-missing-vs-in-big-data-viability-and-value/

[19] Grimes S. Big data: Avoid 'Wanna V' confusion. Information Week [Internet]. 2013. Available from: http://www.informationweek.com/big-data/big-data-analytics/big-data-avoid-wanna-v-confusion/d/d-id/1111077?

[20] Marr B. Why Only One of the 5 Vs of Big Data Really Matters IBM Big Data & Analytics Hub: IBM. 2015. Available from: http://www.ibmbigdatahub.com/blog/why-only-one-5-vs-big-data-really-matters

[21] Zeng J, Glaister KW. Value creation from big data: Looking inside the black box. Strategic Organization. 2017;**16**(2): 105-140

[22] Jin X, Wah BW, Cheng X, Wang Y. Significance and challenges of big data research. Big Data Research. 2015;**2**(2): 59-64

[23] Menz M. Functional top management team members. Journal of Management. 2012;**38**(1):45-80

[24] PwC. Great expectations: The evolution of the chief data officer pwc.com: pwc.com. 2015. Available from: https://www.pwc.com/us/en/financial-services/publications/viewpoints/assets/pwc-chief-data-officer-cdo.pdf

[25] Mithas S, Ramasubbu N, Sambamurthy V. How information management capability influences firm performance. MIS Quarterly. 2011; **35**(1):237-256

[26] LaValle S, Lesser E, Shockley R, Hopkins M, Kruschwitz N. Big data, analytics and the path from insights to value. MIT Sloan Management Review. 2011;**52**(2):21-34

[27] Mazzei MJ, Noble D. Big data dreams: A framework for corporate strategy. Business Horizons. 2017;**60**(3):405-414

[28] Davenport TH, Barth P, Bean R. How 'big data' is different. MIT Sloan Management Review. 2012;**54**(1):43-46

[29] Porter ME, Heppelmann JE. How smart, connected products are transforming companies. Harvard Business Review. 2015;**93**(10):96-114

[30] Weill P, Woerner SL. Thriving in an increasingly digital ecosystem. MIT Sloan Management Review. 2015;**56**(4): 26-34

[31] Bharadwaj A, El Sawy OA, Pavlou PA, Venkatraman N. Digital business strategy: Toward a next generation of insights. MIS Quarterly. 2013;**37**(2): 471-482

[32] Barney JB. Firm resources and sustained competitive advantage. Journal of Management. 1991;**17**(1): 99-120

[33] Penrose ET. The Theory of the Growth of the Firm. 4th ed. Oxford, UK: Oxford University Press; 1959

[34] Teece DJ. The foundations of entreprise performance: Dynamic and ordinary capabilities in an (economic) theory of firms. Academy of Management Perspectives. 2014;**28**(4): 328-352

[35] Lewis A, McKone D. To get more value from your data, sell it. Harvard Business Review [Internet]. 2016. Available from: https://hbr.org/2016/10/to-get-more-value-from-your-data-sell-it

[36] Dee S. How Does Capital One Differentiate Itself in the Card Industry? 2015. Available from: http://www.forbes.com/sites/greatspeculations/2015/09/11/how-does-capital-one-differentiate-itself-in-the-card-industry/#661f617e1edc

[37] National Association of Insurance Commissioners. Usage-Based Insurance and Telematics. 2015. Available from:

http://www.naic.org/cipr_topics/topic_usage_based_insurance.htm

[38] Weier MH. Coke's RFID-Based Dispensers Redefine Business Intelligence. 2009. Available from: http://www.informationweek.com/mobile/mobile-devices/cokes-rfid-based-dispensers-redefine-business-intelligence-/d/d-id/1080236?

[39] March JG. Exploration and exploitation in organizational learning. Organization Science. 1991;**2**(1):71-87

[40] Huber GP. Organizational learning: The contributing processes and the literatures. Organization Science. 1991; **2**(1):88-115

[41] Crossan MM, Lane HW, White RE. An organizational learning framework: From intuition to institution. Academy of Management Review. 1999;**24**(3): 522-537

[42] Nonaka I. A dynamic theory of organizational knowledge creation. Organization Science. 1994;**5**(1):14-37

[43] Argote L, McEvily B, Reagans R. Managing knowledge in organizations: An integrative framework and review of emerging themes. Management Science. 2003;**49**(4):571-582

[44] Argote L, Ingram P. Knowledge transfer: A basis for competitive advantage in firms. Organizational Behavior and Human Decision Processes. 2000;**82**(1):150-169

[45] Favaro K. Still Searching for the Strategy in Alphabet [nee Google]. 2015. Available from: http://www.forbes.com/sites/kenfavaro/2015/09/07/still-searching-for-the-strategy-in-alphabet-nee-google/#2925929376e5

[46] Adner R. Amazon vs. Apple: Competing Ecosystem Strategies. 2012. Available from: https://hbr.org/2012/03/amazon-vs-apple-competing-ecos

[47] Tushman ML, O'Reilly CA. Ambidextrous organizations: Managing evolutionary and revolutionary change. California Management Review. 1996; **38**(4):8-30

[48] Baculard L-P. To lead a digital transformation, CEOs must prioritize. Harvard Business Review [Internet]. 2017. Available from: https://hbr.org/2017/01/to-lead-a-digital-transformation-ceos-must-prioritize

[49] McShea C, Oakley D, Mazzei C. The reason so many analytics efforts fall short. Harvard Business Review [Internet]. 2016. Available from: https://hbr.org/2016/08/the-reason-so-many-analytics-efforts-fall-short

[50] Wilder-James E. Breaking down data silos. Harvard Business Review [Internet]. 2016. Available from: https://hbr.org/2016/12/breaking-down-data-silos

[51] Tobaccowala R, Gupta S. Extracting insights from vast stores of data. Harvard Business Review [Internet]. 2016. Available from: https://hbr.org/2016/08/extracting-insights-from-vast-stores-of-data

[52] Henke N, Bughin J, Chui M. Most industries are nowhere close to realizing the potential of analytics. Harvard Business Review [Internet]. 2016. Available from: https://hbr.org/2016/12/most-industries-are-nowhere-close-to-realizing-the-potential-of-analytics

[53] Drnevich PL, Croson DC. Information technology and business-level strategy: Toward an integrated theoretical perspective. MIS Quarterly. 2013;**37**(2):483-509

[54] Tippins MJ, Sohi RS. IT competency and firm performance: Is organizational learning a missing link? Strategic Management Journal. 2003;**24**(8): 745-761

[55] Powell TC, Dent-Micallef A. Information technology as competitive advantage: The role of human, business, and technology resources. Strategic Management Journal. 1997;**18**(5): 375-405

[56] Economist.com. Management theory is becoming a compendium of dead ideas. The Economist [Internet]. 2016. Available from: http://www.economist.com/news/business/21711909-what-martin-luther-did-catholic-church-needs-be-done-business-gurus-management

Chapter 5

Underlying Forces of Organisational Control on Administrative Behavioural Theoretical Insights

Abstract

Control, for a long time, has been a constitutive aspect of organisational sociology. However, much of the scholarly account on the concept has overlooked a critical character of discretion in organisational discourse. By meticulous application of Herbert Simon's theory of administrative behaviour, this theoretical piece reveals the interesting dynamics of organisational control to bring the enduring significance of discretion in the control of subordinates at work. The analysis draws on the idea that control is not merely about the predetermination of goals that are achieved at the lower level. In views of this, the research advances a primary conceptualisation of control as double-edged model, adding the application of discretion that, occasionally, makes subordinates lead and encourage vital control practices that drive the life of the organisation.

Keywords: control, rationality, authority, training, organisational loyalty

1. Introduction

Instances of organisational control exist in varied manifestations [1, 2], and its appreciation in view of mediated interaction [3] can be driven by a motely of underlying themes in administrative behavioural analytical perspectives. However, scholarly views on control in terms of administrative behavioural theoretical insights appear to have been overlooked in the mainstream human resource management (HRM) literature [4]. Some of the sociological theories that readily come to mind to possibly offer explanations into the phenomena under investigation now are institutional theory [5, 6], agency theory [7, 8], structuration theory [9], actor-network theory [10], and information processing theory [11], among many others.

Particularly, structuration and institutional theories have the possibility of assisting in shedding lights on the routines and norms of sanction against both organisational and individual actions over a stated period. Usually, these theories provide some form of assistance, nevertheless, in giving extensive interpretation and analysis of the purposeful orientations and psychological reinforcements necessary to appreciate the individual and organisational undertakings in their application of systems of technology. Structuration theory in its basic formulation indicates restricted sense to address issues of technology use [12]. On the other hand, institutional theory has the inclination to over-accentuate the even patterns that exemplify predictable organisational praxis unless exogenous factors induce a transformation of the status quo [13]. By virtue of these elucidations, these theories are hardly ever substantial in their ability to give the real-world outlook instrumental to stimulating our thoughtful consideration into a realistic understanding of individual and organisational behaviour in their categorical versions of functional complexity.

For example, vital matters like organisational recognition, identification and loyalty, the instrumental role of authority, the psychology undergirding administrative decisions, channels of communication and the manner of efficiency hardly get any worthy attention from the theory of administrative behaviour. Notwithstanding this, it would be appropriate to suggest that administrative theoretical framework has the capability to challenge our current stock of knowledge and understanding on individual and organisational behaviour in everyday experience, especially from the standpoint of control in contemporary organisational interactions. Consultation on certain technology-oriented theories could not be relied upon to offer any encouraging attraction despite their near-balanced attention to behavioural and technology issues within the sphere of control in administrative behaviour. By the same account, socio-technical theory (STT) and task-technology fit (TTF) theory could not be applied as both theories have a very limited way of contributing to control and its varied implications for organisational configuration (see, for example, [14–16]).

However, given the rationale of this scholarly piece—to understand control and its manifestations and ramifications from the standpoint of administrative behaviour in contemporary organisational discourse—I have decided to apply the theory of administrative behaviour [17] to this compendium. The reasons for this stance are not far-fetched, to enable an extensive exegesis on the issues meant to be explicated.

Firstly, the theory of administrative behaviour provides a far superior explanatory power for doing a detailed discussion and analysis of organisational control in collaborative engagements. Secondly, the theory of administrative behaviour has a better explanatory power by means of the diverse thematic ideas that are well situated to offer the hands-on use and the additional repercussions for control. Worker, customer loyalty and discretionary actions are some of the occurrences of the associated consequences of contemporary organisational discourse in accommodating the subtleties of organisational control. Thirdly, administrative behaviour is relevant to afford philosophical and psychological commitment and understanding crucial to formulating ideas that intimately account for the inspiration driving the appropriation of mediated artefacts in daily organisational interactions.

In other words, the psychosomatic and theoretical models found in the theory make it not only exemplary but also practical in projecting a thorough execution of organisational control in organisational discourse. Last, but not least, applying administrative behaviour in a fundamentally diverse organisational milieu can give a typical test to the appropriateness of the theory and, probably, demonstrate its shortcomings on studies related to control in organisational discourse from the viewpoint of administrative behaviour.

In what follows, I introduce the theory of administrative behaviour and demonstrate how elucidation of its primary precepts and indispensable concepts leave us with no doubt as to its significance in articulating control from the standpoint of modern organisational interactions in administrative behaviour. In the pursuance of this objective, the epistemological path plus a sketch of administrative behaviour are showcased by means of a discourse on the elementary and cross-disciplinary ideas from which the theory originated. The mechanisms of organisational influence are elaborated by teasing out such themes as the exercise of authority in organisations, and the structural constituents of authority. That provides the opportunity to further consider the triangular structure of authority with respect to responsibility, coordination and specialisation, all analysed as the various categorical versions of control in administrative behaviour. The rest of the paper reflects the vital importance of training in securing individual and group commitment to the course of the organisation. Lastly, the psychology of administrative behaviour is scrutinised to highlight such principles as rationality, organisational loyalty and routinisation of work as a consideration of future research directions on the subject of control in administrative behaviour.

2. Philosophical foundations of administrative behaviour

The history of administrative behaviour is traceable to Herbert Alexander Simon, who coined the expression to describe the practices persons embrace to work in organisations. To be put simply, Simon investigated the multifaceted purposes of firms through the administrative behaviour template. The justification and drive that led to the theory of administrative behaviour (TAB) can be associated with Simon's original work on decision-making in organisation. Simon's determination to clarify—in intensely brief way—the practices linked with the administration of people and the cherished procedures relevant to the working of organisations prior to their existence foreshadowed the theory of administrative behaviour. Roundly persuaded that satisfactory terminology was not forthcoming in the field of the suitable schemes for reasoned treatise on organisations; Simon pursued an academic expedition that investigated the constructs worthy of support to organisational sociology.

With this academic expedition, Simon firmed up the means of target formalisation and task assignment procedures plus genuine organisational performance. The control of subordinate actions emphasises, though obliquely, the manner of administrative behaviour in varied situational scenarios. Nevertheless, with the overriding attention the setting of goals and their achievement receive in the theory, it is appealing to understand control as being relegated to the peripherals. Perrow [18] made references to this view in his suggestion that the notion underscores unassuming subordinate control in terms of their interactions in information exchange, norms and standards as well as in preparation. This tool of control is accentuated by stipulating the procedures for realising determined aims, however, contradictory to a person's (the individual under control) knowledge of likely alternative decision choices.

Administrative behaviour theorises the idea that determinations with 'higher value component' originate from the highest level of the structure of the organisation while subordinate at the bottom part make decisions rich in factual content [19]. The top-end choices stresses the *what*, but the factual content underscores the *how* part of subordinate judgements. Altogether, this dualistic nature of decision-making presents a bird's eye view of the concept of administrative behaviour. Thus, the entirety of decisions in organisations is a mixture of value premises (beliefs of all the means necessary) and factual premises (the practical situation). In this scenario, the real and applications of administrative behaviour are shown [20].

'*Choice of ends*' and '*choice of means*' constitute the chief tenets of administrative behaviour as Simon espouses to signify the nature (what) and functions (how) of decisions, respectively. Organisational actions at the highest managerial level are manifested via consensus building or fiat decisions connected with choice of ends. In this scenario, goal-led decisions characterise choice of ends since it determines obvious conditions for realising certain organisational aims at the top level of management. Choice of means connects with the resulting subordinate judgement driven by realistic and emergent occurrences. Simon identifies the realistic and emergent circumstances that confront subordinate decision-making at the point of performance as 'the observable world and the way in which it operates' ([17, 19], p. 55).

It is the very uncertain character of the observable world that encourages subordinate discretionary decisions in the course of performance. The rationale could be that value premises might be inconsistent with factual premises at the moment a performance is necessary, as factual premises are driven as well as inspired by situations completely directed by nascent and uncertain forces. Nonetheless, the final subordinate action is also inspired by the inclusive intentions of the organisation [19], as aberration from these unequivocal objectives in terms of the controlled (the subordinate) may induce sanctions or punishment from the organisation's upper level.

As per the techniques of organisational decision-making, it seems lower level employees and their bosses run on two ever-opposing wavelengths of decision-making. However, the final purpose of these decision-making functions is the attainment of a shared aims of the organisation. To this end, the complete organisational hierarchy 'can be viewed as a congealed set of means-end chains promoting consistency of decisions and activities throughout the organisation' ([21], p. 46). Simon [22] articulated the making of decisions and managerial processes by which advance determination of goals and the establishment of control schemes motivate sensible organisational behaviour. Simon discounted Henry Fayol's idea of 'economic man' and substituted it with 'administrative man', who is somewhat aware of all the possible options of his choices and so is ready to go with those that produce satisfactory approval.

To him, the notion of optimisation is quite misrepresentative as the prospects of attaining the utmost possible result seems characteristically elusive. Drawing on March and Simon's [23] considerations on bounded rationality, Simon shows the parameters in the intellectual talent of decision-makers. Simon championed the use of 'uncertainty' in organisational decision-making due to the real impossibility to derive total and complete information at any particular period during the decision-making process. While this may not be altogether a new idea, it is fair to consider that Simon initiated that notion and that later won him the 1978 Nobel Prize in this field.

The notional devices that Simon applied to comprehend the cosmic system intersects with a broad gamut of disciplines, such as, administrative theory, public administration, political science, organisation theory, economics, psychology, sociology, philosophy, computer science and cognitive science [4]. Reconsideration of the principled impression of making decision with particular allusion to reasonableness took a substantial share of his time. Consequently, rationality became the underlying logic in almost all the fields of enquiry he was related to because the idea encircled and occupied the broader structure of society. Hence, his efforts to dilate on rationality predictably got him to varied theoretical perceptions on economics, philosophy, psychology, sociology and politics. The relationships involving information, decision-making and technology appeared to be Simon's key research attention during the final part of the 1950s [24].

Notwithstanding Simon's multi-layered-disciplinary orientation to administrative behaviour, problem-solving and decision-making, he did not restrict his allegiance to any one specific discipline. To be sure, he indicated in a discussion cited in ([4], p. 583) that 'If you see any one of these disciplines dominating you, you join the opposition and you fight it for a while'. The core of Simon's influence was on problem-solving and decision-making in the specific aspects of individuals, organisations and societies. For example, Simon's [25–27] cases are of such works. 'Logical positivism', explained simply by Simon as possessing a similar meaning as empiricism ([19], p. 68), is apparently the crucial recurring argument in the work of administrative behaviour. Administrative behaviour has at its centre the searching of perceptible organisational consideration driven by the rigours of organised approaches. In view of this, subjects like philosophy, the social sciences and mathematics are practically considered along with the study of administrative behaviour [28].

3. Control in organisations

Control in administration invariably denotes shaping the character of the governed, transforming and guiding their operations to be favourable and aligned with the ambitions of group and the firm's aspirations. The foregoing logic demonstrates, as it does, at least, three central ideas, namely, authority, training and organisational loyalty, that profoundly undergird the workings of organisational control. Each of these fundamentally affects and encroaches on personal engagements resulting from different situational exigencies. When social agents become formal members of an organisation, the organisation is confronted with the problematic situation of how to modify the members' behaviour consistent with the overall organisational frame of its activities. A couple of internal and external influences by way of stimuli are applied to deal with these behavioural checks. These are 'the stimuli with which the organisation seeks to influence the individual and the psychological "set" of the individual, which determines his response to the stimuli' ([19], p. 432).

Influencing the organisational agents places their character on a commonly recognised form in two basic categorical forms. The sets of influence are qualified as 'internal' and 'external' and each category drives, to a more or less degree, all the main means by which organisational dominance is achieved, namely, authority, training, identification or organisational loyalty and communication.

3.1 Authority orientation in organisations

Among the means of influencing personal and group actions and leading behaviour in organisations, authority seems to be the one that evidently and principally sets apart the behaviour of individuals as actors within the organisation from that of their behaviour outside of it. Authority identifies the official structures for the organisation on which the other expressions of organisational influence depend. It is pertinent we firm up a sense of what authority represents, as far as its explanation so as to set up the frame for the various manifestations of its effect within the organisational setting. To this end, Simon purely submits authority as 'the power to make decisions which guide the actions of another' ([19], p. 179). However, in the interest of thorough analysis and more all-inclusive understanding of the notion of authority, drawing on Barnard's view provides enhanced and enriched explication.

Barnard's view suggests a clarification that affords a necessary association that highlights the actual essence of authority within the context of the organisation. The account provides a hint of the frontiers for the impression of suitable personal organisational behaviour contingent on a crucial level of relationship. This relationship portends substantial logical reasoning for appreciating mediated control in ICT-driven interactions as instructions or guidelines designed for the realisation of organisational aims largely shift from the upper part of organisational ladder to those at the bottom level of the organisational structure. The lines of authority can also start from one department to another, not essentially in a hierarchical order. Prior to an individual's familiarisation with the numerous dominant instructions, they must have been provided with clear guidelines pertaining to the conditions placed on their conduct. The settings and conditions delineating such conduct and the terms by which they are showcased must be unfailing, and be consistent, with the complete desires of the ideals of the organisation.

A parallel interpretation of authority is theorised by Simon that noticeably portrays the subject-object duality of authority. The subject-object duality underscores the senior/junior spectacle intrinsic to authority relationships, which Simon expounds as mainly hinging on 'objective and behaviouristic terms'.

The shared expressions of desired behaviour between the boss and the subordinate account for the presence of authority. Thus, the subordinate must recognise and perform legitimate directives of the superior for authority to triumph. Perrow succinctly conveys this idea when he considers that in a situation where a subordinate declines to carry out legitimate instructions from an authority above, the superior loses their authority ([18], p. 71).

The rational supposition from the preceding quote indicates that in a circumstance where the desires and anticipations of the superior are not adhered to, authority would not be deemed to exist. The behaviour configuration of the subordinate on other hand is affected by specific considerations for engaging in some form of operation. Consequently, the matter of discretion is brought into the decision-making processes of the subordinate before undertaking a given assignment. Thus, the subordinate subjects his private agenda by projecting the wishes and command of their superior as a basis of his action ([19], p. 179).

To Chester I. Barnard's mind, authority flourishes on two primary levels, namely, the subjective and objective phases. While the subjective phase involves the 'personal, the *accepting*[1] of a communication as authoritative, the latter relates to the character in the communication by virtue of which it is accepted' ([19], p. 163). Chester's objective-subjective dichotomy on authority supports a vital analytical device for this piece as it provides a comprehensive means to appreciating the foundations and functions of organisational control. It offers superior clue that shared influence is intrinsic and essential to any control commitments. Subordinates must be ready to embrace guidelines and instructions for goal-centric results to be obtained. By a similar account, superiors should be able to embrace and encourage the proposals and creativeness of subordinates in the interest of stated organisational goals. A scenario where a subordinate declines to obey reasonable orders issued from a superior undercuts the true pillars on which authority rests. The maintenance of authority is subject to the dominant ideas of the people whose decisive goal is to have specific operations undertaken for their joint advantage.

For authority to be purposeful, it is crucial to guarantee the relevant involvement in terms of private efforts aimed at common targets. There should be the presence of structured individual efforts inextricably linked with prompt dynamic interests at any stated period with the aim of maintaining the reliability of the prevalent organisational authority insofar as instructions lie within the purview of, what Chester labels as, 'zone of indifference'. By zone of indifference, Barnard [29] attempts to illustrate a situation where lower ranked employees incontestably accommodate the guidelines or directives for carrying out a goal-oriented duty. Disparities exist in the zone of indifference. The disparities reveal diverse forms of broadness and narrowness subject to the extent to which inducements exceed the 'burdens and sacrifices' that describe a person's loyalty and attachment to the organisation.

Authority possesses bi-modal source, all of which seem to complement rather than contest with the technological and social components. The establishment of

[1] Italics in the original

authority in an organisational environment is, therefore, dependent on these same technological and social apparatuses. There is a reciprocal shaping of both social and technological components in the expression of authority. For example, technology is as vital in putting structures of authority in place and effecting behaviour just as much as the social (human) devices in the realisation of expected behaviour and motivating predetermined results. Both work hand-in-hand as each has its field of operational emphasis. In view of this, individuals aver their allegiance to human authority systems in pretty much the same way as they submit to the demands of technology-led cooperative and control systems. Controlling group, varying private behaviour and influencing organisational objectives and requirements imply modifying the mechanisms that convey the demands for the performance of certain operations. With these analytical notions of authority, it is possible to delineate the nature of authority through which these features manifest as well as the procedures that underlie its operations.

3.2 Structural apparatus of authority

Authority can be said to rely on three basic stakes of operationally interlocking equivalents of responsibility, specialisation and coordination [29]. It is compelling to accentuate the role of each of these structural apparatuses and explore how they, together, operate in concert to offer some novel insights into the appreciation of control. It is vital to highlight this dimension as it assists to widen the scope by which social agents, with motley organisational agendas can purposefully be understood. Each of these dimensions of authority merits some consideration in turn, because controlling the activities of subordinates by means of both output and behavioural expectations, demands a significant degree of responsibility, specialisation and coordination. Responsibility defines performance expectations, specialisation clarifies the degree of discretion and coordination stipulates the synchronisation of individual (superior and subordinate) endeavours. Now I turn attention to focus on how these concepts become implicated in control in organisational discourse from the viewpoint of administrative behaviour.

3.2.1 Responsibility

A primary aim of authority that appears to win the attention of administrative behaviour enthusiasts is its purpose to assert group and individual acceptance of the principles of standards of behaviour established by those at the upper levels of authority [30]. Responsibility suggests the power of a 'particular private code of morals to control the conduct of the individual in the presence of strong contrary desires or impulses' ([31], p. 263). To a greater extent, a particular conduct is administered by diverse private codes. Such codes could be high, simple low, complex, sketchy or comprehensive, based on a person's ethical status. Logically, general tendencies exist whereby people act in consonance with private interests and contrary to determined organisational ideologies. In view of this, 'elaborate set of sanctions may be evoked and applied against the recalcitrant member' ([19], p.187) upon contravention or disobedience to established instructions, rubrics, standards and recognised principles in the carrying out of specified operations. In Barnard's view, the clash of codes of behaviour has serious repercussions. The risk or enduring fear occasionally present in the use of disciplinary tools can go as far as to offer people some opportunity to engage in manoeuvres favourable to their private agenda.

In Gaus' view [32], it is almost assuredly unconceivable to think about authority in the administration of organisations without encouraging its analogous considerations on the structures that invite different grades of the hierarchy of organisations to justify their operations.

3.2.2 Coordination

Essentially, coordination aims to guarantee a cohesive sense of purpose towards a shared direction [33]. In other words, the particular application of coordination is 'the adoption by all the members of the group of the same decision, or more precisely, of mutually consistent decisions in combination attaining the established goal' ([19], p. 190). The duty of compliance with a mutual command and objective makes communication a challenge to, and a crucial aspect of, coordination. Coordination advocates the incorporation of the various 'islands of automation' to accomplish the overall efforts of the organisation. ([34], p. 511). Varied private and team events are unified to attain a common organisation-inspired ends. Communication is the vital factor that secures that functional differences are synchronised to reflect the collective contributions of all the participants in the organisation. From a philosophical viewpoint, authority functions as a harmonising device [35]. Authority endorses the establishment of command structures and communication channels by which individual commitments are coordinated towards the attainment of a common aim. The communication avenues strengthen interdependences among different organisational entities [36]. Coordination could be evident in two deeply separate types, in the form of procedural and substantive. Procedural coordination tries to highlight a sketch of the extensive amplification of the actions and associations of the members in an organisation, while substantive coordination connects with the functional endeavours of the firm.

In Simon's view, the delineation of the chains of command with directives establishing the constraints on individual agents epitomises procedural coordination, although schemes for the creation of specific goods and services characterise substantive coordination. The core of coordination buttresses the conviction that allows people in a harmonised entity expect the probable conduct of their associates. To realise the highest degree of coordination, Gulick recommends the execution of a couple of primary pragmatic necessities.

By organisation, that is, by interconnecting the sub-categorisation of job roles by assigning them to people who are connected in a line of authority. The rationale is for purposeful coordination of work by the orders of bosses to subordinates, moving from the top to the bottom of the whole enterprise.

3.2.3 Specialisation

Specialisation as an expression of authority inspires the vital worth of administrative proficiency, the spirit of which resides in the awareness that organisational entities differ in their expertise, experience, proficiency, capability and appeal. This belief is informed by the propensity of specialisation to enhance output by boosting profitability [37]. Crucial to specialisation is the notion of division of labour in which 'the work of the organisation is subdivided, so far as possible, in such a way that all processes requiring a particular skill can be performed by persons possessing that skill' ([19], p. 189). Specialisation has its attendant continuous reciprocal fine-tuning by agents in collaborative efforts. Barnard [29] sketches five dynamically interconnected benchmarks by which specialisation gets implicated in constituting organisational activities, which include *specialisation by location*, *time*, *expertise*, *artefacts* and *methods*. None of these separations avoids the part technology plays in carrying out and underlining the particular demands of their corresponding operations.

Specialisation by location connects with the terrestrial area where job is undertaken. Spatial organisation of job by way of accommodation, air-conditioning, compartmentalisation, etc. offers a notion of individuality for finishing certain tasks. Time-induced specialisation is necessary for arranging the procedures and patterns of composite operations, principally in places where work is done in the mode of day-and-night to offer accelerated and premium service. The coordination test for the period of synchronisation at which work is completed has repercussions for promptness and stability in the course of work. Lost time, unobtainability of the relevant resources at the appropriate moment and engaging in things in an unsuitable manner are some of the real-world problematic scenarios to time-led specialisation.

Know-how as an expression of specialisation underscores the vitality of entities in organisation that performs various specialised tasks. Training and selection processes are led by proficiency and readiness to adhere to uncompromising time timetable of structured arrangements so as to ensure the needed practical skill [38]. Specialisation is also evidenced in the devices and objects applied to complete a given task. In this case, certain accoutrements and technological artefacts may be favoured ahead of others in certain task performance, such that the processes may result in various effects of the final outcome. For example, telephone may be desired for instantaneous response on unmediated interaction to email. Lastly, aspect by means of which specialisation can take place is the processes or modalities that agents apply for the attainment of their operations. The efficiency of such process-inspired specialisation is subject to the adroitness and the expected flexibility of agents involved.

The following figure (**Figure 1**) is initiated as a proxy to Barnard's exposition on the functional nature of authority.

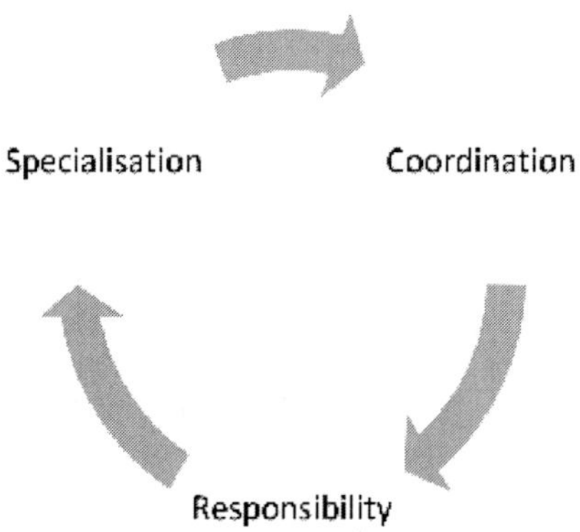

Figure 1.
The authority triad based on Chester Barnard's [31] analysis of the concept.

4. Training in organisational influence

Training offers one of the means that assists organisations to effect the character, practice and attitude of their staffs. As a style of organisational stimulus, training changes social agents 'from the inside out' ([19], p. 13) and as such, shapes their choices and judgements sympathetic to the functional competence and administrative fidelity. Key to this notion is the system of indoctrination, which gets employees to do away with unhelpful conduct and features while instantaneously picking up other traits and abilities that come between them and productive output [39] via learning. Accordingly, training stresses the importance of developing capacity. Getting employees ready to handle the challenging exigencies linked with given tasks is a crucial component of training. The notion of training could be to diminish the regularity with which directions and rules are given to guide subordinate behaviour. In this case, training 'prepares the organization member to reach satisfactory decisions himself, without the need for the constant exercise of authority or advice' ([19], p. 13). Logically, even though training assumes a substitutive control mechanism by which to shape the judgments and choices of employees, it could also be considered as, what I call, a discretion-granting channel. Reinforcing the discretion-granting construct, Simon directs our focus on the point that minimal supervision is necessary after the time of training.

Perfecting the specifics for carrying out a given duty with the slightest degree of faults and blunders is the trademark of, and the logic driving, many training arrangements in organisations. Training, thus, encourages a certain extent of delegation of duty as a vital link of shaping character at different levels of the organisational ladder. The decentralising process conditions the context for employee thinking and activities, driven by wide structural instructions designed to inform and pattern behaviour at the subordinate level of the organisational structure. Training understood in this sense is a prospective basis for encouraging consistency and dependability [40] plus imbuing poise and courage in worker decision-making in terms of their acceptable operational efforts.

Regardless of its promise to diminish the extent of mistakes, coupled with the assertions of reinforcing the ideals of requisite variety to certify dependability among social agents, training is thought to be the source of several unsatisfactory circumstances [40]. Without a doubt, training fails to uncover all the likely circumstances that social agents are expected to experience in the normal period of their legitimate tasks. It is plausible to concur with Weick that training packages in many situations fail to match up with the factual situational happenings that real-life settings provoke [41]. The ensuing struggle between training experience and exposure to actual exigencies may cause even competent staffs to recoil and cling to deep-rooted behaviour [42] much to the detriment of organisational strategizing.

This could be troubling, and could therefore condition the awareness and determination of social agents with unfriendly repercussions, typically the prospect of undesirable outcomes on objectives and proficient performance. Again, when training is fruitful, familiarity through experience brings little certainty for employees to deal with the fleeting and changeable forms of work the moment they take up the demands of their tasks. Put bluntly, employees are barely offered an identical setting they received for their training 'once they actually operate the system' (Weick, p. 332). The ramifications of this scenario could be irritatingly unsatisfactory and occasion work-associated tension by harming the emotional balance of employees thus placing them in a situation less able to cope with impending challenges.

Directing attention on training in the control of employees in administrative behaviour could be a definitive means of accepting the essential antecedents and consequences of the rationale training occasionally fails to achieve its ideals. This failure can act as a true source for probing into the perceptual narrative meant for this unpleasant situation. It could also highlight an operational realignment of the forces that condition the facilitating environment for effective training efforts. It could also mark a preliminary point for studying the crucial dimension of technology mediating artefacts in deciding their usefulness in training arrangements. On account of this, the necessary relationships can be recognised between the difficulties connected with reality and the ordered nature of training settings. This would lead to a legitimate call for the motivating factors of the strategic management of training approaches to fit organisational control strategies. Against this situation, some form of validity would be brought to bear on the evidence of mediated control in collaborative work environments.

5. The mindset of administrative behaviour

To appreciate the relevance of administrative behaviour to this essay to any substantial mark, it is critical that the appropriate cognisance is afforded to the degree to which the mentality of the individual gets accounted for in the entire realm of organisational operations. This is meant to envision how the organisation modifies and alters their attitudinal trajectory. Giving some thought to this part of the theory is vitally important because one of the primary jobs organisations undertake is to 'place the organization members in a psychological environment that will adapt their decisions to the organisation objectives and will provide them with the information needed to make these decisions correctly' ([19], p. 92). The mindset of administrative behaviour is befitting for analysing control in mediated interaction due to the fact that notions such as rationality and organisational loyalty can be applicable to different motivations for control in organisational interaction. Ways by which these can be ascertained are the idiosyncratic explanations for the application of mediated interaction and the degree to which these same mediated interaction exercises encourage employee loyalty or disaffection.

5.1 Rationality

Rationality is considered a basic and significant frame in administrative theory. And it is relevant to link it with mediated control to figure out the kind of forces that drive the choices and actions of subordinates in undertaking their given obligations. It should be pointed out in advance that paying attention to rationality is not meant to illustrate employees, as is habitually supposed, as primarily logical, an understanding that overshadowed much of economic theory. To be sure, rationality should be encouraged to mirror the entire conclusions reached by social agents in situations connected with their precise organisational commitments even though such ultimate decisions may be inaccurate to the 'objective bystander'. In other words, rationality in this situation has more of a strict application than its conventional dictionary implication of 'agreeable to reason: not absurd, preposterous, extravagant, foolish, fanciful or the like, intelligent and sensible' ([43], p. 2).

Furthermore, rationality in this instance is not only regarded as a preserve of humans, material agency [44, 45] can also be ascribed as rational to the extent that 'structural arrangements within organisations are conceived as tools deliberately designed for the efficient realisation of ends ... Rationality resides in the structure itself, ... – in rules that assure participants that evaluate performance and detect deviance, in reward systems that motivate participants are selected, replaced, or promoted ...' ([46], p. 78).

In view of this, rationality is generalised to embrace organised systems of processes and directions intended to permit the sound advancement of flow of work from a process or condition to another. Rationality in this study, fundamentally, reinforces control in its claim. Rationality appears to encompass three crucial cognitive processes of intuition, reasoning and perception. These cognitive processes are contingent beliefs, opinions and preferences and that commonly motivate and drive individual action. At least one of the primary cognitive processes is stimulated in arriving at conclusion before carrying out a preferred course of action. Rationality can then be deployed to appreciate flexible activities as far as mediated control.

Accordingly, rationality concerns itself with the practice of 'means-end' series of arrangements or levels of objectives. The means-end angle illustrates the technology or material component part of rationality. The technology bit, which, as a matter of convenience, can be designated as system, projects the incorporation of behaviour by which the sub-entities in the whole system work to disclose the general purpose for which the system was intended. Rationality requires evaluating calculated choices for obtaining the crucial goal. It should be feasible to advise consistent with Simon [19] that rationality is dependent on 'useful purpose' for an individual or organisation in undertaking a given exercise.

In rationality, mindful or determined act and unplanned activity become obvious in the thought processes of making decisions. However, an inadvertent act can be considered once the particulars for performance have been learned to the extent that it becomes programmed and automatic to the individual. Behaviour can be altogether subjectively and objectively rational based on the dimension of scrutiny. Subjective rationality underscores the belief pattern and inclinations of the individual while objective rationality emphasises the perceptions ascribed to the intrinsic value of the decision depending on the result of the completed task. This perception suggests that even though some particular medicines cannot treat a certain type of ailment, the truth about its efficacy makes it objectively rational. From a subjective orientation, the belief that a medicine can cure a disease is adequate and indubitable evidence of its disease-curing competencies. The preceding analysis offers the basis for outdooring 'qualifiers' to illuminate the almost baffling difficulties linked with the notion of rationality.

To start with, objective rationality claims the suitable behaviour for ensuring the greatest advantage in a specified condition. Furthermore, subjective rationality points to attaining the maximum rewards from the viewpoint of the people concerned. Yet still, conscious rationality identifies a scenario where the outcome and mean tension is a cognitive course. Finally, deliberate rationality situates a scenario that individuals totally occupy their psychology in exemplifying a certain behaviour. It must be pointed out that altogether these distinctions of rationality can show up in contemporary organisations. It can soundly be argued that there is the prospect for social agents to undertake operations without the consciousness of the fundamental aim for their action. Rationality in an organisation involves the systems of structures and procedures for amending and inspiring tolerable behaviour together with the techniques and methods for their creation, thus making rationality altogether a process and consequence of individual, group and organisational commitment. The rationality of the individual member in the organisation can have an enduring consequence for their loyalty within the framework of the organisation's endeavours.

5.2 Understanding organisational loyalty

It is vitally important to recognise the means by which social agents progressively, albeit fairly reliably, become associated with the issues of the organisation. Fundamentally, the organisation's aims are enforced on individuals in the course of administering authority and control. Regarding organisational discourse from the viewpoint of administrative theory could shed light on crafting a conceptual outline that could shape our opinions of mediated control. Administrative theory assists in the clarification and explanation of the means by which individuals get to be assimilated and turn out to be deeply attached to the organisation in unalloyed loyalty. This loyalty to the organisation, as Simon suggests, derives its origins from a couple of different patterns of behaviour of individuals. Tendency in the direction of an obligation to 'the service of the organization' and an 'attachment to the conservation and growth of the organization itself' ([19], p. 278). The course through which employees in organisations acquire 'organisation personality' pretty unlike their individual personality is ...through his subjection to organizationally determined goals, and through the gradual absorption of these goals into his own attitudes ... ([19]).

The aforementioned quote entails a means whereby the organisation apportions explicit roles to individuals and recommends the principles, beliefs, choices and facts against which their judgements, choices, decisions and actions in the organisation should be moulded and recognised. Minimising the options within which a person's actions are to function, the organisation—to a logical degree—restricts the tests and possibilities of his judgements and actions to a manageable extent. Forfeiting a person's own predilections plus subduing one's private values in an attempt to follow organisational demands may be mentally trying. It provides the scenery of two divergent forces drawing the individual apart, each requiring similar attention.

The vigorous tussle can lead to the individual preferring either his private inclinations, morals, decisions or largely overlooking the training in respect to the requirements of his role. However, Simon notes that as soon as the frame for actions and decisions has been determined, a person is left with but one 'best' alternative that mirrors the values of the organisation and situational exigencies. Ignoring the prospect of accounting for a person's intentions in the final decision-making and ultimate action could diminish any hints of discretionary choices of the individual in matters of their benefits.

Admitting the limits on his own exposition, Simon observes that there are occasions when a person might not work to the benefit of the organisation, whereby 'personal motives reassert themselves, and the organisation, to that extent, ceases to exist' ([19], p. 283), at that material period when the judgement and the probable consequent action are considered. As a result, the individual trades the scale of values of the organisation for their private one as the crucial benchmark for the relevance of his decision. A considerable and leading avenue of administrative behaviour by which a person mentally joins their emotions with the purpose of the organisation is identification. Identification can result in a condition by which 'a person identifies himself with a group when, in making a decision, he evaluates the several alternatives of choice in terms of their consequences for the specified group' ([19], p, 284).

It seems reasonably sound to report that identification is a needed tool for group solidarity. The psychological devices for explicating the identification experience, per Simon's view, goes under three separate groupings of personal interest in organisational success, transfer of private-management psychology and focus of attention. These distinctions are taken one after the other to demonstrate their corresponding zones of logical concentration. Individual interest in the triumph of the organisation as a result of loyalty to it thereof is driven by personal motivations. Personal motives are not the only reason for a person's established relationship with the organisation but also 'the growth, prestige or the success of the organisation itself'. These afford sufficient chances for enhanced compensation, upgrade, manpower progression plans and the application of superior obligation so that a person looks over and above the difficulties and unfavourable situations linked with his job functions. In view of this, a more profound sense of engagement grows with troubling conditions to attain the complete specified goals of the organisation.

The shift of private-management thinking empowers the individual in the organisation to recondition their mentality and regard the organisation as theirs.

The transfer in mental attitude drives people in the organisation to employ such personal pronouns as 'my' unit, 'my' group, 'my' business, etc., a suggestion that they have a stake in the worries of the organisation as well as in its ambitions and beliefs. The application of these grammatical constructs also serves the indication that organisational members possess a shared fate since they possess a communal sense of 'ownership'. Focus of attention, as a tool of mental proof of identity, leads the administrator's endeavours at those beliefs and those people within the organisational outfit who are expected to be not obliquely affected by the administrative agenda. In short, focus of attention reassures the subordinate to modify what they do towards the goals and targets of the organisation.

Considered against these viewpoints, identification provides an operative means for regulating persons and groups in the organisation so as to build their welfares, desires and individual proclivities in the direction of the organisation's general targets. The planned tools of the organisation for identification permit for extensive redesign of the organisation to normalise and guide the operations of persons known to be contributors to the full organisational processes. Therefore, this promotes rationality to go further than the constraints brought upon it by a diminished span of attention.

6. Final thoughts

As a lens for analysing the dynamics of administrative behaviour from the standpoint of organisational mediated control, this write-up has considered the diverse and searching views offered by administrative behaviour on the matter at hand. The piece surveyed the mechanics of organisational influence, emphasising the approaches by which authority is constituted and applied. Training was observed as a tool for both influencing behaviour on the one hand and an avenue for permitting discretionary opportunities on the other, all aimed at facilitating enhanced job performance and organisational efficiency.

The closing segment then concentrates on the psychology of administrative behaviour by drawing comprehensively on such notions as rationality and organisational loyalty and how they impact shared collaborative endeavours in technology-mediated control. Together, these interweaving impressions disclose the variety of understanding probable to be acquired by examining some of the critical facets of administrative behaviour. The philosophical explanations put forward by the theory of administrative behaviour etched naturally from the discussions of Herbert A Simon proffer a favourable and thorough framework for probing mediated control from the viewpoint of organisational discourse. It remains the wish of this piece to have an empirical data the juxtaposition of which should tease out the different dimensions by which organisational efficiency, allegiance, meaningful interaction and dynamic relationship between the organisation and its external world are brought to bear on its normal operational endeavours.

References

[1] Garland D. The Culture of Control: Crime and Social Order in Contemporary Society. Oxford: Oxford University Press; 2001

[2] Garland D. What is a "history of the present"? On Foucault's genealogies and their critical preconditions. Punishment & Society. 2014;**16**(4):365-384

[3] Rettie R. Mobile phone communication: Extending Goffman to mediated interaction. Sociology. 2009;**43**(3):421-438

[4] Augier M, Frank KF. Introduction: Herbert A. Simon (1916-2001). Industrial and Corporate Change. 2002;**11**(3):583-586

[5] Scott RW. Institutions and Organizations. Thousand Oaks: Sage; 1995

[6] Selznick P. TVA and the Grass Roots. Berkley, CA: University of California Press; 1949

[7] Eisenhardt KM. Agency theory: An assessment and review. Academy of Management Review. 1989;**14**(1):57-74

[8] Williamson O. Markets and Hierarchies: Analysis and Antitrust Implications. New York: Free Press; 1975

[9] Giddens A. The Constitution of Society: Outline of the Theory of Structuration. Berkeley: University of California Press; 1984

[10] Latour B. Reassembling the Social: An Introduction to Actor-Network Theory. Oxford: Oxford University Press; 2005

[11] Miller GA. The magical number seven, plus or minus two: Some limits on our capacity for processing information. Psychological Review. 1956;**63**:81-97

[12] Jones M. Structuration theory and IT. In: Currie WL, Galliers RD, editors. Rethinking Management Information Systems: An Interdisciplinary Perspective. Oxford: Oxford University Press; 1999. pp. 103-135

[13] DiMaggio PJ. Interest and agency in institutional theory. In: Zucker L, editor. Institutional Patterns and Organizations: Culture and Environment. Cambridge, MA: Ballinger; 1988. pp. 3-21

[14] Avgerou C, Ciborra C, Land FF, editors. The Social Study of Information and Communication Technology: Innovation, Actors and Context. Oxford: Oxford University Press; 2004

[15] Bostrom R, Heinen JS. MIS problems and failures: A socio-technical perspective. MIS Quarterly. 1977;**1**(3):17-32

[16] Land FF. Social aspects of information systems. In: Piercy N, editor. Management Information Systems: The Technological Challenge. Beckenham: Croom-Helm; 1987. pp. 11-57

[17] Simon H. Administrative Behaviour: A Study of Decision-Making Processes in Administrative Organizations. New York: The Free Press; 1997a

[18] Perrow C. Complex Organizations: A Critical Essay. New York: Random House; 1986

[19] Simon H. Administrative Behaviour: A Study of Decision-Making Processes in Administrative Organizations. 4th ed. New York: The Free Press; 1997b

[20] Simon AH. Reason in Human Affairs. Stanford, California: Stanford University Press; 1983

[21] Scott RW. Organizations: Rational, Natural, and Open Systems. 4th ed. Upper Saddle River, New Jersey: Prentice-Hall; 1998

[22] Simon AH. Administrative Behavior. 3rd ed. New York: Macmillan; 1976

[23] March JG, Simon AH. Organizations. New York: Wiley; 1958

[24] Waring SP. Taylorism Transformed. Chapel Hill, NC: University of North Carolina Press; 1991

[25] Simon AH. Administrative Behavior. New York: Free Press; 1947

[26] Simon AH. The Architecture of Complexity. Paper Presented at the Proceedings of the American Philosophical Society. 1962

[27] Simon AH. Altruism and economics. American Economic Review. 1993;**83**:156-161

[28] Kerr G. The development history and philosophical sources of Herbert Simon's administrative behavior. Journal of Management History. 2007;**13**(3):255-268

[29] Barnard C. The Functions of the Executive. Cambridge, Massachusetts: Harvard University Press; 1956

[30] Friedrich CJ. Responsible Bureaucracy. Cambridge: Harvard University Press; 1932

[31] Barnard C. The Functions of the Executive. Cambridge, Massachusetts: Harvard University Press; 1938

[32] Gaus MJ. The responsibility of public administration. In: Gaus W, Dimock ME, editors. The Frontiers of Public Administration. Chicago: University of Chicago Press; 1936. pp. 26-44

[33] Daft RL. New Era of Management. South-Western: Cengage Learning; 2012

[34] Kling R, Kraemer K, Allen L, Bakos J, Gurbaxani V, King J. Information systems in manufacturing coordination: Economic and social perspectives. In: Paper Presented at the Proceedings of the Thirteenth International Conference on Information Systems, Dallas, TX. 1992

[35] Simon AH. Organizations and markets. The Journal of Economic Perspectives. 1991;**5**(2):25-44

[36] Kling R. Cooperation, coordination and control in computer-supported work. Communications of the ACM. 1991;**34**(12):83-88

[37] Gulick L. Notes on the theory of organization: With special reference to government in the United States. In: Gulick L, Urwick L, editors. Papers on the Science of Administration. New York: Institute of Public Administration; 1937. pp. 1-46

[38] Taylor FW. The Principles of Scientific Management. New York: Harper & Bros; 1911

[39] Terpstra DE, Rozell EJ. The relationship of staffing practices to organizational level measures of performance. Personnel Psychology. 1993;**46**:27-48

[40] Weick K. Making Sense of the Organization. Malden, MA: Blackwell Publishing; 2001

[41] Weick KE. The collapse of sense making in organizations: The Mann gulch disaster. Administrative Science Quarterly. 1993;**38**:628-652

[42] Weick KE. A stress analysis of future battlefields. In: Hunt JG, Blair JD, editors. Leadership on the Future Battlefields. Washington, DC: Pergamon; 1985. pp. 32-46

[43] Simon AH. Rationality as process and as product of thought. The American Economic Review. 1978;**68**(2):1-16

[44] Orlikowski W, Scott SV. The algorithm and the crowd: Considering the materiality of service innovation. MIS Quarterly. 2015;**39**(1):201-216

[45] Winter S, Berente N, Howison J, Butler B. Beyond the organizational 'container': Conceptualizing 21st century sociotechnical work. Information and Organization. 2014;**24**:250-269

[46] Scott RW. Organizations: Rational, Natural, and Open Systems. Englewood Cliffs: Prentice-Hall; 1981

Chapter 6

Developing Entrepreneurship in Digital Economy: The Ecosystem Strategy for Startups Growth

Abstract

The transition of the economies toward the digital era is determining the arising of a type of entrepreneurship based on factors and features quite different from established game rules. These changes disclose a series of opportunities for those firms which will be able to adapt at the new parameters and functionalities related to digital technologies diffusion. This contribution underlines some dynamics that should be considered from policy makers who aspire, on the one hand, to promote the emergence of a significant number of startups operating in the digital field and, on the other hand, to nurture the growth process of startups into scale ups. Due to social and economic troubles of many western areas, this latter aspect is even more important. According to a flourishing research stream on entrepreneurship, an interpretative approach for achieving the dual objective is to implement a specific strategy to create an appropriate regional ecosystem. The ecosystem represents a clear challenge within the traditional entrepreneurial policies frame, whose results have so far often been unsatisfactory. Despite its initially selective approach, from an ecosystem, many potential benefits can descend. However, creating an ecosystem for digital startup is a complex and burdensome task, which requires a safe and competent guidance, as well as the active involvement of many local actors.

Keywords: entrepreneurship, digital technology, ecosystem, high-growth firm, startup

1. Introduction

Since 1980s, in many western countries, the focus of industrial choices has changed substantially as consequence of the transition from SMEs policies to entrepreneurship policies. More recently, to react to the deep economic and financial crisis of 2008 and to sustain the diffusion of ICT, industrial policy measures have been fundamentally finalized at providing instruments increasing starting-up and the emergence of the self-employment in general, by spreading entrepreneurial culture and stimulating the direct participation of citizens in entrepreneurial process.

New ventures have been believed as a pathway for increase employment, especially for youth suffering from a disproportionate lack of job opportunities [1–3], while the startups, considered as innovation-based new ventures, have been spurred by the ambition of accelerating the adoption and diffusion of border line technologies, in doing so counteracting the competition of Eastern countries benefiting of lower production costs [4, 5].

These purposes have been sustained by measures improving the business environments, trying to make them economically conducive for firm emergence. Among these new measures, there are R&D grants and tax benefits, business accelerators and incubators, incentives and facilities for university-based spin-offs, financing of risk initiatives, and so on.

Nevertheless, this strategy has often led to unsatisfactory results, notably as regard to the contribution to territorial economic growth, innovations spreading, and dissemination of skills and competencies. Even in local contexts where high ventures birth rates were registered, there have been no relevant increases of key economic indicators, such as gross income, firms' survival, or profit level (e.g., [6–8]). A managerial and business research stream [9–11] argues that the weak impact of the mentioned measures on local economy development could be linked to three main aspects.

Firstly, a nebula idea of the entrepreneurship concept exists. A wide range of economic activities is used to be included in this term, even if the scientific literature has been clarifying its real meaning since many decades [12, 13], as detailed later.

Secondly, usually new firms are considered in a similar manner and often equated at startups. But not all new firms necessarily are startup, as well as startups are dissimilar in terms of value generation or job creation [14, 15]. A basilar matter is that too few startups are able to become high growth firms, which are able to assure a tangible contribution to the territorial context in terms of employment, income, investment, knowledge, and competencies [16, 17]. Indeed, startups are unsteady activities, with high probability of failure or destined to remain small business, when not simple micro-firms or self-employment activities. In the last circumstances, the contribution to regional growth is rather limited, if it exists [18, 19].

Thirdly, an excessive emphasis on technological innovation exists. Technological innovation in itself is not a panacea as it is risky and normally takes a long time to deploy its effects and to be fully appreciated. These peculiarities contrast with the typical weaknesses of new ventures, when they are not able to evolve in more established societal or legal forms [20–22]. The overwhelming focus on technologies innovation might acquire an ambiguous meaning when related to startups [23]. Firms operating into the so-called traditional sectors (automotive, domestic appliances, furnishings, etc.) of Western countries often exhibit higher growth rates than firms placed at the technological border. The capacity to propose, over the time, more and more effective business models could, therefore, overcome the prominence of technological factor [24]. Hence, all high growth firms are neither necessarily high-tech startups nor a new business in general.

With this in mind, the incoming of digital technologies in the realm of entrepreneurship represents a new challenge for entrepreneurs and policy makers [25]. When applied to manufacturing, digital technologies (such as social media, mobile computing, data analytics, 3d printing, cloud, and cyber solutions) lead to a remodeling of productive patterns originating new market opportunities, higher revenue streams, faster time-to-market, enhanced service provision, and increased productivity [25, 26]. Moreover, digital technologies also deeply modify the boundaries of products and processes, in doing so transforming the nature of uncertainty inherent entrepreneurial processes and outcomes, as well as the ways of dealing with such uncertainty [27]. All these changings are shifting the traditional way of creating and doing business, determining the emergence of a new specific type of entrepreneurship, the *digital entrepreneurship* (Nambisan, 2017).

Broadly defined as creating new ventures and transforming existing businesses by developing novel digital technologies and/or novel usage of such technologies [27], digital entrepreneurship needs to be properly fueled and enabled in many directions. Among these, European Commission [25] suggests the creation of specific digital knowledge base and ICT markets, the creation of digital business environments, an easier access to finance facilitations, the diffusion of digital skills, the creation of e-leadership, and the creation of entrepreneurial culture. These complex aims assume a heuristic and wide-ranging approach that, presumably, requests a reconsideration of the logic that leads to the emergence and development of startups operating in the digital setting.

This chapter aims primarily to discuss how the current focus on startups could be addressed, so that the digital era becomes a source of opportunities more than risks. Specifically, the paper is consistent with an up-warding audience of scholars [28–31] according to the best answer for collecting the business opportunities and channeling the benefits for local areas appears the creation of ecosystems able to support scale ups; that is, startups with high potentiality to grow-up [32].

The debate on the importance of these companies for local development and growth is really dated. The novelty is that, instead of an undifferentiated starting-up, a selective approach centered on startups with the better potentialities is now explored by creating specific business environments aligned to the purpose of systematizing, promoting, and sustaining their growth [3, 33, 34].

The chapter is organized as follows. After this introduction, Section 2 specifies the concept of entrepreneurship oriented for the purpose of the regional economic development. Afterward, the notions of startup and scale ups are clarified in Section 3. Section 4 deepens the dynamic meaning of an entrepreneurial ecosystem functional to scale ups development. Section 5 identifies the link existing among the challenges linked to digital technologies and the advantages provided by ecosystems. Some conclusive remarks are showed in the last section.

2. Entrepreneurship and entrepreneurialism

An aspect systematically ignored by policies concerns the concept of entrepreneurship, often considered as an undifferentiated phenomenon whose only evaluable output is the birth of new ventures. This is because, on one side, a shared definition of entrepreneurship is missing, as well as a precise knowledge of its boundaries and factors from which it originates. On the other side, it descends from the fact that, by logic, this concept can only derive from that of entrepreneur [13]. In turn, the figure of entrepreneur is ambiguous, confused with other economic roles such as the owner or the capitalist, not always easy to identify inside the firm, and whose assignments and tasks are not easily framed. Not by chance, the *Huffalump* metaphor, the imaginary animal impossible to capture [35], was introduced.

However, more recently, entrepreneurship literature has shed much light on these aspects. But these advances do not seem fully absorbed in determining policy measures. So that, even if a propulsive thrust of economy is expected from the entrance in the digital economy ([27], Nambisan, 2017), there is a real possibility that not all contexts will be able to benefit from the emerging opportunities.

In this view, this chapter emphasizes the thesis for which standardized policy actions addressed to support an undifferentiated starting-up risk to obtain limited, when not counterproductive effects. Investigations on firms' turnover have showed that an increasing birth rate is often accompanied by an almost similar increase of death rate. This faster turnover has not a positive impact on the social and economic context if the surviving ventures remain micro or individual firms [1, 2, 36]. In other words, just favoring a high *entrepreneurial activity*—the percentage of adults involved in the process of the creation or management of an enterprise—does not necessarily ensure the emergence of a sufficient share of companies that are able to succeed in the medium or long term with a positive impact on local context.

This assumption is coherent with the supposed *U-shaped relationship* between the entrepreneurial activity of a country and its per-capita Gross National Product (GNP). Leading scholars belonging to the *Global Entrepreneurship Monitoring* [4, 37] explain that the entrepreneurship activity is higher for countries with either a low or a high GNP per capita.

In countries with low GNP per capita, entrepreneurship activity is higher owing to the lack of professional alternatives and other revenue sources—'necessity' driven entrepreneurship rather than 'opportunity' [38]. When GNP per capita grows, countries with middle-income, activity gradually decrease up to a certain minimum point. That is because the emergence of scale-intensive firms operating in mid-technology sectors offers stable employment perspectives, which reduce the motivation toward starting up. After this point, activity newly increases. In areas with a higher GNP per capita, the presence of advanced technology and scale economies allows larger and established companies to meet the growing demand of expanding markets, exerting a positive attraction to would-be entrepreneurs. In these circumstances, high startups rates are predictable. They could begin an economic virtuous circle.

This theory, therefore, supports the existence of an *equilibrium rate* of entrepreneurial activity, which varies consistently in line with the degree of national development. This rate is considered "an 'optimal' industry structure, operationalized either in terms of the number of business owners or in terms of the small-firm share in value-of shipments" ([1], p. 3). Deviations from the equilibrium rate caused by cultural forces, institutional changes, and economic trends risk to cause negative consequences for national growth, since "economies can have both too few and too many businesses and both situations can imply a growth penalty" ([36], p. 285). A too low equilibrium rate may imply few stimuli toward innovation and change. A too high rate could determinate the failure to exploit scale and scope economies, a reduction in R&D expenditure, or an excess of price-based competition, forcing firms to reduce output/input quality or resorting to shadow economy. Consequently, regions deviating from the level of entrepreneurial activity compatible with their GNP, risk to obtain lower rates of overall economic growth.

The optimal equilibrium rate is dependent on both the *weight* of sectors, —dynamism in services business is statistically much greater than in manufacturing industry—and the *type* of entrepreneurship created. Hence, generic starting up policies could not be a panacea for local economic and social troubles, neither present nor future. This statement is supported by many evidences.

One of the most quoted scholar of entrepreneurship states that new firms do not always have an innovation propensity higher than incumbent firms, "even for a developed country such as the United States, only a very small fraction of new startups is really innovative" ([39], p. 8). Without innovative capacity, in a contestable market, these firms have limited chance to growth.

Likewise, usually the large majority of incumbents firms are destined to remain a small firm or even a self-employment venture. This possibility is more likely when the entrepreneurs' teams that manage such firms do not possess an adequate level of entrepreneurship, but only *business entrepreneurialism*, that is, a generic spirit or state of acting in an entrepreneurial manner in the broader sense [38]. A pioneer in the field of entrepreneurship research and education [40] explains that there is a "continuum" along which each entrepreneur or aspiring entrepreneur has a different increasing subjective level of entrepreneurial capabilities. In addition, the more the business is small, the more the relationship among entrepreneur's potentialities and firm's performance tends to be stronger.

Generally, policies do not care or are not able to select aspiring entrepreneurs with the better potentialities. Hence, it is surprising to discover neither high failure rates nor large share of micro-firms from policies directed to favor undifferentiated startups. While firms which are unable to grow and develop rarely can disseminate knowledge or innovations, high failure rates are associated with a possible dispersion of public funds and sunk costs.

These contingencies introduce the specific problem regarding the *quality* of the arising entrepreneurship: "business ownership and entrepreneurship are not synonymous ... entrepreneurs are a small fraction of the business owners" ([36], p. 275). It is worth to underline that a seminal article on the nature and quality of entrepreneurship goes back to Carland et al. [12].

Authors distinguish entrepreneurs with the highest level of entrepreneurship and capabilities, identified as *true entrepreneurs in the Schumpeterian sense*, from other typologies of entrepreneurs with a lower level of entrepreneurship. Among the latter, there is the *small business owner* ("an individual who establishes for the principal purpose of furthering personal goals ... the owner perceives the business as an extension of his/her personality, intricately bound with family needs and desire") ([12], p. 358) and the *self-employer*, a personal response to the lack of professional alternatives, implying a low entrepreneurial level [38]. Businesses undertaken by small business owners and self-employers who "are not dominant in their field, and don't engage in any new marketing or innovative practices" ([12], p. 358) usually exhibit a low propensity for expansion, change, and knowledge adoption, while we have a high probability of failure. Often these entrepreneurs "have incomes below the poverty line" (Stam, 2015, p. 123).

On the contrary, a true entrepreneur is an individual who creates an *entrepreneurial venture* in Schumpeterian sense. That is a venture "characterized by innovative strategic practices ... employ strategic management practices in the business" ([12], p. 358). An entrepreneurial venture does not necessarily mean a large firm, but a business able to develop and to reach profitability and success, thereby having a relevant and stable impact on local growth. The ability to found and manage an entrepreneurial venture mirrors entrepreneurs' subjective predispositions, personal traits, experiences, knowledge and competences, innate or acquired, that shape their capabilities in a business's management, as well as in lifestyle [41].

The logic of this brief exposition concerns the opportunity, in some circumstances, to abandon policies that aim to support generic entrepreneurial activity by proposing top-down measures, such as granting subsidies or facilitations. The simple improving of the environmental framework risks to favor an undifferentiated creation of new businesses and/or startups, as well as the survival of incumbents no more competitive.

As researchers agree to sustain that the entrepreneurial process is the result of a complex interaction between individuals, cultural, social, and environmental factors, the alternative that is intended to endorse is to concentrate efforts on entrepreneurs/aspiring entrepreneurs who show the best business plans, the preeminent entrepreneurial features, and the ability to withstand market difficulties [3, 28, 34, 42]. These entrepreneurs have the higher probability of founding and managing *entrepreneurial ventures*.

3. The transition from startups to scale up

3.1 The concept of startup

A focus of entrepreneurship policies has been, as explained, increasing the number of startups and spreading the entrepreneurial culture by providing tangible (grants, real services, and facilitations) and intangible tools (training, incubators, consultancies). The corner stone of this policy sinks its roots in the belief that the startups are a powerful tool for spreading innovations and knowledge locally [21].

It is therefore essential to clarify what the startups are. Alike other social and economic phenomena based on individual or collective behaviors, different interpretations of startup exist. Each one offers a viewing angle for reading, analyzing, and evaluating the startup process.

This chapter follows and deepens one of the best known definitions of startup: "a temporary organization searching for a repeatable and scalable business model [32]." Although extremely concise, this definition is very widespread and effective.

A startup is an "organization" that is a systematic complex of human, material, and financial resources, tangible and intangible assets, coordinated by someone with a rough business idea for reaching a unitary scope. Often, it is a venture which is trying to become something to evolve in a steady enterprise. There is no certainty about a happy end of this process. This organization is designed to create a new product or service works under conditions of extreme uncertainty; hence, it is "searching." Statistically, it is more likely that the founders decide to abandon the project or to sell the idea they were working on. Then, a startup can and must evolve into an enterprise, or fail, or dissolve. This is why it is "temporary." Behind the possibility of becoming a company, however, there must be the perspective of transforming a business idea into a business model. Of course, this contingency does not imply that a startup will become a big company. It can remain a small firm with few employees or even an individual firm.

Consistent with the pillar of Schumpeterian theories, the focus of a startup is expected to be on innovation. Innovation understood as a positive change compared to a pre-existing situation, therefore not only technological but also managerial, organizational, productive, or technical, who allows and sustains a company in the proposition of a profitable business model. The latter has to be "repeatable." It means that the way in which company creates, delivers, and captures value has to be sustainable with recurring profit. Startup also has to be "scalable." It implies that the company must be able to serve profitably an increasing number of customers. Some business models can be repeatable but not scalable or scalable but not repeatable; but only when they are in the meantime both repeatable and scalable, they can catch the interest of venture capitalists [32]. The role of venture capitalists is essential for the startup dynamic because, often, traditional banks have neither the instruments to finance the starting-up processes nor competencies to judge business model potentialities.

As reminded by Blank [32], a scalable startup created from the very beginning by founders who believe that their proposal could change the world is different from a startup created by people just aspiring to become self-employed or to satisfy family need through a small business which is not designed to scale. In short, scalability is the basilar feature which distinguishes a startup with potentialities from other types of enterprises generically defined newborn ventures. This potentiality to profitably expand their boundaries is a crucial aspect which allows to clarify some doubt about the overall startups policies efficacy for the territorial development.

Some researchers [9, 14, 23] are quite skeptical about the advantages of the starting-up in general, describing a blanket policy focus on startups as "bad public policy." It occurs when startups born, thank to public facilitations and supports, and limit themselves at crowding-out existing companies that have not benefited from support or when they replicate existing business model taking advantage of greater operational and management slenderness by virtue of learning by others mistakes ("copycat") or if they absorb all the resources allocated for policy measures. Moreover, high startups death rate could determinate relevant sunk costs for society and aspiring entrepreneurs. In these circumstances, "evidence suggests the contribution of entrepreneurial startups to the economy is limited and in some cases can be potentially damaging" ([15], p. 136).

Moreover, some types of startups normally offer a lower contribution to local economy development. Among them, there are [32] *buyable startups*, namely startups born to be bought; *large company startups*, for answering to changes in customer preferences, new technologies, legislation issues, competitors pressure; or *social startups*, whose mission is to make the world a better place for a welfare purpose. Hence, to consider startups in a similar and undifferentiated way is a limit of industrial policy.

3.2 The concept of scale up

If entrepreneurship literature is rather skeptical about the effectiveness of startups, it agrees to sustain that the so-called high growth firms (henceforth HGFs) have significant spill-over effects: "small businesses that become middle-sized and ultimately large businesses, over a comparatively short period of time, are central to economic prosperity" ([14], p. 208). That is because HGFs are the preferential channel in the net jobs creation [6] and are beneficial to the development of other enterprises placed in the same context [43], as well as in industrial clusters [44], as they provide meaningful stimulus within economies by increasing competition, promoting innovation, and improving the efficient allocation of resources [23]. Not by chance, HGFs tend to exhibit high levels of productivity, innovation, export-orientation, internationalization, and investments in human capital [29, 43, 45]. Consequently, "the ability of a country to nurture the growth of such businesses is probably the most important element in enterprise development" ([14], p. 208).

HGFs are neither exclusively young businesses [18] nor predominantly in high tech sectors [6], and just few are venture capital backed [8]. Moreover, only episodically exhibit a linear growth, while they can expand organically or with external acquisition [23]. In line with these assumptions, a thriving stream of research stresses the necessity to favor the emerging of *scale ups* [22, 28, 29].

A univocal definition of scale up company still does not exist since the metrics, that is, the characteristics that distinguish it from the startup, vary according to the size of the reference context, the type of sector in which they operate, and the business model (usually b2c or b2b) [46]. Consistent with Blank [32], a scale ups can be framed as fast growing startups that have already overcome some phases on which the activity of the startup is focused. In particular, the scale up is a company that has developed its product or service, has defined its business model (scalable and repeatable), and can therefore focus on its growth on the market to take it forward in a controlled and sustainable manner. Hence, terminologically and consistent with the previous startup definition, only startups can become scale ups, while incumbent ventures can become HGFs; often just for a limited period of time [16].

A scale up stands out for some parameters attesting its success like market traction, 1–10 million € turnover annually, at least 1 million users (in the b2c), 20% growth in revenues or headcount for 3 years running after at least 10 people and $ 1 million in revenues, and 20% of the turnover from the foreign market [47]. Their highest ambition is to become a "centaurus"—valued more than 100 million dollars—or an "unicorns"—valued over 1 billion dollars.

3.3 Favoring scale ups diffusion

As other entrepreneurial ventures, the possibility that scale ups come to light is strictly linked to their intrinsic capacity to discover, to exploit, and to successfully manage economic opportunities. The incoming of digital era certainly is a source of uncountable opportunities. A new wave of economic openings linked to the Industry 4.0, where digital platforms will be coupled and connected with sophisticated infrastructures of sensors, cyber-physical systems, and robots, is expected [48]. Furthermore, digital innovations are bringing substantial new challenges on how to handle with technology, management, government policies, stakeholders' engagement, and so on [49]. Hence, the digital economy represents for ventures both a challenge and a requirement for conformity. It is a challenge, if they wish to set out a developmental pathway; it is a duty, if ventures are forced to adapt their organizational and productive pattern in order to remain competitive.

To look for strategies that are able to increase the presence of scale ups engaged into digital economy should be a primary aim for researchers and policy makers of many western countries. In this perspective, literature (Brown and Mason, 2012) [19, 34] specifies that this possibility is linked to the capacity to create a specific business environment consistent with scale ups needs. Only when effectively planned, this framework provides consistent outcomes. In Italy, for instance, the low number of scale ups created is not believed to depend on the lack of quality startups but mainly on their need to move abroad to find sufficient risk capital investments for tackling scaling, as well as for the shortage of connections with external actors [47].

Hence, new policy measures are requested, as the environments in which scale ups prosper are distinct from those which have high rates of startups [17, 21] (Brown and Mason, 2013). Scale ups also need to access to specialized resources that differ significantly from those supporting new firms [28, 32]
(Brown and Mason, 2012).

To this purpose, the necessity to create a distinctive type of supportive economic and social framework emerges. It should be planned to captivate entrepreneurs with wide economic potential [16, 19, 42]; to establish steady and productive relationships among all the local stakeholders; to provide relational forms of support (such as network building, institutional alignment of priorities, strategic guidance, leadership development, and mentoring) ([20], p. 2016), instead of money-based facilities (from grants to tax incentives or subsidies) that have showed limited impact [10]; to attract different businesses funding resource (such as debt finance, crowd-funding, and peer to peer) targeted to the specific requirements of the businesses [43]; to nurture the developing of the innovation system joining local customers end users, suppliers, universities, and so on [50]; to guarantee the recognition of unprotected and open sources innovations, respect on technological innovations and the protection of intellectual property rights [46]; and to limit its action at regional or local level [33].

The specific environments and the specialized resources scale ups and HGFs need are usually defined *ecosystems* (Napier and Hansen, 2011) [24].

4. An ecosystem for the emerging of scale ups

4.1 The basilar features

In the last decade, the *entrepreneurship ecosystem approach* has emerged as response for the propagation of scale ups and HGFs in general (e.g. [11, 28]). An ecosystem encloses the "set of interconnected entrepreneurial actors (both potential and existing), entrepreneurial organizations (e.g. firms, venture capitalists, business angels, banks), institutions (universities, public sector agencies, financial bodies) and entrepreneurial processes (e.g. the business birth rate, numbers of high growth firms, levels of 'blockbuster entrepreneurship', number of serial entrepreneurs, degree of sell-out mentality within firms and levels of entrepreneurial ambition) which formally and informally coalesce to connect, mediate and govern the performance within the local entrepreneurial environment" ([8], p. 5).

There are more models of entrepreneurial ecosystems, but each one is unique, that emerge under an inimitable set of conditions and circumstance and only where it finds fertile soil [31]. However, ecosystems usually share some common crucial features.

Firstly, an ecosystem cannot come to light in a vacuum [24] but generally arises where there are place-based assets, such as a previous strategic location of other industrial activities, even if of traditional type, or cluster [8]. This is not a surprising assumption, as researches indicate that firms that are located in "clusters" exhibit higher growth than those in other locations [44], and that in clusters usually have high number of graduates in technical disciplines who support the adoption of innovations [50]. However, the entrepreneurial ecosystem approach offers a distinctive perspective on the clustering of economic activities respect to the original concept of Porter [51].

Notably, the core of a thriving ecosystem is the presence of one or more large successful established businesses, preferably knowledge based. Their primary role is to deliberately cultivate the ecosystem itself [31]. Large companies provide outcomes of their R&D, are magnets of skilled workers, provide a market for local subcontractors, and shape specialized personnel who can decide to leave the firm to assume other roles (entrepreneur, mentor, angel investor, etc.) in the same context. These companies also invest in the local territory financing universities, research centers, and social initiatives and attract specialized suppliers that fertilize the context spreading knowledge [8, 11].

About the *cross-fertilization* process, it is crucial to underline the so-called entrepreneurial *recycling* process. It is fostered by entrepreneurs whose successful business idea/startup (*blockbusters*) was taken over from another firms or who, having already reached entrepreneurial significant goals, decide to remain in the cluster reinvesting their profit, time, wealth, experience, and expertise in supporting new entrepreneurial activities as serial entrepreneurs, venture investors, advisors, or manager of other firms [52]. The spillover effect of these entrepreneurs is particularly significant in the developmental process of the ecosystem, and these businesses in turn are the source of further waves of spinoff activity (Mason, 2009) [29]. Hence, potential entrepreneurs are themselves important players in creating the ecosystem and keeping it healthy [53].

Another key role is played by *deal-makers*, "individuals with valuable social capital, who have deep fiduciary ties within regional economies and act in the role of mediating relationships, making connections and facilitating new firm formation" ([54], p. 24). They can be entrepreneurs, investors, or service providers who are well-connected, qualified, and experienced who informally or with a fidelity role offer support to young firms and startups, helping them to develop their potential [29]. *Deal-makers* also support information sharing process. This is consistent with a relevant feature of the ecosystem, that is, an information-rich environment in which knowledge is both accessible and shared according to the principle of open innovation and cooperation for tacit dissemination. For successful entrepreneurship, the presence of dealmakers is more important than the measures supporting local entrepreneurship or investors networks, and it is a valid predictor of the health state of the regional entrepreneurial economy [54].

For the effectiveness of an entrepreneurship ecosystem, a prominent role is also due to the presence of universities and other research centers. The most significant lapel is not as much the research output transfers as the predictable presence of innovative spinoffs and startups that spread knowledge in the ecosystem itself.

Evidence shows that ecosystems have typically emerged in places that already have an established and highly regarded knowledge base which employs significant numbers of scientists and engineers. Universities and research and corporate R&D laboratories are a primary source of skilled personnel who can found innovative startups [55]. Anyway, sometimes the substantive disconnection between universities and their surrounding local entrepreneurial and innovation ecosystem belittles entrepreneurial spillovers from universities [50].

Another propulsive role is played by services providers that perform no-core activities which are outsourced. Three types of services facilitating the process of business startup and growth by enabling new firms to focus on their area of expertise can be highlighted: (1) specialist business services (law, marketing, accountability, management, consultants familiar with the unique needs of technology startups, technology marketing and assessment consultants, and PR firms), (2) technical services offering precision machining, prototyping, testing, and so on, (3) finance providers, such as venture capital firms or investment banks.

From financial perspective, the most important aspect concerns the availability of a critical mass of seeds and connections with local and foreign investors and venture capital funds [10], while the importance attributed to venture capitalists tends to be minor, as most firms are initially funded through a combination of self-financing, loans from family and friends, and bootstrapping. Despite a cluster is likely to stagnate or decline without these actors [44], in ecosystems venture capital seems lags, rather than stimulate, the emergence of entrepreneurial activity (Mason, Brown, 2014). This type of financing is more suitable for high growth technology-based firms [10].

4.2 The entrepreneurial enablers

An ecosystem has to be planned and managed. Often traditional decision makers of political origin have not suitable and enough technical and economic competencies to follow the implementation of the ecosystem: "however challenging the encouragement of entrepreneurship may seem, it is truly too important to be left to policy specialists" ([10], p. 264). In this regard, Isenberg [28] argues it would be better to establish new organizations with a 'sell-by date' composed of experts with specific entrepreneurial competencies—*entrepreneurial enablers*.

The tasks of these temporary organizations are to assure a holistic approach that considers especially bottom-up measures, as the major needs for the firms belonging to the entrepreneurial ecosystem do not concern the offering of grant and subsidies. The latter could have self-defeating effects respect on a Darwinist natural and spontaneous selection of the best firms and business models [5, 28]. As explained, ecosystem is chiefly founded on the active input coming from the entrepreneurial community. Hence, the involved firms require *relational* rather than *transactional* assistance during the different stages they run across, with the provision of intensive support and mentoring, as well as facilitations for startups through business incubators. The latter provides business advice, networking with mentors, business angels, banks, and service providers. The purpose is to build "bridges" between different actors through the creation of communities of best practices or entrepreneurial networks [8, 21]. Therefore, it is important primarily to establish steady and effective *connections* among all the involved actors and networking linkages.

These tools answer to the essential presence of startups which aspire to expand and develop. Sometimes, in the early stages of establishing an ecosystem, to stress on supporting the starting up processes helping these ventures with organizational and human capital development, internationalization support and access to growth capital could be necessary. But a mature ecosystem needs to focus its efforts on companies with the greatest potential. Entrepreneurial enablers should possess the ability to understand the right moment to shift the focus of their intervention. In addition, as the creation of an ecosystem occurs by phases which evolve over time, the organization's experts have to be able to determinate metric to evaluate strength, weakness, and bottlenecks of the ecosystem through a continue monitoring, identifying whether and how to intervene, and verifying over time the effectiveness of such interventions. Consistent with the described selective approach, they should also have the political strength to concentrate resources (public and/or private) primarily on a small number of high-potential early stage firms to accelerate their development [6, 46]. As success breeds, resources have to be granted in a selective way and not equally distributed [28].

Among the enablers duties, another vital aspect concerns the creation and diffusion of a specific *culture*. There is the necessity to plan initiatives acting on the cultural pattern of the territory, stimulating universities and school to focus on entrepreneurial education and promoting events which celebrate local entrepreneurship and innovation. The purpose is to valorize the entrepreneurial choice among citizens favoring a mentality changing and stimulating imitation. In this perspective, it would be significant to already have in the ecosystem HGFs or other successful examples to imitate. In parallel, as basic informal rule, an ecosystem should be characterized by the acceptance of failure as a normal outcome of entrepreneurial activity. The consequence is that there is no diffidence to employ workers coming from other companies, even if they have failed [11]. Being based on largely trustworthy relationships, the ecosystem has also to be pervaded by the typical optimistic and positive business climate which feeds of self-confidence among entrepreneurs [41].

Last but not least, a prosperous ecosystem also depends on innovations diffusion and industry conditions. For instance, even if riskier, technological advances of disruptive nature, which create "discontinuities," are believed to produce the largest opportunities [27, 50]. Consequently, often the emergence of an entrepreneurial ecosystem depends on the development of markets for newer technologies [8, 55]. Digital technologies are a remarkable example of this type, with a lot of opportunity that could be disclosed for new would-be entrepreneurs and the local context [48]. From this last perspective, entrepreneurial enablers have a great responsibility in connecting the ecosystem to the technological and innovation dynamics. To collect all these changes and challenges, the business environment has to show a high social capital [54], while firms show a high level of intellectual capital, in form of the three interrelated human, relational, and organizational components [56].

The overture described is in line with the increasingly widespread theses according to which economic behavior can be better understood within its historical, temporal, institutional, spatial, and social contexts. Contexts provide individuals with opportunities and set boundaries for their actions and influence entrepreneurial choices, helping to understand who, when, how, and why someone becomes involved. But also entrepreneurship impacts on context, modifying its features [3]. Consistent with some influential experts [57], the next shift in policies will lead from "regional entrepreneurship policy" to "policy for an entrepreneurial regional economy," that is the ecosystem approach.

5. Perspectives for digital startups birth and scale ups diffusion

5.1 The digital technologies

Observing the transformations taking place in the industrial system, it is clearer how, on the one hand, technology becomes much more pervasive by entering more and more directly and intensely in production processes, products, and services. From the other hand, the technology-based competition is intensified, with new comer countries that force Western countries to continuously renew the bases of their technological and competitive advantage. This dynamic makes R&S activity and the related ability to propose innovations increasingly necessary [49].

With specific regard to digital technologies, "the biggest transformation in business the world has seen in over a century" ([48], p. 5), they are radically changing the way people live, work, communicate, and play. Their pervasive diffusion is also causing significant repercussions on the dynamics of companies in European countries: 2.6 new digital job for each job destroyed is expected, manufacturing can achieve growth from 15 to 20% by 2030 if digitalized, revenue coming from digital technologies will growth of 2% for year, big data technology and services are expected to grow worldwide to USD 16.9 billion in 2015 at a compound annual growth rate of 40%, while companies using that data become 5–6% more productive [48]. Also, the way of carrying out many of the traditional production processes is modifying considerably, as well as consolidated theoretical approaches regarding the methods of supplying resources, the product management, and service offered are questioned. Indeed, the possibility of constantly introducing new functionalities for a product or service, even in remotely, would seem to alter the validity of theories on the product life cycle, on the genesis of the innovation, or on the product development process [25, 26].

Consequently, by proceeding with digital technologies adoption and implementation, an almost infinite number of economic opportunities for existing or new ventures is emerging, waiting to be grasped. Even more by considering that the boundaries of digital technologies in the three interrelated components of digital *artifacts*, *platforms*, and *infrastructures* are still unexplored, and every innovation such as cloud computing, data analytics, online communities, social media, 3D printing, and digital makerspaces contains indefinite applications.

The magnitude of this change is so significant and visible that a specialized literature has arisen—the *digital entrepreneurship*. It analyzes the effects of digitalization on the traditional methods of conducting a business to success. For instance, about the digital artifacts (the digital components, applications or media content that are part of a new product/service and offers a specific functionality or value to the end-user), the decoupling of information from its related physical form or device has led to the gradual infusion of such digital artifacts into a wide range of products and services and discloses a plethora of business occasions for different industrial sectors [58]. Digital artifacts are continually embedded in wider and constantly shifting ecosystems, such that they become increasingly editable, interactive, reprogrammable, and distributable [59]. Similarly, digital technology that offers communication, collaboration, and/or computing capabilities to support innovation digital infrastructures requires new personnel with different roles (customers, investors, partners, etc.) in all stages of entrepreneurial process, from opportunity exploration to venture launch [59].

Furthermore, "digital infrastructures (digital technology tools and systems that offer communication, collaboration, and/or computing capabilities to support innovation and entrepreneurship) infuse a level of fluidity or variability into entrepreneurial processes, allowing them to unfold in a nonlinear fashion across time and space" (Nambisan, 2017, p. 6), making less stable boundaries in both entrepreneurial outcomes and processes. This, in turn, leads to changes in behaviors and actions among digital entrepreneurs. Indeed, digital firm's success tends to step away from the exploiting of a certain opportunity, or the execution of a detailed value proposition, as it needs to follow a continuously evolving value proposition, namely actions that leverage the potential of a continuous re-scoping of business model [27].

The continuous changes associated with the implementation of digital technologies also support a transformation in the figure of the entrepreneur and his orientation to primarily seek economic performance. On one side, in fact, the most important aspect of the firm, especially if in the initial stages of life, becomes the validity of the business idea that it intends to develop and the consistency with the skills already possessed. The goal is to ensure the future competitiveness of venture or its attractiveness toward larger companies that might decide to buy it. On the other side, the focus of the decision-making process could depend on the pool of employees, probably coetaneous of the entrepreneur but with more digital skills, who are able to identify and collect market opportunities and transforming in business [26].

In the meantime, less importance of funding sources is expected in favor of the role of connections. In fact, unreleased opportunities to resort to financing with methods such as crowdfunding or crowdsourcing or obtaining support from customers and suppliers are arising. In this way, the traditional funding gaps for new businesses, particularly in technology sectors, normally looking for small amounts of finance, can also be easily filled [43].

On closer inspection, these changes are intrinsic conditions and functionalities belonging to the entrepreneurship ecosystem approach. In ecosystems, the goal of profit is fundamentally subordinated to the desire for self-realization or experimentation with innovative ideas of aspiring entrepreneurs (the pleasure of discovery), while the presence of networks of stakeholders along the productive process and the supply chain is believed crucial. Likewise, a continuous rotation of employees who pushed by personal objectives of income, job satisfaction, or self-efficacy tends to offer their competencies to other neighboring companies or to create their own startup, is judged spontaneous.

These behaviors improve not only the processes of dissemination of knowledge and innovative ideas within the ecosystem but also their propagation speed. This high fluidity of people and resources within the ecosystem is considered a strategic lever for its success [28]. But fluidity is also a key feature of digital technologies which often have low access barriers and are cheap to adopt and exploit.

In addition, re-programmability and re-combinability of digital artifacts and platforms, on their own and in conjunction with other factors, enable the introduction of new functionalities in different market contexts, thereby refashioning existing pathways or opening new chances to create value, i.e., rendering existing market offerings less bounded from already existing opportunities. Digital firms could not feasibly operate without the Internet-enabled digital platforms (shared, common set of services and architecture that serves to host complementary offerings, including digital artifacts), which meet producers and consumers and facilitate the exchange of goods, services, or social currency, also enabling value creation for all through the digital landscape [25]. The difficulty to establish boundaries for digital platforms is therefore confirmed. In addition, the interaction of digital artifact properties with other contextual features resulting from the challenges linked to digital technologies (e.g., new legislative regulations, new pricing mechanisms, etc) also can radically change the definition of value in a market, proposing new further functionalities or business opportunities [59].

5.2 The role of ecosystem

On these premises, ecosystems could assure a fundamental contribution facilitating the developmental pathway for digital startups. Indeed, an ecosystem guarantees the passage of the traditional business environment to one no longer linked to individual or company factors but to a network of specialized partners with a wide availability of knowledge and open innovations.

Due to the presence of research centers disseminating knowledge, universities forming graduates in technical disciplines, and consultants, it is highly probable that these specific environments are linked to regional or urban areas. Not by chance, some authors (e.g., [33, 60]) put cities as the key organizing unit for innovation, entrepreneurship, and economic growth and argue about how digital startups and scale ups may take in place in cities and, sometime, require them as preferential ecosystem that help lever their development [58, 60].

Even the ecosystem tendency to the concentration of activities is coherent with the nature of digital companies. Their location choices do not depend on factors such as proximity to the market or availability of tangible inputs or from the availability of large physical space difficult to find in an urban area. As digital companies include online retailers but exclude retailers which have a physical presence on the 'high street' and are linked to the generation and diffusion of knowledge, as well as to the presence of specific support services or specialized human capital and venture capital, they should give priority to the agglomerations of competencies typical of urban context with the presence of universities and research centers [8, 61].

Belonging to an ecosystem presents another advantage for digital companies. In the ecosystem, the innovative and creative processes are no longer centered on the individuals or on the ventures, but looks at the entire regional context meant as fertile environment from which economic opportunities can arise. Therefore, the innovative and entrepreneurial critical processes become linked to the entire external environment, considered as a place of aggregation of individuals, companies, individual talents, institutions and support services [28]. This feature is consistent with the needs of digital entrepreneurship, where the most important productive factors are the availability of specialized personnel, of venture capitalists, and knowledge generation sources. To be placed in an ecosystem also could help all the memberships companies to obtain legislative rules that ensure, for example, the ownership of the innovations introduced and the cyber security of client companies, in doing so encouraging the adoption of the same technologies [62].

Anyway, to grow, digital startups must incorporate quickly new management functions, from operations to marketing, evolving from an unstructured chaotic day-to-day to an evolving structure, mature, and dynamic organization. Consequently, they have to bring out the need of new competencies, especially of digital nature. They have to be able to possess, manage, dominate, and develop digital technologies and the inherent knowledge. These competencies enclose hard skills (from the ability to use computer programs and packages to the use of specific machines and tools for production such as social, mobile, analytics, cloud, artificial intelligence, robotics, Internet of Things, and cybersecurity) and soft skills (linked to relationships and behaviors of people enabling the effective use of new digital tools such as problem solving, knowledge networking, the new media literacy, etc.) [63]. Consistent with the ecosystem features reminded in the previous sections, even from this last perspective, the ecosystem approach seems the more suitable for digital startups and their growth.

6. Conclusive remarks

The diffusion of digital technologies with their still undefined boundaries announces a new era in entrepreneurship, where traditional ways and forms of pursuing entrepreneurial opportunities will be increasingly reshaped. A new horizon of business opportunities only waits for being discovered and then managed profitably [27, 48, 57].

Relevant changes also are involving the basilar criteria of management and organization of companies and the ways to compete globally. From these modifications, new criteria to start a business and pathways for its development and growth descend: the emergence of *digital entrepreneurship* [25, 62].

For policy makers, the main challenge is to assure both that the domestic ventures are able to collect digital business opportunities successfully and to provide benefits for the whole territorial context, along a development route stable and persistent in terms of net employment, income, and cross fertilization. A flourishing entrepreneurship research stream believes that a chance to reach the above objectives lies in the ability to implement specific business environments called *ecosystems*. These are targeted on selective measure supporting the emerging of ventures with innovative business models but also their development and growth ([24]; Napier and Hansens, 2011). While, according to empirical evidence, policies only focused in favoring the firms birth rate may not be the best solution to the problems of employment and growth of many Western countries.

Anyway to support scale ups and high growth firms in general is a hard task that must be carried out by specialized personnel and with the appropriate skills. This is because there are not many cases of good practice to follow, but only a basic logic according to which all the domains (a favorable culture, enabling policies, availability of adequate financing, high-quality human capital, safety-friendly markets for products, institutional supports, etc.) that make up an ecosystem must be aligned and coordinated (*holistic approach*). Moreover, the ecosystem needs to involve, since the beginning, many stakeholders/actors (at least an interested large corporation, policy makers, local bankers, and venture capitalists, people acting on the local culture, local universities, etc.) [24, 54]. The more intense the cooperation among these key actors is, the more likely the ecosystem will be to succeed.

Nevertheless, both domains and actors are characterized by proximity and include hundreds of variables interacting in highly complex and idiosyncratic ways. They should be able to converge toward a set of shared objectives according to a series of priorities [31] (SEP, 2018).

Despite the complexity to create an ecosystem, its features and functionalities seem well-suited with digital enterprises features, as they focus on the development of the *intellectual capital*, which has to sustain the growth of firms operating with a new disruptive technology [8, 56]. Indeed, the roots of a well-operating ecosystem lie in a specialized and motivated *human capital*, open to innovation and with a widespread entrepreneurial culture. It is also founded on a dynamic system of connections among all the stakeholders of a context who are interested into its development, the *networking capital*. Again, the ecosystem rests its strength on the quality of the firms enclosed in terms of values, managerial philosophy, organizational patterns, and informative systems; in other word, the *organizational capital*.

To this aim, therefore, policy makers are called to sustain a great effort. Not by the chance, up to now a lot of attempts aiming at creating conducive environments failed. Moreover, there is an effective risk that the entrepreneurial ecosystem remains a tautological concept (Stam, 2015): entrepreneurial ecosystems produce successful entrepreneurship, but where there is a lot of successful entrepreneurship, there is apparently a good entrepreneurial ecosystem.

Beyond this theoretical-conceptual paper, aimed to connect the increasing sector of digital firms with a specific business environment, future surveys should focus their analyses at least on three directions. Firstly, a clear individuation of the needs and resources requested by digital firms and startups in the light of their own specificities; secondly, the detailed examination of the operative mechanisms of existing ecosystems precisely focused on digital technologies; and lastly, an investigations on the coherence among digital technologies with the local background of competencies and knowledge to individuate possible gaps to fill.

References

[1] van Stel A, Carree MA, Thurik R. The effect of entrepreneurial activity on national economic growth. Small Business Economics. 2005;**24**(3):311-321

[2] Audretsch DB, Keilbach MC, Lehmann EE. Entrepreneurship and Economic Growth. New York: Oxford University Press; 2008

[3] Autio E, Kenney M, Mustar P, Siegel D, Wright M. Entrepreneurial innovation: The importance of context. Research Policy. 2014;**43**(7):1097-1108

[4] Bosma N, Acs ZJ, Autio E, Coduras A, Levie J, Global Entrepreneurship Monitor. Global Report. Babson Park, MA, USA: Babson College; 2008. p. 2009

[5] OECD. An international benchmarking analysis of public programmes for high-growth firms. In: LEED Programme; Paris. 2013

[6] Henrekson M, Johansson D. Gazelles as job creators: A survey and interpretation of the evidence. Small Business Economics. 2010;**35**:227-244

[7] Hathaway I, Litan R. Declining Business Dynamism in the United States: A Look at States and Metros. Washington, D.C.: The Brookings Institution; 2014

[8] Mason C, Brown R. Entrepreneurial Ecosystems and Growth Oriented Entrepreneurship. The Hague, Netherlands: OECD; 2014

[9] Shane S. Why encouraging more people to become entrepreneurs is bad public policy. Small Business Economics. 2009;**33**(2):141-149

[10] Lerner J. The future of public efforts to boost entrepreneurship and venture capital. Small Business Economics. 2010;**35**:255-264

[11] Feld B. Startup Communities: Building an Entrepreneurial Ecosystem in Your City. New York: Wiley; 2012

[12] Carland JW, Hoy FS, Boulton WR, Carland JC. Differentiating entrepreneurs from small business owner: A conceptualization. Academy of Management Review. 1984;**9**(2):354-358

[13] Gartner WB. What are we talking about when we talk about entrepreneurship? Journal of Business Venturing. 1990;**5**(1):15-28

[14] Storey DJ, Greene F. Small Business and Entrepreneurship. Harlow: Prentice Hall; 2010

[15] Nightingale P, Coad A. Muppets and gazelles: Political and methodological biases in entrepreneurship research. Industrial and Corporate Change. 2014;**23**:113-143

[16] OECD. High-growth Enterprises: What Governments Can Do to Make a Difference. Paris: OECD Studies on SMEs and Entrepreneurship; 2010

[17] OECD. Financing High Growth Firms: The Role of Angel Investors. Paris: OECD Publishing; 2011

[18] Acs ZJ, Muller P. Employment effects of business dynamics: Mice, gazelles and elephants. Small Business Economics. 2008;**30**(1):85-100

[19] Mason C, Brown R. Creating good public policy to support high growth firms. Small Business Economics. 2013;**40**:211-225

[20] Brown R, Mason C. Inside the high-tech black box: A critique of technology entrepreneurship policy. Technovation. 2014;**3412**:773-784

[21] Passaro R, Quinto I, Thomas A. Start-up competitions as

learning environment to Foster the entrepreneurial process. International Journal of Entrepreneurial Behaviour & Research. 2017;**23**(3):426-445

[22] SEP (Startup Europe Changing). Startup and Scaleup Ecosystem Recommendations for Policy Change. 2018. Available from: https://startupeuropepartnership.eu/

[23] Brown R, Mawson S, Mason C. Myth-busting and entrepreneurship policy: The case of high growth firms. Entrepreneurship & Regional Development. 2017;**29**(5-6)

[24] Isenberg DJ. How to start an entrepreneurial revolution. Harvard Business Review. 2010;**88**(6):41-49

[25] EC (European Commission). Digital Entrepreneurship Scoreboard 2015. Brussels: Directorate-General for Internal Market, Industry, Entrepreneurship and SMEs; 2016

[26] EC (European Commission). Fuelling Digital Entrepreneurship in Europe. Background Paper. 2014. file:///C:/Users/utente/Desktop/file%20scaricati/Digital%20Entrepreneurship.pdf

[27] Nambisan S, Baron RA. Entrepreneurship in innovation ecosystems: Entrepreneurs' self-regulatory processes and their implications for new venture success. Entrepreneurship Theory and Practice. 2013;**37**(5):1071-1097

[28] Isenberg D. The Entrepreneurship Ecosystem Strategy as a New Paradigm for Economic Policy: Principles for Cultivating Entrepreneurship. Babson Park: Babson College; 2011

[29] Napier G, Hansen C. Ecosystems for Young Scaleable Firms. FORA Group; 2011. www.kauffman.org/~/media/kauffman_org/z_archive/resource/2012/5/irpr_2012_napier.pdf

[30] Brown R, Mawson S. Targeted support for high growth firms: Theoretical constraints, unintended consequences and future policy challenges. Environment and Planning C: Government and Policy. 2016;**34**(5):816-836

[31] Isenberg D, Onyemah V. Fostering scale up ecosystems for regional economic growth. Innovations: Technology, Governance, Globalization. 2016;**11**(1-2):60-79

[32] Blank S. The Four Steps to the Epiphany: Successful Strategies for Products that Win. Pescadero (US) K & S Ranch; 2013

[33] Bosma NS, Sternberg R. Entrepreneurship as an urban event? Empirical evidence from European cities. Regional Studies. 2014;**48**(6):1016-1033

[34] Audretsch DB, Belitski M. Entrepreneurial ecosystems in cities: Establishing the framework conditions. The Journal of Technology Transfer. 2017;**42**(5):1030-1051

[35] Kilby P. Hunting the heffalump. In: Ibidem, editor. Entrepreneurship and Economic Development. New York: The Free Press; 1971

[36] Carree MA, van Stel A, Thurik AR, Wennekers S. Economic development and business ownership: An analysis using data of 23 OECD countries in the period 1976-1996. Small Business Economics. 2002;**19**(3):271-290

[37] Acs ZJ, Arenius P, Hay M, Minniti M. Global Entrepreneurship Monitor 2004 Global Report. Babson Park, MA, USA: Babson College. p. 2005

[38] Reynolds PD, Bygrave WD, Autio E. Global Entrepreneurship Monitor GEM. Executive Report. Babson Park, MA: Babson College; 2003

[39] Audretsch DB. Entrepreneurship: A Survey of the Literature. Brussels: European Commission: Enterprise Directorate General; 2002

[40] Vesper KH. New Venture Strategies. Englewood Cliffs: Prentice-Hall; 1990

[41] Thomas A, Passaro R. Entrepreneurship and firm performance. An approach based on entrepreneurs' subjective characteristics. In: Dossena G, editor. Entrepreneurship Today. Milan: McGraw-Hill; 2010. pp. 99-122

[42] Thomas A, Passaro R, Marinangeli B. Entrepreneurial Behaviors and strategic paths in innovative SMEs: Evidence from Italy's Campania region. Global Business and Organizational Excellence. 2015;**34**(5):51-62

[43] Mason C. Public policy support for the informal venture capital market: A critical review. International Journal of Small Business. 2009;**27**:536-556

[44] Feldman MA, Francis J, Bercovitz J. Creating a cluster while building a firm: Entrepreneurs and the formation of industrial clusters. Regional Studies. 2005;**39**:129-141

[45] Brown R, Mawson S. Trigger points and high-growth firms: A conceptualization and review of public policy implications. Journal of Small Business and Enterprise Development. 2013;**20**:279-295

[46] Brown R, Mason C. Raising the batting average: Re-orientating regional industrial policy to generate more high growth firms. Local Economy. 2012;**27**:33-49

[47] ScaleIT. 2018. Available from: www.scaleit.biz/

[48] EC (European Commission). Digital Transformation of European Industry and Enterprises. DG Internal Market, Industry, Entrepreneurship and SMEs; 2015

[49] Brynjolfsson E, McAfee A. The Second Machine Age: Work, Progress, and Prosperity in a Time of Brilliant Technologies. New York: WW Norton & Company; 2014

[50] Brown R. Mission impossible? Entrepreneurial universities and peripheral regional innovation systems. Industry and Innovation. 2016;**23**(2):189-205

[51] Delgado M, Porter ME, Stern S. Clusters and Entrepreneurship. Journal of Economic Geography. 2010;**10**(4):95-518

[52] Mason C, Harrison RT. After the exit: Acquisitions, entrepreneurial recycling. Regional Studies. 2006;**40**:55-73

[53] Stam E. Entrepreneurial ecosystems and regional policy: A sympathetic critique. European Planning Studies. 2015;**23**(9):1759-1769

[54] Feldman MP, Zoller T. Dealmakers in place: Social capital connections in regional entrepreneurial economies. Regional Studies. 2012;**46**:23-37

[55] Isenberg D. Worthless, Impossible and Stupid: How Contrarian Entrepreneurs Create and Capture Extraordinary Value. Cambridge: Harvard Business Review Press; 2013

[56] Passaro R, Quinto I, Thomas A. The impact of higher education on entrepreneurial intention and human capital. Journal of Intellectual Capital. 2018;**19**(1):135-156

[57] Thurik R, Stam E, Audretsch D. The rise of the entrepreneurial economy and the future of dynamic capitalism. Technovation. 2013;**33**(8-9):302-310

[58] Lusch RF, Nambisan S. Service innovation: A service-dominant logic perspective. MIS Quarterly. 2015;**39**(1):155-175

[59] Kallinikos J, Aaltonen A, Marton A. The ambivalent ontology of digital artifacts. MIS Quarterly. 2013;**37**(2):357-370

[60] Florida R, Adler P, Mellander C. The city as innovation machine. Regional Studies. 2017;**51**(1):86-96

[61] Malecki EJ. Connecting local entrepreneurial ecosystems to global innovation networks: Open innovation, double networks and knowledge integration. International Journal of Entrepreneurship and Innovation Management. 2011;**14**:36-59

[62] Nambisan S. Digital entrepreneurship: Toward a digital technology perspective of entrepreneurship. Entrepreneurship Theory and Practice. 2017;**41**(6):1029-1055

[63] Iordache C, Mariën I, Baelden D. Developing digital skills and competences: A QuickScan analysis of 13 digital literacy models. Italian Journal of Sociology of Education. 2017;**9**(1):6-30

Chapter 7

Strategic Use of Zero-rating of Mobile Data

Abstract

The digital economy, characterised by goods exhibiting high instantiation and low reproduction costs frequently created and distributed over multisided platforms, poses challenges for the pricing of products and services. As convergence occurs between applications and transport, flexible ways of pricing internet access and content are being developed. One frequently used pricing strategy is 'zero-rating'—where traffic for specific applications is not counted against the 'cap' in an internet user's monthly access plan. This pricing strategy has drawn much criticism from net neutrality advocates, but it is far from clear that the policy is harmful. Using an economic analysis based upon relaxing assumptions in the simple model of perfect competition, so that it more closely reflects the complex internet ecosystem, we assess the extent to which it is plausible for zero-rating to be used to harm competition, consumer welfare and incentives for application innovation. We develop five questions to assist inquiry into the potential harm or benefits arising, which can be applied by competition authorities, regulators and the firms concerned to assist in sorting the cases less likely to be harmful from those that warrant further investigation.

Keywords: zero-rating, economic analysis, regulation, competition, strategic interaction

1. Introduction

The digital economy, characterised by goods exhibiting high instantiation and low reproduction costs frequently created and distributed over multisided platforms, poses challenges for the pricing of products and services. Unlike for most physical goods, it no longer follows that the optimal price for any individual item will be a simple function of its cost of production, or even that the individual consuming the product or service should be the one that pays for it [1].

Information goods providers are increasingly adopting strategies subsidising the consumption of information goods by bundling them with other goods, or by utilising multisided platforms whereby revenues in excess of costs raised in transactions with customers of one product type (or side of the platform) are used to subsidise below-cost purchases by consumers of another product type (or side of the platform). For example, consumers receive 'free' (or discounted) newspapers, television and radio channels when advertising revenues offset the costs of providing the printing and broadcasting infrastructure required for the content to reach consumers. 'Virtuous cycles' arise as advertising revenues subsidise the costs of readers or viewers accessing content, thereby increasing consumer welfare, at the same time as having more readers and viewers increases the value to advertisers and hence the price that platform operators can charge them [2]. So long as there is careful balancing of demand elasticities on both sides of the platform, having prices varying from marginal cost on both sides can be both profit- and welfare enhancing [3, 4, 24].

Such practices have, however, proved particularly challenging for regulators and competition authorities entrusted with the pursuit and protection of competitive markets for the long-term benefits of consumers. Successfully engaging in above-cost pricing in at least one market requires the firm to have some degree of market power, while using the surpluses to subsidise another potentially alters the competitive dynamics in that market as well [5]. Inevitably, the interests of consumers of one product must be traded off against those of another. Furthermore, in the context of increasing disintermediation of once-integrated firms and their replacement by complex contractually co-ordinated supply chains for the relevant products and services, it is no longer obvious that one specific firm or even one market is the appropriate focus for attention. While a mandate clearly exists for competition authorities and regulators to be interested, it is far less clear that their historic precedents and inquiry methods based on historic structure-conduct-performance (SCP) models of industrial organisation established to deal with single firm or markets and non-information goods are suitable for governing commercial interactions in the new context.

The complexities are highlighted by 'zero-rating'. This occurs when internet service providers (ISPs) do not count the data traffic used to service specific applications (supplied typically by third-party content and application providers—CAPs—who may also be using advertising revenues to subsidise production costs) against the data traffic 'cap' allowed in an internet user's access (subscription) plan. Data transmissions for these applications are effectively 'free to the user', whereas data transmissions serving other applications incur an effective positive price. Regulators and telecommunication authorities in many jurisdictions have been required to adjudicate allegations of the use of zero-rating to harm competition in both the ISP and CAP markets, and thereby to cause harm to consumers collectively, and disproportionately to different consumer groups. Telecommunications regulators have been lobbied to impose rules prohibiting its use entirely, or at least permitting it only in very restricted circumstances.

To date, regulators and competition authorities have generally responded cautiously, by eschewing outright prohibition of zero-rating in favour of case-by-case analysis, as was explicitly required in the United States Federal Communications Commission's (FCC) subsequently repealed 2015 Open Internet Rule [6]. Following repeal, case-by-case jurisdiction has persisted under generic competition law overseen by the Federal Trade Commission, as occurred prior to 2015, and has always prevailed in countries such as Australia and New Zealand, where no specific net neutrality regulations have been introduced. In contrast, the European Union's approach, encapsulated in its 2016 Net Neutrality Regulation, is more prescriptive.

Nonetheless, even with case-by-case evaluation, regulators and competition authorities face many difficulties in assessing economic harms and benefits. Not least is defining the relevant market(s). Benefits and harms may accrue in multiple markets, many of which may be far-removed from both that in which the firm engaging in the pricing practice is deemed to be operating (e.g., in CAP markets not ISP markets) and the territory over which the relevant authority has jurisdiction (e.g., a CAP operating from a different country to the ISP). Further decision-making complications exist due to extensive use of bundling of internet and content access with other products and services (e.g., with fixed and mobile voice applications, and pay television, in classic 'triple' and 'quadruple' play subscriptions), and the fact that little may yet be known about consumer valuations and preferences in markets for products that are comparatively new [7]. While the Body of European Regulators for Electronic Communications (BEREC) has endeavoured to address this complexity by issuing a set of guidelines for member state regulators to assist in implementing the European Net Neutrality Regulation [8], they have proven problematic. Their focus on legal compliance with the directive rather than detailed assessment of the economic harms and benefits in different circumstances has resulted in considerable variation between member state regulators' interpretation and application of the rule, creating both controversy and uncertainty about the acceptability of zero-rating pricing strategies across the notional single communications market to which the commission aspires [9].

Given the levels of economic complexity invoked by zero-rating, and the lack of theoretical and empirical evidence to date to inform both firms seeking to adopt the practice and regulators and competition authorities seeking to maintain fair and competitive markets (on balance, most that has been produced finds the practice NOT harmful), the development of some general economic principles for evaluating its effects is indicated. This chapter represents a first step in this direction. The contribution is five questions, which can be used as a preliminary filter to assess the likelihood of a specific instance of zero-rating being harmful to total welfare, thereby necessitating either caution on the part of a firm potentially implementing it, or justification on the part of competition authorities and regulators contemplating expending their scarce resources on a more intensive investigation.

We begin by outlining the general arguments for and against the use of zero-rating. Next, we summarise key economic characteristics of the internet ecosystem in which zero-rating offers are being made. Then, beginning with the models of perfect competition upon which theories of competitive harm were developed in classical SCP thinking, we demonstrate how successively relaxing the model assumptions when it is applied to the commercial interaction between ISPs and end users leads to the identification of circumstances where zero-rating may be more or less harmful to total welfare. The theoretical economic methodology used for this inquiry draws upon and extends the similar approach used by Greenstein et al. [21] and Gans and Katz [10, 11] in their inquiries into specific examples of zero-rating. The result is the five questions, which are summarised in our conclusion.

2. Zero-rating, net neutrality and competitive harms

Calls for the banning of zero-rating offers have arisen in the context of wider advocacy for increased regulation of ISPs to impose a particular view of an internet where ISPs are required to treat every data packet equally—in regard to both technical and financial characteristics. Calls for ISPs (but not the providers of content and applications used on the infrastructure) to operate in this neutral, non-discriminatory manner—so-called net neutrality—derived from Wu's [12] seminal paper.

Particular concerns have been voiced about ISPs charging some content and applications providers (CAPs) but not others to deliver their traffic to end consumers, even when those payments are not associated with traffic prioritisation (so fall outside the so-called 'hard' network neutrality regulations [13] precluding such behaviour). ISPs, however, are continually looking for new revenues in order to finance the newer, more capable networks required to transport a burgeoning volume of content and application data between CAPs and end users, in addition to winning new customers and amortising general network costs.

Some neutral internet proponents (e.g., [14, 15, 28]) have argued that 'zero-rated' internet access plans, frequently offered by mobile providers, should be prohibited.

These plans do not count data used for selected ('zero-rated') applications against the data downloading 'cap' specified within the monthly access fee. End users face a lower effective price for using the selected application than for other applications that are not 'zero-rated'. The ISP may or may not charge the selected CAPs to recover the costs of delivering their data to end users. 'Zero-rated' plans are seen by net neutrality proponents as a form of unfair price discrimination[1] against those internet users who do not access the selected content. It is also argued that when ISPs selectively zero-rate data relating to large established CAPs, smaller and newer rivals will be foreclosed, thereby harming incentives for application innovation, regardless of whether or not ISPs charge CAPs. A further argument is that application variety will be harmed because smaller, newer providers may not have the resources to pay ISPs to zero-rate their traffic, leading to their applications being eschewed by end users preferring the zero-rated options.

Others, however (e.g., [10, 16, 17, 25, 27]), contend that preventing all instances of zero-rating will necessarily rule out some cases (e.g., those analogous to advertising in newspapers) where payments on both sides of a two-sided market may be necessary for both an application and the additional infrastructure needed to service demand for it to be commercially viable in the first place. They also suggest that zero-rating will facilitate higher internet use in total (and therefore higher welfare) than if payments were restricted to only one 'side' of the internet platform. The potential welfare gains from higher internet use may be especially valuable in developing countries where the ability to pay for additional data use is very low [18]. They argue for a more nuanced approach, where each case is considered on its merits, so that the interests of all participants in highly complex internet-enabled ecosystems can be assessed [9, 19, 29, 30].

To date, no consistent view has emerged amongst regulators and competition authorities of what constitutes anti-competitive use of zero-rating. In the United States, much press has been directed at T-Mobile's zero-rating of its Binge-On application, but the FCC has found no harm. In Europe, the Belgian regulator found Proximus use acceptable according to the BEREC guidelines [31], and two National Regulatory Authorities (NRAs)—Austria and Croatia—found zero-rating acceptable when assessed against BEREC's commercial criteria. However, the Dutch NRA found Deutsche Telecom had infringed in zero-rating its free music service. The decision was struck down on appeal, but on grounds that the NRA decision exceeded EU law, rather than on its commercial merits.[2]

3. The internet ecosystem and zero-rating

Zero-rating offers take place in a complex internet-enabled ecosystem consisting of multiple intertwined two-sided platforms, of which ISPs are just one of many in the commercial chain linking senders and receivers of data [20, 21, 32]. **Figure 1** illustrates how in this ecosystem, payment flows need not necessarily follow data flows. The systemic interaction of payments and data flows means that actions at any one segment of the ecosystem can have material consequences at any other part.

[1] A distinction needs to be made between legal definitions of discrimination—where two people with observable differences are treated differently (e.g., racial or gender discrimination) and economic discrimination—where two people with different economic characteristics are treated differently (e.g., where those with low willingness-to-pay are charged a low price and those with high willingness-to-pay a high price). The latter case may frequently lead to a more efficient outcome. However, in the former, the individuals may have identical economic characteristics, so charging different prices is not welfare-enhancing.

[2] Autoriteit Consument & Markt, "ACM Not to Appeal Ruling on Net Neutrality | ACM.Nl," News, May 23, 2017, /en/publications/publication/17267/ACM-not-to-appeal-ruling-on-net-neutrality.

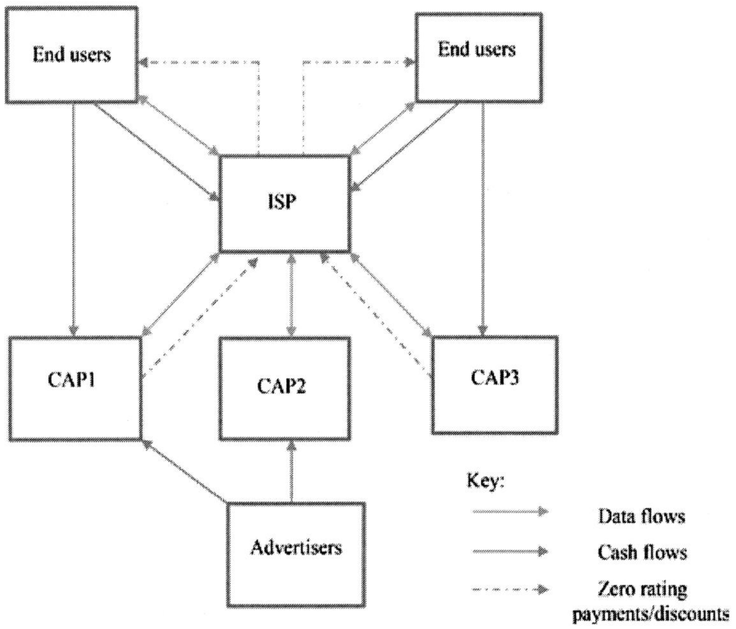

Figure 1.
The internet-enabled ecosystem.

3.1 Complex interactions

Net neutrality advocates assert that innovation at the CAP 'edge' of the ecosystem unconditionally dominates innovation at the ISP core. In this view, ISPs' sole commercial functions are to serve the internet data transmission requirements of their end users. ISPs should not have commercial interactions with CAPs—thereby precluding any possibility that selected CAPs can pay ISPs to prioritise (i.e., discriminate against) traffic related to their applications over that of their rivals. By extension, any arrangements whereby ISPs discount the charges relating to specific applications (i.e., zero-rating) are seen as price discrimination. Both practices are seen to discriminate amongst CAPs, so are antithetic to the objective of promoting the internet ecosystem as an engine of innovation [22]. Van Schewick [15] uses this argument to question the efficacy of T-Mobile's zero-rating of content on Binge-On, as do critics of Facebook's Free Basics. Indeed, Lemley and Lessig go so far as to suggest that ISPs should not charge CAPs for data delivery as a form of subsidy for application development activities.

In contrast, ISPs claim that they have been required to build ever-more-capable networks (for example, from 2G to 3G, 4G and now 5G mobile, and fixed fibre and wireless) to serve the vastly increased demands placed on them to deliver ever-larger amounts of data at ever-faster speeds to meet the demands of specific applications [26]. A handful of application types—notably audio and video streaming—require vastly more sophisticated network capabilities than others—for example, simple websites. As not all consumers use these applications equally, and some applications—for example, those relating to time-critical bilateral interactions—need to be treated differently from others—e.g., one-way streamed data—then some degree of discrimination (both in terms of traffic management and pricing, such as charging CAPs in some instances as well as ends users) is essential if their networks are to be operated efficiently and effectively.

Regulators and competition authorities are charged with promoting competition in each of the relevant markets in order to protect the long-term interests of consumers. This dynamic welfare criterion is predicated upon the assumption that the long-term interests of consumers in each of these markets are a suitable proxy for the long-term interests of the ecosystem as a whole. Thus, balance is required between short-term and long-term factors. Furthermore, what is optimal at one time of the ecosystem lifecycle may not be optimal at another [33, 34]. To the extent that social preferences may override the economic considerations, then the costs of imposing those preferences must be recognised in both the total welfare foregone, and the transfers that those preferences engender between ecosystem stakeholders. Moreover, a single stakeholder may participate in the ecosystem in multiple capacities, and these may vary over the ecosystem lifecycle. The dilemma for regulators and policy-makers is to decide what to take into account when developing a framework for assessing cases of zero-rating, and deciding how and when to intervene.

3.2 Derived demands

The dilemma is exacerbated because end-users' demands for ISP services are not determined solely by their own interaction. An ISP connection is of no value to an end user if it is not used to access internet applications. ISPs operate two-sided platforms connecting CAPs and end users. The relevant products for any zero-rating inquiry are the complex bundles of internet access and application use that end users consume. Internet connection value cannot be considered in isolation—it is dependent upon the value the consumer places on the applications accessed. The ISP may supply some of these applications, but for the most part, consumers' value of the connection is contingent upon being able to access a vast range of applications provided by third-party CAPs.

A nontrivial observation arising is that, for the most part, ISPs do not have strong incentives to impede their consumers' access to the preferred applications, for fear of losing them—and their revenues—to rival ISPs [21]. If favouring one application harms access to or use of another, then likewise this will likely reduce both the number of ISP customers and the ability of the relevant CAP to earn subscription and advertising revenues. Ipso facto, this reduces the incentives for ISPs to use pricing to strategically foreclose selected third-party applications—especially those consumers valued highly—unless they are compensated by the CAP. However, as the market power (measured by the consumer base) of highly valued CAPs vastly exceeds that of any individual ISP, and they have very wide (global) reach whereas ISPs are geographically specific, it is most unlikely that they will engage in contracting in each of the vast number of local geographic ISP markets in order to foreclose their CAP rivals. It cannot be discounted that locally specific CAPs might find such a strategy advantageous with regard to a rival facing the same geographic limitations.

3.3 Complex tariffs

ISPs can charge consumers a flat fee, a usage-based fee or a combination of the two for internet access. Consumers' internet access purchases are determined by trading off the fixed price paid for access and any usage charge against the benefits of accessing and utilising applications. Menus of two-part tariffs bundling access and usage charges are generally welfare enhancing relative to a single flat-rate or solely usage-based tariff as they allow users with different valuations associated with different usage levels of even a single application to self-select the tariff that gives them most surplus [35].

A zero-rated tariff applied to a specific application is simply a tariff with no usage-based component—that is, a flat fee. Flat fees are most advantageous for those with the highest expected usage, (e.g., video gaming) as they will utilise it up to the point where no further benefits will be obtained. This is necessarily more than if usage is charged at marginal cost (noting that network congestion is a significant externality proportional to utilisation that is imposed by users when utilising applications). If the higher costs associated with higher usage levels are to be recovered in user fees, a single flat-rate tariff will be higher where usage is higher that when it is lower. Metered tariffs (including plans with flat-rates within a given data cap, that rise as the data cap increases) are an efficient means by which ISPs may recover revenues from each consumer rising in proportion with the costs that usage imposes on the ISP (including the costs of congestion that lower service quality for all users).

3.4 Heterogeneous end users

However, metered tariffs will arise in practice only if consumers are heterogeneous in their valuations of application usage. If all consumers value their connections identically, then there will be one tariff that is efficient for all users, and there will be no incentive for ISPs to offer any other tariff. Consumers' valuations of internet application usage are inherently heterogeneous because different users will prefer to use different applications for different purposes. Some will prefer applications requiring high usage (e.g., video streaming) while others will prefer applications with lower resource demands (e.g., web browsing, email). Even consumers preferring a single application will vary in their use of it due to personal preferences and resource constraints—for example, time to watch streamed video and the cash to pay for the connection.

Consequently, internet access as sold by ISPs is not a homogeneous good—it varies with the application preferences of the consumers using it. Consumers with higher valuations for a single application will consume more resources than those with lower valuations. If metered tariffs are intended to recover higher revenues from higher-using consumers of a single application, then offering a zero-rated tariff for that application is inconsistent with the ISP's objective to recover its costs in usage fees. Assuming that the ISP does not recover the revenues lost from zero-rating application usage from the application provider, and it costs the same to deliver a unit of each application to the end user, then it is strategically illogical for the ISP to charge for the usage of one application and zero-rate usage of the other. Costs remain unchanged, but revenues will fall.

Hence, in the simplest case, as zero-rating by an ISP discounts revenues received from selected end users on the consumer side of the ISP platform, it must necessarily be associated with compensatory revenue streams—for example, higher fees charged to non-selected users, charges on the CAP side of the platform, or revenues from other sources, such as taxation or advertising—if in the long run the ISP wishes to remain solvent.

4. Competition: relaxing the assumptions

The principal arguments against zero-rating promulgated by net neutrality advocates rest on the one-sided logic that all end users should pay the same price for internet access, regardless of whether the market for the product in question conforms to the assumptions of perfect competition. In this model, the marginal unit supplied will be sold at its marginal cost of production, and this cost will determine the price paid for all other units sold. This leads to a statically efficient outcome, with maximum total welfare.

However, for this to be achieved, other specific market conditions must be met. Importantly, the product sold must be perfectly homogeneous, there must be perfect information, no transaction costs, no externalities, and no barriers to firms entering or leaving the market. There must be perfectly divisible output (i.e., no scale economies). All participants are price-takers—that is, no firm can charge more than the efficient price and remain in the market, and consumers must pay that price if they value the product at that price or above.

Requiring all units to be sold at the same price does not of itself make a market more competitive (i.e., render the perfectly competitive outcome) unless all of the other conditions are met. In this section, we will demonstrate that as practically none of these assumptions prevail in the complex market for internet access discussed in the previous section, simplistic calls to prevent zero-rating are insufficient to guide decision-making.

First, we show that when the assumption of homogeneous goods is relaxed, it is most unlikely that zero-rated tariffs can be used to foreclose rival applications. Instead, we demonstrate that requiring the same price to be charged for accessing products costing different amounts to produce obscures crucial underlying differences in costs on the supply side and user preferences on the demand side. This leads to our first three questions to be posed by those undertaking case-by-case assessments of zero-rating examples. Next, we relax the assumptions of perfect information and absence of transaction costs in the exchanges between ISPs and their end consumers, and their effects on barriers to entry for new CAPs and ISPs. This leads us to question the competitive positioning of the party objecting to an ISP using zero-rating prices—and our fourth question for assessors. It also leads to our final consideration—how the presence of transaction costs creates barriers to entry that lead to entrants and not incumbents favouring zero-rating policies. This leads to our fifth question, regarding the strategic options available to CAPs and ISPs that render financial transactions between them an adjunct to zero-rating that makes the strategy not only pro-competitive but also welfare-enhancing.

We note that in this analysis we are considering only instances of pricing of data transfer as a strategy for zero-rating. We do not consider cases of payments for data prioritisation. The examples we consider therefore have the appearance of the price discrimination to which Wu [12] and Van Schewick [15] raise objections, rather than being artefacts of paid data management, which are considered in other literature.

4.1 Relaxing the constraints: homogeneous products and heterogeneous users

In net neutrality discourse, ISPs could strategically zero-rate a selected application to steer end users away from using another application and towards the favoured one. This could occur if the ISP is also the CAP for the favoured application, whereby it could foreclose another ISP offering a similar application, or to foreclose a rival stand-alone CAP. However, such foreclosure can only occur only if the end users perceive the applications as perfect substitutes: that is, the applications are homogeneous.

If the two applications offer materially different value propositions to end consumers (i.e., the assumption of homogeneous products in the perfect competition model is relaxed), then the zero-priced application will not be able to force the positive-priced one from the market so long as there are consumers who prefer the positive-priced one over the zero-rated one by more than the discount embedded in the zero-rating offer [11]. As demonstrated above, as end users are also inherently heterogeneous in their content preferences, it is quite unlikely that the requisite conditions for foreclosure will occur unless the applications concerned are indistinguishable.

The inability for 'free' offerings to foreclose those with a positive price is observed with broadcast television and newspaper providers. Free-to-air television and free newspapers have not foreclosed pay television and newspaper subscriptions. Indeed, some consumers willingly consume both, even when some of the content overlaps, because the additional value offered by the pay version is sufficiently high enough that it overcomes the price differential. Arguably, the presence of the two different newspaper forms has led to greater content variety, with subscriber newspapers providing a professional journalist-based news service, and free newspapers relying more upon content generated by readers (e.g., local school and sports reports) and advertisers.

This leads to our first question to be posed about zero-rating offers.

Question 1. What very close or perfectly substitute applications accessible over the ISP's connection, costing the same to deliver, are likely to be foreclosed by the zero-rated application(s)?

The closer are the non-zero-rated application(s) to the zero-rated one(s) in the perception of the end users, then the more likely it is that the non-zero-rated applications will be crowded out. However, there are very few applications meeting this requirement that are truly close substitutes. For the most part, CAPs such as Netflix and Hulu are not close or perfect substitutes for each other because they contain different bundles of content for which end users have distinct preferences. The applications themselves are differentiated; even if it costs the ISP the same to deliver a Hulu movie and a Netflix one of equivalent specifications. If a consumer preferring Netflix is not prevented from paying the higher usage fee to watch Hulu content if the content available only on Hulu is sufficiently highly valued, then Hulu will not be foreclosed, even in respect of the subset of Hulu-preferring consumers on the discriminating ISP's network.

It might be a concern, however, if the applications in consideration were, for example, two identical cloud storage applications. The zero-rated application will have an unequivocal advantage over the non-zero-rated one, leading to all consumers with a non-zero valuation of using cloud storage opting for the lower-cost one. However, for foreclosure to occur, it is necessary for the applications to be undifferentiated—that is, homogeneous products. Foreclosure of differentiated products will be a function of the degree of differentiation—the more similar they are, the more likely it is that foreclosure will occur.

The logic applied in this simple illustration leads to the conclusion that without some non-neutral pricing signals, over-much (inefficient) investment in CAP variety is possible if equalising the prices faced by consumers and application providers conceals underlying real differences in costs and user preferences.

4.2 Equalising prices conceals underlying cost and valuation differences

Assume now that the two applications are perfectly homogeneous, but one actually costs less to deliver than the other. This could be because the ISP has been able to customise the delivery of one application within its own networks so that it costs less (or causes less congestion) than an otherwise-equivalent one that has not been customised. It could also be that one class of applications can be processed via a different operational process that is less costly, as occurred in Australia and New Zealand in the mid-1990s, when the internet was first becoming popular. At the time, international bandwidth capacity on the PACNET sub-oceanic cable was constrained. Due to asymmetric data flows, Australian and New Zealand ISPs purchased PACNET capacity under transit arrangements rather than peering. Traffic to and from end consumers over PACNET was more costly to handle than traffic handled under local peering arrangements. The original retail internet plans metered international (PACNET) traffic by volume, but offered unmetered (i.e., zero-rated) local traffic.

In this instance, zero-rating low-cost local traffic but metering high-cost international traffic reflected real differences in underlying costs. Zero-rating that diverts consumers' usage of substitutable applications towards lower cost applications raises efficiency.

This leads to our second question for regulators and adjudicators.

Question 2. Does usage of the zero-rated applications actually cost the ISP less than equivalent usage of non-zero-rated applications?

If the answer to this question is 'yes', then zero-rating would be less harmful to total welfare than the alternative of requiring all usage to be charged at a single price. Under the two-price arrangement, more usage than efficient would be made of the low-cost application, and the high-price usage tariff would have to be above cost to subsidise the additional low-cost usage. Arguably, this could lead to some low-cost applications surviving that would not otherwise be viable if their usage was charged at cost—that is, inefficient over-supply of application variety [11].

However, the alternative of a single positive usage price that does not signal the different underlying costs will lead to more usage of the high-cost application than if it was charged at cost. This usage would have to be subsidised by users of the low-cost application. Increasing the price of using the low-cost application above its cost to subsidise the high-cost usage leads to less usage of the lower-cost application, and at the margin some consumers will give up their internet connections entirely because they no longer receive utility higher than the combined price of access and usage. Without the fixed revenues of these low-cost consumers to offset the higher usage costs of the consumers paying below cost, the average usage cost per unit of traffic handled increases, leading to even higher usage fees and a second depressing effect on the usage of and fees generated by low-cost users. That is, a 'waterbed effect' emerges [23].

Hence, zero-rating of applications with lower costs than non-zero-rated applications is not equivalent in its effects to zero-rating applications with the same costs as their zero-rated counterparts. The difference is material. In a perfectly competitive market, it is necessary for the price signals associated with lower costs to be sent to consumers so that efficiency-raising changes in purchasing behaviours can take place. Concealing information about cost differences (e.g., by averaging the prices for two or more applications) prevents consumers making efficiency-raising choices.

We note, however, that in the New Zealand case, discounting local applications did not crowd out content from foreign origins because they were not substitutes. Indeed, foreign content and applications were overwhelmingly preferred by end users, even though they were more costly.

4.3 Differentiated price and product offers to low-valuers

We now turn to the argument of pro-net neutrality advocates that zero-rating should not be allowed when it enables free or discounted access to a narrow range of internet applications or applications with some functionality removed, when the ISP charges a higher fee for unrestricted access to the 'full service' applications. This restriction is claimed for ISPs, even though the same practice is widespread in the software industry—for example, Microsoft's Office available as a low-price, restricted student version and a high-price, full service professional version.

The advocates claim that restricted offer users cannot participate equally with unrestricted users in a supposed 'right' to access the full potential benefits of all applications and content available on the entire internet. Any arrangement that allows differentiated access to that content is seen as an infringement of that right. Zero-rating that reduces access charges in exchange for reduced functionality is therefore 'unfair discrimination'. Free Basics, where potential internet users in developing countries are offered free access to a restricted range of applications, but can access the full versions when paying a monthly internet access subscription, is frequently cited as such an infringement.

In principle, zero-rating access to a restricted-functionality application is no different to an application provider choosing to make some content available freely, and releasing other content only when some other obligations—for example, paying a fee, or sharing personal information—have been met. Access providers can set different tariffs for using different versions of the application if they really do invoke lower costs (e.g., stripped-down versions with lower data consumption), as per question 2. However, these versions may also be associated with compensation from the CAP to the ISP, especially if the low-cost version stimulates more low-value consumers to purchase connections, increasing the value available to the CAP from advertising. Furthermore, it is the application provider and not the ISP who makes the decision about restricting the application range to self-selecting end users. Preventing application providers from offering these discount arrangements appears at odds to the net neutrality argument that edge providers and not ISPs exercise control over internet content. If the range of content is restricted by applications providers—for example to foreclose other application providers—then it would seem more properly a matter to be addressed by generic antitrust provisions rather than internet access regulation.

Moreover, the presumption that all end users should pay identical prices to access the same applications ignores economic realities. The expectation that all consumers pay the same price for a product is an artefact of perfectly competitive markets. If all consumers pay the same price, then those with higher valuations of the bundle receive more surplus than those with lower valuations. Perfect equity in access prices for homogeneous good cements in place extreme inequities in surplus distribution. Price discrimination (different prices for the homogeneous good) effectively transfers surplus from high-valuers to low-valuers and leads to higher total consumer numbers without reducing total welfare. Where scale economies are present (as occurs in both ISP services and most CAP products, as they are mostly digital products with near-zero reproduction costs), then total welfare increases as well. Product differentiation (e.g., offering a subset of functionality for a lower price) leads to higher consumer numbers in total than with a single price for the undifferentiated good. Price discrimination and product differentiation therefore both appear consistent with (or at least are not per se harmful to) increased product variety, larger total numbers of internet users and ongoing innovation in the internet ecosystem. That does not mean that the practices might not, in some circumstances, lead to negative outcomes. Rather, it reinforces the merits of a case-by-case analysis rather than prescriptive prohibitions.

Price and product differentiation are important ways of enabling individuals with low valuations of internet use, or facing significant financial constraints, to become internet users, The former case occurs in mature markets, when the last-remaining individuals have not yet connected because the value they place on the connection is less than even a very modest single price charged. The latter case arises in developing economies, where income constraints pose significant barriers to purchase for large numbers of individuals. While subsidising connection fees through a tax and redistribution system may induce purchase in the former group, subsidising via applications may be more effective because the application is the primary determinant of the value derived. It also offers a superior means of subsidising in the latter case, because surpluses generated by users in developed economies can be transferred via the application and access bundle to subsidise those in developing economies. Thus, wealth transfers across national borders can occur without the need for government intervention.

This gives rise to our third question for regulators and adjudicators.

Question 3. Is zero-rated access to a subset of applications primarily intended to increase the number of individuals using the internet?

The purpose of this question is to separate out instances of zero-rating that are more likely to lead to positive network effects arising from larger total numbers of internet connections from instances that may arise from other motivations—for example to change the range and usage of applications by individuals already purchasing internet connections.

4.4 Relaxing the constraints: perfect information and no transaction costs

Having considered the implications of relaxing the constraints of product (and consumer) homogeneity, we now turn to the assumptions of perfect information and zero transaction costs that attend the perfect competition model, and their effects on barriers to entry and exit.

Imposing the assumption of consumer homogeneity reduces the amount of information available to both ISPs and CAPs to customise their offerings to individual consumer preferences. Information that would otherwise have been efficiently signalled or screened in customised offers can only be obtained subsequently by other means—inevitably with higher transaction costs. In the long run, this would seem to impose impediments to, rather than incentives for, the development of new applications and contracting arrangements. That is, banning zero-rating because the practice may pose entry barriers for new application providers must be balanced against the entry barriers that will be created if information about underlying consumer heterogeneity that would be efficiently signalled, screened and shared if zero-rating proceeds cannot emerge due to regulatory intervention banning the practice.

While banning zero-rating has been justified by the potential for ISPs to raise the costs for new application providers, it is equally plausible that banning prevents both application developers and ISPs from learning about and creating offers that cater to these underlying differences. Thus, existing ISPs and CAPs might prefer the information not to be surfaced if in doing so, opportunities were created for new entrants to take advantage of consumer heterogeneity to create new offers, attract consumers away from the exiting providers and appropriate a disproportionate share of the new consumers yet to purchase internet connections. Likewise, existing end users obtaining high surpluses under a single price might be unwilling to share those surpluses with new consumers who will participate only with implicit subsidies.

This gives rise to our fourth question for regulators and adjudicators.

Question 4. Who has requested that an instance of zero-rating be investigated?

If the request has come from existing ISPs, then it is plausible that the motivation may be to foreclose competitive entry by rival ISPs. If it has come from existing CAPs, then the motivation may be to foreclose competitive entry by new applications provides. If it comes from existing end users, then the motivation may be to lock in existing surpluses and not have to share them with new or future internet consumers. On the other hand, if the request to investigate has come from new or potential ISPs or CAPs then the claim that it creates an entry barrier may be credible. It seems most unlikely that a non-end user would ask for an inquiry about the legality of a zero-rating offer that would cost less than the alternative price. Similarly, it is also unlikely that a low-valuing existing end user who would be better-off using the restricted zero-price offer would request an inquiry.

4.5 Positive search costs and barriers to entry

In markets with heterogeneous products, consumers with different preferences, and information asymmetries that make it costly, if not impossible for consumers to identify the attributes of the products or the fit with their preferences before they have been consumed, a more appropriate model for analysing interaction is monopolistic competition. In this model, within a range of products there will be one that will be the best match for a given consumer with given preferences. At any given price, this product gives the consumer the highest possible surplus.

However, the consumer cannot identify in advance, which is the best match. Nor can the provider accurately identify the best consumers for the offer. The consumer can select one offer at random—so long as the surplus from this purchase is not negative, the consumer has gained at least some increase in surplus. Where the consumer will use a service multiple times (or make multiple purchases), the gain from purchasing the same product/service is known. There may be a better match available (higher gain) from buying a different product next time—but there is also a risk that the different product is a worse match than the existing one. The consumer could have had higher surplus if instead the first product had been purchased. There may also be switching, learning and adjustment and other investment (transaction) costs associated with each product. Buying from a second supplier means a second set of these costs—which is avoided if second and subsequent purchases are made from the first supplier. Together, these comprise 'search costs' (a form of transaction costs). The larger are the search costs, and the smaller is the expected benefit of the second product over the first, the less likely it is that the consumer will try to find a better match, even though there is definitely a better one out there. Thus, high search costs lead to suppliers having some market power over their existing customers—akin to monopoly—even though there are many different variants of the product—competitors—available for consumers to choose from.

Almost certainly, the markets for internet application adoption and usage are monopolistically competitive. Customers make investments in using specific applications (learning costs, emotional investments, etc.) that make them reluctant to try new variants. When a new application enters a market where customer preferences are already well established, overcoming these high search costs is likely one of the most significant barriers faced. The more mature is the application market, the more established are these preferences and the harder it will be to overcome them. Even if the new product is superior to all others in the market, customers will be reluctant to try it, because they do not know that it is better for them until they have tried it. If the same price is charged for the new and existing products, the new product will attract very few new customers, because of the high search costs customers face. In this case, the only way that the new product will attract new customers is by charging less than the existing products—that is, undertaking to meet the search costs incurred by the customers. For this reason, new products in markets exhibiting these characteristics are typically introduced with free trials.

However, if a new internet application is offered free of charge to consumers, because the costs are recovered from advertising or other sponsored revenues (e.g., donations, tax funding), it is not possible to discount the application cost to encourage switching. The only way that potential customers' search and switching costs can be reduced is by reducing the internet access charge. Hence, zero-rating may be the only viable way of inducing existing consumers to try a new application. Not being able to offer zero-rating thus constitutes an entry barrier to new applications seeking to compete with established ones. Just as in question four, it will be existing applications providers, and not new entrants, who would prefer that zero-rating not be allowed. However, it is important to note that there are two different reasons for coming to this conclusion.

This gives rise to our fifth question for regulators and adjudicators.

Question 5. Do consumers of the zero-rated application and its rivals make payments to applications providers separate from their payments to ISPs?

If the answer to this question is 'no', then the party with the most plausible reason to use a zero-rating strategy may be a new entrant. Preventing zero-rating then may lead to barriers to entry that protect incumbents. If the answer is "yes', then the situation is more complex, and further investigation is warranted.

5. Conclusion

In sum, therefore, the economic analysis reveals that the strategic motivations for using zero-rating are complex, and turn on a wide range of contextual factors, across all parts of the internet ecosystem. The five questions posed here tease out some factors to inform all ecosystem participants, but especially policy-makers and regulators.

The questions both draw upon, and highlight the fact that, the internet ecosystem is as complex, dynamic and adaptive system that defies simplistic definitions, and cannot easily be analysed or governed using simple frameworks developed for an environment with simple, linear relationships where cash flows closely followed product flows. To the extent that the ecosystem closely intertwines the activities of ISPs and CAPs with end users, it is no longer sufficient for regulators and competition authorities to consider zero-rating as solely an activity governed by the strategic intentions of ISPs alone. The questions posed in this chapter are not intended to substitute for detailed case-by-case analysis based upon economic principles of welfare maximisation, but rather stand as a complement to the frameworks currently being used in regulatory and judicial processes to assess likely harms and benefits.

There is much still to learn about competition and regulation of this complex ecosystem, but the questions here go some way to ensuring that scarce resources are used to investigate the cases most likely to be welfare harming.

References

[1] Evans D, Schmalansee R. The antitrust analysis of multi-sided platform businesses. In: Coase-Sandor Working Paper Series in Law and Economics, 623. 2012

[2] Shapiro C, Varian H. Information Rules: A Strategic Guide to the Network Economy, Boston. Massachusetts: Harvard University Press; 1999

[3] Parker G, van Alstyne M. Two-sided network effects: A theory of information product design. Management Science. 2005;**51**(10):1449-1592

[4] Rochet J-C, Tirole J. Two-sided markets: A progress report. The Rand Journal of Economics. 2006;**37**(3):645-667

[5] Carlton D, Perloff J. Modern Industrial Organization. 4th ed. Boston: Addison & Wesley; 2005

[6] Bring D, Leighton W, LoPiccalo K, Matraves C, Schwarz J, Waterman D. The year in economics at the FCC, 2014-2015. Review of Industrial Organization. 2015;**47**(4):437-462

[7] Howell B, Potgieter P. Bundles of trouble: Can competition law adapt to digital pricing innovation? Competition and Regulation of Network Industries. 2018;**19**(1-2):3-24

[8] Body of European Regulators for Electronic Communications. Draft BEREC Guidelines on implementation by National Regulators of European net neutrality rules. 2016. Retrieved from: file:///C:/Users/howellbr/Downloads/6075-draft-berec-guidelines-on-implementation_0.pdf [Accessed: July 27]

[9] Howell B, Layton R. Differentiating Neutrality and Non-Discrimination: A Politico-Techno-Economic Evolutionary History of the Internet and the Network Neutrality Debate. American Enterprise Institute, forthcoming; 2016

[10] Gans J, Katz M. Weak versus strong net neutrality: Corrections and extensions. Journal of Regulatory Economics. 2016;**50**(1):99-110

[11] Gans J, Katz M. Net neutrality, pricing instruments and incentives. NBER Working Paper 22040. 2016

[12] Wu T. Network neutrality, broadband discrimination. Journal of Telecommunications and High Technology Law. 2003;**2**:141-178

[13] Gans J. Weak versus strong net neutrality. Journal of Regulatory Economics. 2015;**47**:183-200

[14] Lee R, Wu T. Subsidizing creativity through network design: Zero-pricing and net neutrality. The Journal of Economic Perspectives. 2009;**23**:61-76

[15] Van Schewick B. T-Mobile's Binge On Violates Key Net Neutrality Principles. Mimeo; 2016. Retrieved from: https://cyberlaw.stanford.edu/downloads/vanSchewick-2016-Binge-On-Report.pdf [31.03.2016]

[16] Frieden R. A primer on network neutrality. Intereconomics. 2008;**43**(1):4-15

[17] Krämer J, Peitz M. A fresh look at zero rating. Telecommunications Policy. 2018;**42**(7):501-513

[18] Elaluf-Calderwood S, Layton R. Zero-rating: Do hard rules protect or harm consumers and Competition? Evidence from Chile, Netherlands & Slovenia. Paper presented at TPRC, August 2015. 2015

[19] Frieden R. Can internet service providers lawfully enhance or degrade third party content. 2017. Retrieved from: https://papers.ssrn.com/sol3/papers.cfm?abstract_id=2935274 [Accessed: 04.12.2018]

[20] Faulhaber G. Economics of net neutrality: A review. Communications & Convergence Review. 2011;**3**:53-64

[21] Greenstein S, Peitz M, Valletti T. Net Neutrality: A fast lane to understanding the trade-offs. NBER Workign Paper 21950. 2016

[22] Lemley M, Lessig L. The end of End-to-End: Preserving the architecture of the internet in the Broadband era. U.C. Berkeley Public Law and Legal Theory Research Papwer No. 36. 2000

[23] Katz M. Wither US. Net Neutrality Regulation? Technology Policy Institute Working Paper. 2016. Retrieved from: https://techpolicyinstitute.org/policy_paper/wither-u-s-net-neutrality-regulation/ [Accessed: 23.07.2016]

[24] Filistrucchi L, Geradin D, van Damme E, Affeldt P. Market definition in two-sided markets: Theory and practice. Journal of Competition Law and Economics. 2014;**10**(2):293-339

[25] Howell B. Non-neutral net neutrality: Asymmetric regulation strikes again! TechPolicyDaily.com. 2016. Retrieved from: http://www.techpolicydaily.com/internet/non-neutral-net-neutrality-asymmetric-regulation-strikes-again/ [Accessed: August 14]

[26] Laffont J, Tirole J. Competition in Telecommunications. Cambridge, Massachusetts: The MIT Press; 2001

[27] Layton R. BEREC's guidelines on zero rating are another "economics-free zone": Populism is the guiding principle. 2016. Retrieved from: http://roslynlayton.com/berecs-guidelines-on-zero-rating-are-another-economics-free-zone-populism-is-the-guiding-principle/ [Accessed: 27.07.2016]

[28] Van Schewick B. Network Neutrality and zero-rating. Attachment to Barbara van Schewick's Ex Parte in the Matter of Protecting and Promoting the Open Internet submitted February 19, 2015 to the Federal Communications Commission GN Dkt. No. 14-28. 2015. http://apps.fcc.gov/ecfs/document/view?id=60001031582

[29] Yoo C. Beyond network neutrality. Harvard Journal of Law & Technology. 2005;**19**(1):1-76

[30] Yoo C. Wickard for the Internet? Network neutrality after verizon v. FCC. Federal Communications Law Journal. 2014;**66**(3):415-466

[31] Belgian Institute for Postal Services and Telecommunications. BIPT analysis of zero rating of apps in the Proximus offers. 2017. Retrieved from: https://www.bipt.be/public/files/en/22099/Report_Zero_rating_Proximus.pdf [Accessed February 2 2019]

[32] Krämer J, Wiewiorra L, Weinhardt C. Net neutrality: A progress report. Telecommunications Policy. 2013;**37**(9):794-813

[33] Yoo C. The changing patterns of internet usage. Federal Communications Law Journal. 2010;**63**(1)

[34] Howell B. Separation anxieties: Structural separation and technological diffusion in nascent fibre networks. New Zealand Institute for the Study of Competition and Regulation Working Paper. 2014. Retrieved from https://www.econstor.eu/bitstream/10419/106840/1/816646821.pdf [accessed 25 July 2019]

[35] Howell B. Flat rate tariffs and competitive entry in telecommunications markets. New Zealand Institute for the Study of Competition and Regulation Working Paper. 2010. Retrieved from https://researcharchive.vuw.ac.nz/xmlui/bitstream/handle/10063/4053/Tariff_Structure_and_Competitive_Entry_BH.pdf?sequence=1 [Accessed 25 July 2019]

Chapter 8

Toward Clarifying Human Information Processing by Analyzing Big Data: Making Criteria for Individual Traits in Digital Society

Abstract

The purpose of this research is to solve those problems in education by indicating criteria for individual differences of cognitive mechanism when students interact using digital devices so that teachers would be able to instruct students with appropriate teaching strategies in collaborative learning. From the results of experiments for clarifying information processing by analyzing students' various data (Big Data processing), there was a tendency of an interaction comparing students' performance with the first and the second semesters between visual type and auditory type.

Keywords: individual differences, human information processing, criteria, cognitive schemas, decision-making, personality, prediction of behavior

1. Introduction

About two decades ago, digital instrument has begun to prevail in society, and the arrival of peoples' cognitive revolution has been forecasted [1]. Teachers also have begun to concern with the behavior of learners, so-called digital kids or students, because the latest technologies and information have been introduced one after another at the present field of education. On the other hand, however, it is questionable whether those technologies and information are understood conveniently.

Practically, it seems difficult for teachers to find out teaching strategies with using appropriate digital devices. It is not clear what has changed since the digital transformation of society and what are the causes of the change and their effects, because the individual differences of cognitive mechanism have not been clarified yet.

Accordingly, we have developed the measurements of individual traits concerning with human information processing as a fundamental research so that teachers might be able to understand those students more and instruct them appropriately depending on the criteria for individual traits.

The experiments of this system have been conducted under conditions of presentations either sound voice or written letters. We have collected and analyzed various data, for instance, their replies and response time (decision-making time), after their listening or silent reading.

In the practical experiments of collaborative learning which have formed depending on students' individual traits, they have continuously had interactive communication among team members, even using text message through learning management system (LMS). Consequently, high-stake assessments of students have become significantly higher than those of previous students formed by traditional methods [2]. On the other hand, we have found that there were differences among teams when we have compared their results.

We have checked students' data concerning learning, for instance, their reports, text message among team members for subjects so that we can analyze those data with reaction time (decision-making time), and the so-called Big Data processing and analysis [3]. The purpose of this Big Data analysis is to clarify the cognitive mechanism during learning processes along with the hypothesis from the model of human information processing.

With results of Big Data analysis, we have found that there are two types of traits (visual type and auditory type) and they have proved the relation between those traits of information processing and learning effects in collaborative learning. For instance, members of an unsuccessful team have formed by the similar traits of information processing (three of four members), in contrast, those of a successful team has consisted of different traits.

Therefore, it is supposed that individual traits such as personality and cognitive style in terms of information processing might help teachers to make collective decisions, for example, instruction and forming team members. Consequently, we would like to propose the results of the measurements and analysis as criteria for teaching strategies so that teachers can make their decision for forming interactive team members from the prediction of students' behavior.

2. Previous study

We will need to refer to the previous study when we address to find the method on how to indicate changing cognitive mechanism caused by transforming to digital society. We have become able to communicate each other in real time from distance by exchanging mails, text message, and other social network system instead of audio media like telephone and videoconference system (**Figure 1**).

Figure 1.
Conceptual diagram of paper vs. digital.

It is supposed from reaction time that it is not the same information processing by communication media of sound voice and letters because the different organs perceive and input various kinds of information which are not transformed to the same digital encoding [4]. Though the same grammar, words, and meaning are consisted in one language, they are used by different media: sound voice and letters. From aspects of grammar and meaning, they are similar media; it might make their features clear when they are compared with decision time which is measured from beginning of presenting a short sentence by each media until individual decision-making of participants, like the comparison of familiarity between them in terms of words [5].

With regard to those learning effects, it is reported that comprehension is higher in reading the texts aloud than silent reading [6]. Moreover, it is reported the experiment, whether participants read letters silently changing them into sound or not, has shown that the former cases are better comprehensions than latter ones [7].

There is another question, however, whether this result is always right or not, because there are two kinds of orthographic in Japanese case, which are kana and kanji (a phonogram and an ideogram) [8, 9]. In the case of an ideogram, we understand the meaning as a symbol without changing to sound phonetically. From those reasons, it is assumed that the orthography like Japanese kanji might bring about individual differences of cognitive style regarding to information processing [10].

3. System

3.1 Model of information processing

According to previous study, the model of information processing for one short sentence is devised (**Figure 2**). At first, information about letters consisted of a sentence presented as a subject would be perceived (a: input), and then they would be conveyed and processed with a series of letters or a block of words in order to be comprehended (b: problem solving). Next, the meaning of the information would be decided (c: decision-making); then the result of the decision for meaning would be encoded to perception which would be processing next information continuously (d: feedback control). The procedure from (a) to (b), (b) to (c), (c) to (d) would be repeatedly until the problem of the subject would be solved and selected the answer (h: decision-making) and then output it (i).

While those processing might be continued repeatedly, another feedback control might transfer the meaning of words from (c) to higher brain functions

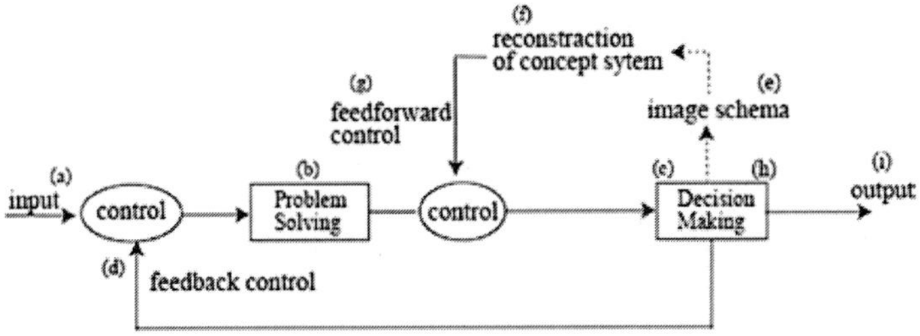

Figure 2.
Model of human information processing system.

by image schema (e) in order to confirm existing meaning or concept of those words or sentences. When those words or sentences are unknown for subjects, they might refer to existing concepts which were constructed by perception of other organs, and then their own new concepts would be reconstructed (f) before decision-making for meaning of words or sentences (c) and adjusted by feed-forward control (g).When you are citing sources, the citations should be set in a numbered format. All the references given in the list of references should be cited in the body of the text. Please set citations in square brackets keeping the below points in mind.

3.2 Hypothesis

There would be two types of traits hypothetically, visual type and auditory type, from the model of information processing. In the case of visual type, information might be mainly processing a circle of (a)→(b)→(c)→(d) repeatedly, and then finally decision-making would be done on (h)→(i) processing. On the other hand, in the case of auditory type, they might add another processing circle of (e)→(f)→(g). In this case, they might be referred to the existed concept which has been constructed by auditory information processing. From those viewpoints.

Hypothesis 1: In the case of auditory type, letters are supposed to be encoded to phonological sound. Consequently, the correlation coefficient between decision time and the number of words or duration of reading aloud (sound voice presentation) might be higher than those of visual type.

Hypothesis 2: The decision time of visual type is faster than those of auditory type because the former ones are supposed to not transform words from letters to sound.

In the next section, we will prove whether those hypotheses are correct or not by experiments.

4. Methods

Questionnaires of personality inventory for a psychological testing (YGPI) have been presented one by one as experimental subjects [Appendices 1 and 2]. YGPI consisted of 120 questionnaires with one short sentence each. Because of making the reliability of the test higher, those questionnaires are presented by reading aloud to subjects in order to fixed interval for selecting answers. It is important for a coefficient of confidence that subjects are brought about replying in time by effort because those regulations make their mental state similar.

For that reason, in the case of testing by paper and pencil, questionnaires of YGPI are not presented by written letters, but sound voice. On the other hand, in the case of testing on display, even presenting them by written letters are controlled the interval of the same condition as sound voice. Accordingly, when we have developed measuring system for cognitive traits of language information processing in terms of written letters, we decided to regulate time of presenting, along with each questionnaire by sound voice.

Participants are required to evaluate their behavior in everyday life whether the questionnaire is the same or not comparing with those of themselves and chose the answer among "yes," "no," and "either one" within 3 s after finishing the presentation of a questionnaire. As an instruction of testing, participants are also required to reply quickly without deliberating on making decision in order to prevent from no choice within the time.

4.1 Pilot

4.1.1 Purpose of pilot experiments

The aim of pilot experiments is to find out what have been changed in digital society from cognitive aspects in education. Along with this purpose, experiments and analysis are planned. In the field of education, we are able to choose media, such as sound voice or written letters, using digital materials, for instance, digital textbook and electronic blackboard. Accordingly, we have planned experiments for two kinds of comparison between sheet (paper)/PC and sound voice/letters.

4.1.2 Experiment 1

(1) Subjects: Three kinds of experiments (presenting questionnaires by sound voice and reply on the sheet (OCR), presenting questionnaires by sound voice and reply on display, and presenting questionnaires by written letters and reply on display). (2) Participants: 29 high school students of the first grade (male 13, female 16).

4.1.3 Experiment 2

(1) Subjects: Three kinds of experiments (presenting questionnaires by written letters and reply on the sheet (OCR), presenting questionnaires by written letters and reply on display, and presenting questionnaires by sound voice and reply on display). (2) Participants: 7 university students (male 5, female 2).

4.2 Preliminary experiments

4.2.1 Purpose of preliminary experiments

The purpose of preliminary experiments is to validate reproducibility concerning with the calibration of measuring system, the method of testing, and the results of analysis (comparison between visual type and auditory type).

4.2.2 Subjects of preliminary experiment

Under the same quality and conditions, experiments of presenting questionnaires by sound voice or written letters and replying on display have planned twice with counterbalance of the order.

4.2.3 Participants

Students of the same university, 28 females of freshmen.

4.2.4 Duration

From January to March in 2015.

4.3 Practical experiment

4.3.1 Purpose of practical experiment

The aim of a practical experiment is to examine the validity of criteria for traits of cognitive style in terms of information processing.

4.3.2 Participants

Students of the same university, 98 females of freshmen.

4.3.3 Method

Before starting classes, two kinds of testing, sound voice and letters, have been planned along with the method of preliminary experiments. The members of teams will be decided for collaborative learning depending on their personality which is measured by sound voice experiment. The observations in class will be recorded on their learning process. The interaction on LMS among members of their team will be also observed and recorded. The other data, for instance, results of performance (high-stake assessments) and reports (low-stake assessments), decision time of YGPI, and so on, will be gathered.

4.3.4 Duration

From April in 2015 to March in 2016.

4.4 Methods of analysis

The purpose of these analyses is to make traits of cognitive type in terms of information processing clear by comparing correlation between the number of words and duration of presenting sound voice (**Table 1**) and decision time.

4.4.1 Pilot

Each average of decision time will be calculated for every number of words; those figures will be shown by graphs. Next, different media such as paper, digital, sound voice, and letters have been compared.

4.4.2 Preliminary experiments

Each average of decision time will be calculated for every number of words; those figures will be shown by graphs. Next, it will be compared by the same media between first and second experiment. And then, it will compare the strength of correlations and variance by standard deviations.

The criteria, which are decided by the correlation coefficient between duration of presenting sound voice and decision time (**Table 2**), will decide the type—whether visual or auditory. Then, the decision time will be compared between those two types.

the Number of Words in Questionnaires	1	2	3	4	5	6	7
Frequency (the Number of Qusetionnaires)	1	12	13	27	25	30	12
Avarge Duration of Presenting Sound Voive (sec.)	0.76	1.01	1.38	1.79	2.18	2.49	2.74

Table 1.
The number of words and its frequency and duration.

	Media	Sound (sheet)	Sound (display)	Letters (display)	the Number of Words	Duration of Sound Voice
Comparison	Sound (sheet)	—	0.39	0.15	0.35	0.43
	Sound (display)	0.39	—	0.34	0.49	0.58
	Letters (display)	0.15	0.34	—	0.17	0.18
	the Number of Words	0.35	0.49	0.17	—	0.86
	Duration of Sound Voice	0.43	0.58	0.18	0.86	—

Table 2.
Correlation coefficient (pilot experiments 1).

4.4.3 Practical experiments

After gathering data of 98 participants by measuring decision time, they will be divided into visual or auditory type depending on the criteria which is decided by the preliminary experiment.

And then, whether this criteria of two types are verified or not by comparing results of decision time between preliminary and practical experiments.

Moreover, the results of students' performance practically will be compared by two types between first and second semesters.

5. Results

5.1 Results of pilot

1. Comparison between digital and paper materials

The average of decision time by digital was faster than those of paper (**Figures 3** and **4**), and the correlations with the number of words of digital were stronger than those of paper (**Tables 2** and **3**).

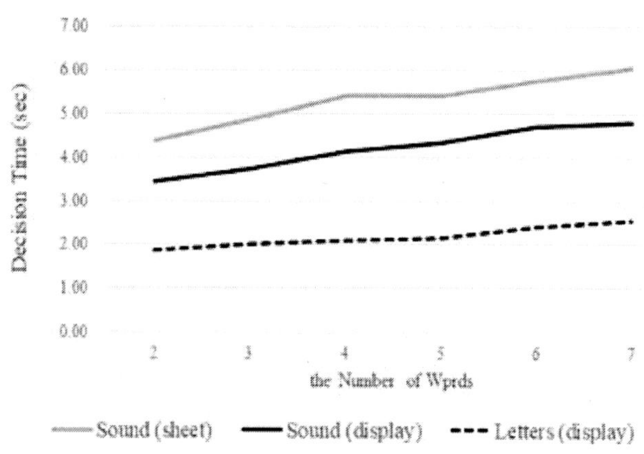

Figure 3.
Comparison of decision time during testing with paper or digital presented questionnaires by sound voice (paper or display) and leteers on display.

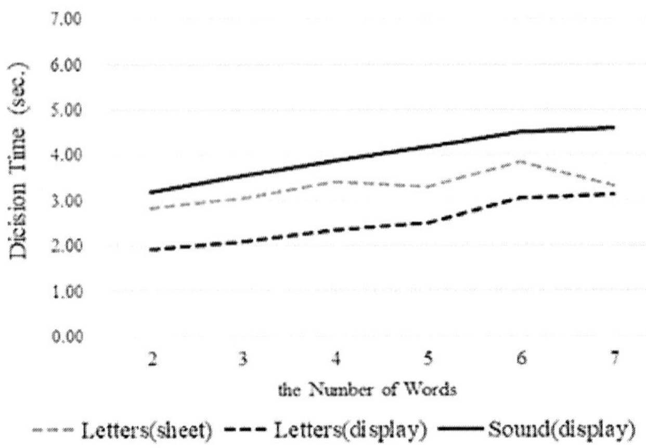

Figure 4.
Comparison of decision time during testing with paper and digital presented questionnaires by letters on paper or display and sound voice with digital.

Media	Letters (sheet)	Letters (display)	Sound (display)	the Number of Words	Duration of Sound Voice
Letters(sheet)	—	0.17	0.16	0.13	0.16
Letters(display)	0.17	—	0.39	0.31	0.30
Sound(display)	0.16	0.39	—	0.53	0.60

Table 3.
Correlation coefficient (pilot experiments 2).

2. Comparison between sound voice and letters media

The average of decision time of sound voice presentation was longer than those of letters (**Figure 4**).

5.2 Results of preliminary experiment

1. Verifying reproducibility

From the results of presentation by sound voice, there were no differences observed in terms of the average of decision time for each number of words between first and second experiment, in addition to correlation coefficient and dispersion (**Figures 5** and **6**). In the case of letter presentation, the results of comparison between the first and the second experiment were similar to those of sound voice, but the second average of decision time was faster than the first ones (**Figure 6**).

It is supposed the dispersion of decision time of letter presentation is larger and caused individual differences when comparing with sound voice presentation.

2. Comparison between visual and auditory type

There was no difference between visual and auditory type regarding the average of decision time and correlation coefficients (**Figure 7**).

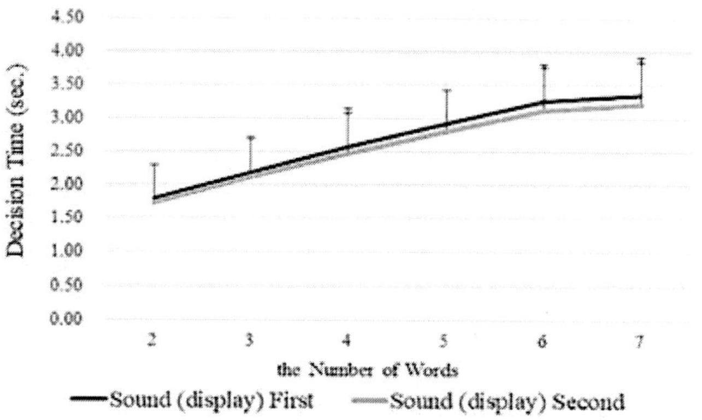

Figure 5.
Comparison of decision time between the first and the second by sound voice.

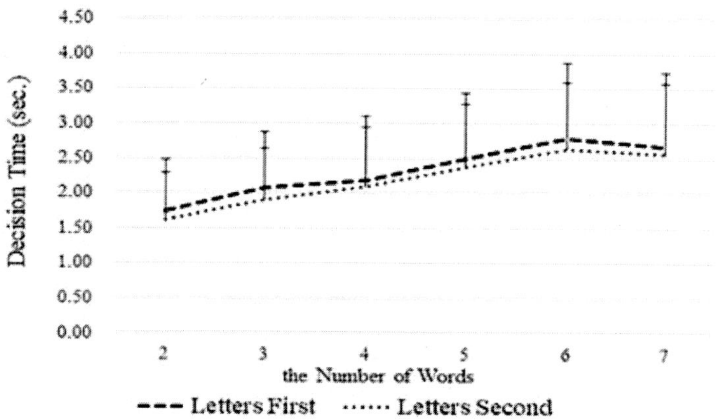

Figure 6.
Comparison of decision time between the first and the second by letters.

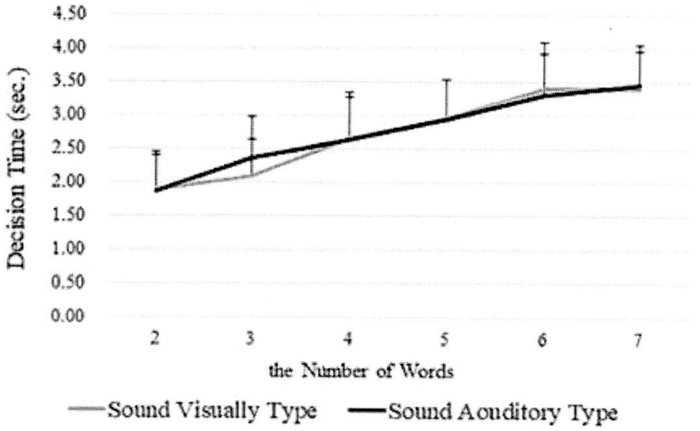

Figure 7.
Comparison of decision time between visual and auditory type by sound voice.

In the presentation of letter case, the average of decision time for visual type was faster than auditory type (**Figure 8, Table 4**).

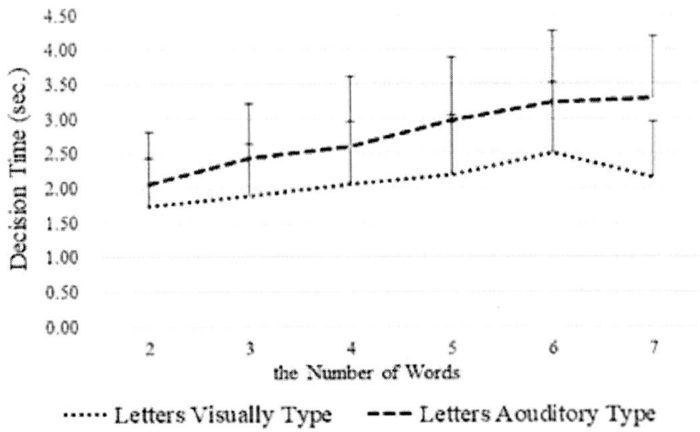

Figure 8.
Comparison of decision time between visual and auditory type presented by letters.

Cognitive Style	Correlation Coefficient
Visual Type	r <0.3
Auditory Type	r >0.5
Intermidiate Type	0.3 =< r <=0.5

Table 4.
Criteria of cognitive style for information processing.

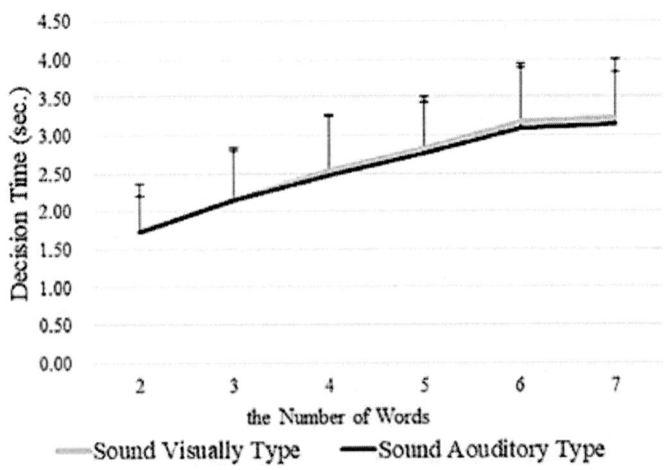

Figure 9.
Comparison of decision time between visual and auditory type presented by sound voice (practical experiment).

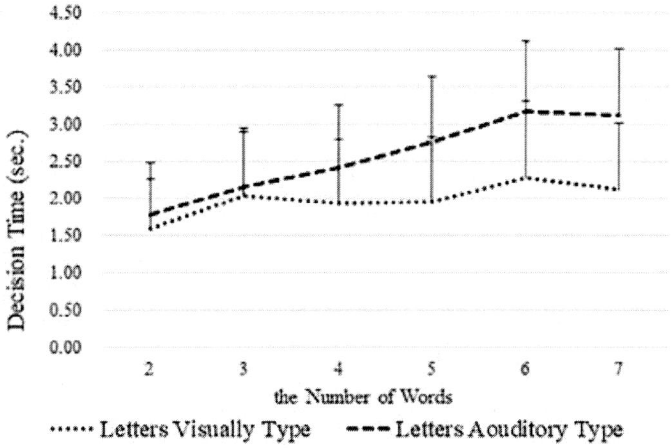

Figure 10.
Comparison of decision time between visual and auditory type presented by letters (practical experiment).

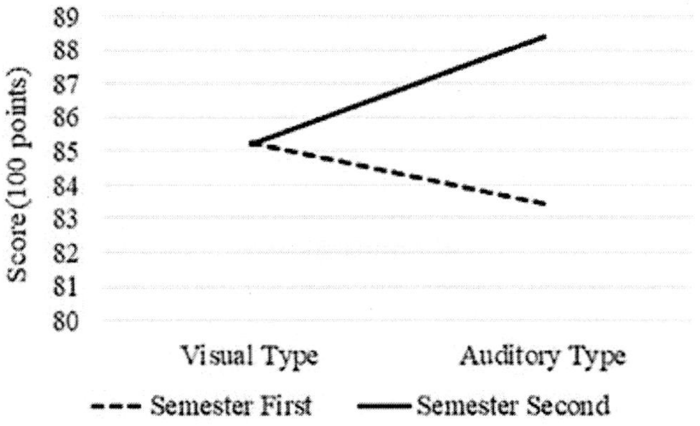

Figure 11.
Comparison of students' performance the first and second semester between visual and auditory type.

Because there were observed similar results between the first and the second experiment, it is supposed the reproducibility of measurements, method of analysis, and the criteria are verified.

5.3 Results of practical experiment

There were 12 students of visual type and 31 students of auditory type, according to the criteria of cognitive type in terms of information processing. There were no differences of the results in sound voice presentation between types regarding to the average of decision time depending on the number of words (**Figure 9**). In contrast, there were differences of the results in letter presentation between two types, regarding the average of decision time and the strength of correlation between decision time and the number of words (**Figure 10**). The tendency of a reciprocation between visual and auditory type concerning with the results of students' performance between the first and the second semester (**Figure 11**) was observed.

6. Discussion

6.1 What has been changed in digital society?

We have implemented the comparative experiments comparing paper and digital materials based on model of information processing (**Figure 2**). The results of measurements of individual decision time by digital materials were observed faster than those of paper. It was supposed to be caused more strongly by time constraints of digital materials than paper ones. In other words, it seems that the periods of time for decision-making were more unrestricted in condition of paper materials than digital ones. In the paper material case, participants were free to fill in their answers on sheets after the next presentation of questionnaire has been begun; on the other hand, in the digital material case, the display has already moved to the next page; then they were not able to reply their previous answer. From this reason, it was supposed the decision time by paper materials is longer than digital ones.

Especially in the presentation of letter case, participants were free to read silent questionnaires on the sheet freely, and then their decision time has become longer than others. In the PC case, each questionnaire is presented on display, and when the next questionnaire is presented, the display is moved to the next page at the same time by automatic migration from the program. From those reasons, in the letter presentation case, participants are not allowed to read previous questionnaires again after the display moved to the next page. It seems that the correlation between decision time and the number of words in digital materials case becomes higher than those of paper.

Through the basis of these results, there is more strict time in the digital material case, and this condition might have effects on decision time. In other words, participants might have been affected on their mental state in the digital material condition because they might feel that they need to decide strictly faster than paper ones. From those results, time bar has been added on display so that participants can feel more comfortable reducing their anxiety.

6.2 Toward clarifying information processing

Preliminary experiments have been conducted to examine the reproducibility for calibration of measurements toward a practical experiment. It is supposed that the reproducibility has been recognized because there were little differences in results regarding to the average of decision time between the first and the second experiments. The correlation coefficient of decision time with period of reading aloud (presented questionnaires by sound voice), comparing between Experiment 1 and Experiment 2, were similar without significantly differences. Concerning with the standard deviation of decision time, the case of letter presentation has been larger than sound voice case. It means that there exist individual differences in traits of cognitive style regarding to information processing.

Accordingly, the criteria of visual and auditory type have been decided provisionally by measurement of decision time depending on correlation coefficients with duration of sound voice presentation time. The results of the examination showed that there were no differences of decision time of sound voice presentation; on the other hand, in the case of letter presentation, the average of decision time for visual type is significantly faster than those of auditory type. Moreover, in the case of auditory type, the correlation coefficients between decision time and duration of sound voice presentation have been higher than visual type. For those results, it is supposed the hypothesis by the model of information processing is examined and proved (**Figure 2**).

6.3 Effects of changing

Those results of preliminary experiments have proved the validity by practical experiments with 98 participants (**Figures 9** and **10**). The indicator of learning effectiveness by high-stake assessment on their performance has shown the tendency of two-factor interaction between visual type and auditory type. From the interpretation on the model of information processing (**Figure 2**), it is supposed that there might be more opportunities for auditory type to reconstruct their concepts from various information when they are learning than visual type.

6.4 Teaching strategies

We have studied about the optimization of forming team members (collective decision-making) by personality (individual decision-making) as teaching strategies [11]. In this case, it is presumed that the learning effect has been improved by interactive communication among team members smoothly, comparing with traditional method of team forming which had decided by order of a student number. On the other hand, when the team members were decided by their personality in order to improve their performance in practical class, there were successful or unsuccessful teams. Looking at cognitive types, the latter has involved the same type of traits (three of four) with regard to the information processing but not personality. From this viewpoint, it is suggested that the method of optimization of forming team members might have been better with criteria for traits of cognitive type in terms of information processing in order to improve learning effectiveness.

7. Conclusion

In this paper, we have conducted experiments toward clarifying human information processing and examined the influence of digital materials in education. Moreover, the criteria for individual differences of information processing have indicated the impact on learning effectiveness. Consequently, the criteria of students' individual traits might help teachers make their plans, such as teaching strategies. It is also supposed that the appropriateness has been proved by the results of analyzing various data concerning with learning, for instance, students' performance, reports, and observation in class. On the whole:

1. What have been changed by digital materials, and what are the causes and how the effects have prevailed?

In education, the materials have been transformed from paper to digital. From the results of our research, it is suggested that the time limitation of digital materials might be strict more strongly than paper and it might have caused their anxiety for learners carrying their mental baggage.

2. There have been increasing opportunities of communication by text media like SNS in real time.

From the results of those experiments, it is assumed that the learning by digital materials with texts might have been caused by clearing individual differences of cognitive style concerning with information processing and effect on learning.

3. From the results of Big Data analyzing, it was assumed that the criteria for traits of cognitive style in terms of information processing by letters might suggest teaching strategies.

A. Appendix 1

the Number of Words	Number	Questionnaires (Letters)	Questionnires (Sound)
2	1	無口である	Mukuch de Aru
	2	感情的である	Kanjyouteki de Aru
	3	心配性である	Sinpaisyo de Aru
3	4	用心深いたちである	Youjinbukai Tachi de Aru
	5	気が変わりやすい	Ki ga Kawari Yasui
	6	人のあつかいがうまい	Hito no Atukai ga Umai
4	7	自分はいつも運がわるい	Jibun ha Atsukai ga Umai
	8	たびたび考えこむくせがある	Jibun ha Knagaekom Kuse ga Aru
	9	気持ちを顔にあらわしやすい	Kimochi wo Kao ni Arwasi Yasui
5	10	色々違う仕事がしてみたい	Iroiro Chigau Shigoto ga Shitemitai
	11	新しい友達はなかなかできない	Attarashii Tomodachi ha Nakanaka Ddekinai
	12	色々な世間の活動がしてみたい	Iroirona Seken no Kadudo ga Shite Mitai
6	13	色々な人と知り合いになるのが楽しみである	Iroirona Hito to Shiriai ni Naru noga Tanoshimi de Aru
	14	人は私を十分認めてくれない	Hito ha Watashi wo Jyubun Mitomete Kure Nai
	15	会話の最中にふと考えこむくせがある	Kiwa no Saichu ni Huto Kangaekomu kuse ga Aru
7	16	理由もなく不安になることが時々ある	Wake mo Naku Huan ni Naru Koto ga Tokidok Aru
	17	実行する前に考えなおしてみることが多い	Jikko Suru Mae ni Kangae Naosite Mirukot ga Oi.
	18	なかなか決心がつかず機会を失うことが多い	Nakanak Kessin ga Tuka zu Kikai wo Usinau Koto ga Oi

B. Appendix 2

the Number of Words	Number	questionnaires (in English)
2	1	I am a reticent person.
	2	I am a sentimental person.
	3	I am a worrier.
3	4	I am an extremely cautious person.
	5	I am capricious.
	6	I am good at dealing with people.
4	7	I am always unluky.
	8	I sometimes tend to think deeply.
	9	I am easy to betray my emotion.
5	10	I would like to do various kinds of jobs.
	11	It is difficult for me to make new frinds.
	12	I would like to be extremely acitve in variety of wolrd.
6	13	I am pleasure of meeting with a lot of people.
	14	People would not accept me adequetly.
	15	I am prove to think deeply during converstion.
7	16	Sometimes I become nervous without any reasons.
	17	I have frequetnly reconsidered before a plan.
	18	I have often lost chances because I could not decide immediately.

References

[1] Gardner H. The Mind's New Science: A History of the Cognitive Revolution. New York: A Member of the Perseus Books Group; 1987. 401 p

[2] Tsujioka K. Development of Support System Modeled on Robot Suit HAL for Personalized Education and Learning. EITT. Society of International Chinese and Education Technology; 2017. pp. 337-338. DOI: 10.1109

[3] Tsujioka K. A Case Study of ICT Used by Big Data Processing in Education: Discuss on Visualization of RE Research Paper. ICIET, Association for Computing Machinery; 2018. pp. 160-164. ISBN: 978-1-4503-4791-4

[4] Card SK, Moran TP, Newell A. The Psychology of Human-Computer Interaction. Hillsdale, NJ: Lawrence Erlbaum Associates; 1983

[5] Amano S, Kondo T. Modality dependency of familiarity ratings of Japanese words. Perception & Psychophysics. 1995;**57**(5):598-603

[6] Elgart DB. Oral reading, silent reading, and listening comprehension: A comparative study. Journal of Reading Behavior. 1978;**10**:203-207

[7] Takahashi M, Tanaka A. Cognitive processing during silent and oral reading: Cognitive load and phonological representation. Cognitive Studies. 2011;**18**(4):595-603 (in Japanese)

[8] Gernsbacher MA. Resolving 20 years of inconsistent interactions between lexical familiarity and orthography, concreteness, and polysemy. Journal of Experimental Psychology. American Psychological Association, Inc. 1984;**113**(2):256-281

[9] Morton J. Interaction of information in word recognition. Psychological Review. 1969;**76**(2):165-178

[10] Kimura Y. Concurrent vocal interference: Its effects on kana and kanji. Quarterly Journal of Experimental Psychology: Section A. Human Excremental Psychology. 1984;**56**

[11] Tsujioka K. A case study of using big data processing in education: The method of matching members by optimizing collaborative learning environment. In: Cano A editor. Social Media and Machine Learning. Account/IBAN number: HR2424840081104542506, in printed

Chapter 9

Evaluating Information Technology Strategic Planning Process: Lesson Learnt from Bruneian Small Businesses

Abstract

The chapter investigates the 85 small and medium organizations in Brunei Darussalam within the context of information technology (IT) strategic planning process. The study results reveal that although the surveyed Bruneian SMEs are familiar with IT strategy basic methods, however, the use of any of the basic IT strategic development process is at the grassroot level. The results further found that only three methods have indirect influence on IT strategy development such as critical success factors, transaction cost, and balanced scorecard. Conclusion from these findings further suggests that no statistical difference exists among SMEs on the basis of organization size and industry sector. These findings are useful for both the researchers and practitioners. For researchers, it helps in building a theoretical foundation in developing the repository of organizational use of IT strategy basic methods and for practitioners to gauge the performance of SMEs in relation with developing IT strategy basic methods in designing the relevant policies.

Keywords: IT strategy, strategic planning methods, small and medium enterprises, Brunei Darussalam

1. Introduction

The adoption of Information Technology among business organizations have entered the maturity stage especially with the advent of Web-based developments, new opportunities have been brought into the organizational functions and business processes that has enabled them to meet the market demands and to sustain their capacity building. However these latest trends and changes in technology have brought several challenges to the businesses especially to the SMEs who are overloaded with global competition, economic downturn, and fierce competition in changing customers' demands that has pushed these SMEs to reengineer their business processes. Such challenges demand effective capabilities and competitive solutions. The business organizations started using information technology as a tool to get strategic and competitive advantages. The organizations started using their resources strategically so as to reduce the cost and gain more profit and become productive in customer relationship. To achieve these strategic options, organizations started deploying various strategic planning processes. While the benefits of adopting strategy as a tool to get the business gains among the big businesses became viable, the SMEs started adopting the similar practices coupled with the Internet technologies, new business approaches like e-business and e-commerce soon became familiar and being widely used across the globe. Information Systems are linked with business strategy, management skills, and decision-making to enhance the competitive advantage to achieve the overall organizational success [1]. Researchers have focused on the process of strategic information systems planning (SISP) since the 1970s [1, 2]. SISP further help business to innovate, create new products, reduce cost, and enhance relationship with customers [3, 4]. Unfortunately, majority of SMEs could not be successful in their business endeavors, mainly due to the reasons that these small businesses are not exploiting their full resources mainly due to lack of strategic planning process. This situation continues to exist in almost all the economies especially in the developing countries. A right choice for SMEs to meet these market-driven forces is to increase using ICT to significantly improve their competitive capabilities [5].

In their study, Bhagwat and Sharma [5] stated that IT has a vital role in an organization's sustainability and growth. This further supports the study that found impact of IT usage on organizational performance is positively related [6]. Azyabi [7] studied IT/IS strategy development among Australian SMEs and that has provided the basic motivation to conduct the study in Brunei. Secondly, up to our knowledge, no prior research was undertaken in Brunei focusing SMEs from IT strategic development point of view. On these rationales, this pioneering study was conducted to investigate the main strategic issues of Bruneian SMEs with two basic objectives:

1. To find out the extent to which the SMEs are using or familiar with IT strategy development methods

2. To investigate the difference in the use of basic strategy development method on the basis of organization size (small or medium) and industry sector (manufacturing and non-manufacturing).

1.1 Role of the SMEs for nation's economy and importance of IT strategy to SMEs

The SMEs are considered as a major backbone for the national economy especially in the developing nations. It is true to the Bruneian business environments as well. The first report on Bruneian SMEs [8] has recommended the enhanced use of information technology to gear up a task of improving SME functionality for the overall economic development. The report has highlighted the slow diffusion of technology and has further recommended the strategic directions in adopting new technology. In their study, they not only considered the adoption of new technologies as a strategic issue but also rated the adoption of new technologies as number 9th critical success factor out of 11 that would be contributing toward the success of SMEs.

In the past, most of the researchers [9–11] have suggested that SMEs have the following characteristics: small management team, strong owner influence, centralized power and control, lack of specialist staff, multifunctional management, lack of control over business environment, limited market share, short-term strategic planning, low employee turnover, and reluctance to take risks. Some other studies [11–13] suggested that most SMEs avoid sophisticated software and applications, lack necessary expertise to fully utilize the benefits of technological innovations, and associate their ongoing success with vendor support and vendor expertise.

While discussing the strategic planning among SMEs, we should consider both the dimensions of strategic planning process: (1) strategic planning process to gauge and monitor the performance of SMEs and (2) strategic information technology planning (SITP) process that includes the planning process for the IT resources. However, in its own context, the term is interrelated as some organizations consider it as one process, whereas other SMEs deploy strategic planning process at the outset and then continue it with SITP. The strategic planning on the performance of SMEs has been discussed extensively in theory and in literature [14–16]. Strategic planning is concerned with the establishment of long-term organizational objectives and the development and implementation of plans to achieve them to further improve the organizational performance [16]. In other words, SMEs not only make long-term planning but also systematically plan at operational level to evaluate both internal (within organization) and external (competitive environments) factors [17].

The focus of this study is not to examine overall strategic planning practices in SMEs but from the Information Technology Strategic Planning (ITSP) process, in particular. Thus examining and evaluating ITSP not only lead to the firms' performance but to find an answer as how the capacity building of the firm in the competitive environment is sustained. Literature provides the full support that most importantly SMEs engage in strategic planning process is less likely to fail [16, 18, 19]. In addition to the above discussion, we should consider the changing business dynamics with the advent of the Internet and Web services including the m-services. These emerging trends have imposed new challenges and change the strategic planning process henceforth.

1.1.1 The Bruneian context

The study focus solely on SMEs located in Brunei Darussalam—small island in South China Sea located at the equator between Singapore and Malaysia with a small population of 0.4 million[1]. About 57% of the population is aged from 20 to 54 years old. The country is ruled by 29th Sultan of Brunei His Majesty Sultan Hassan-ul Bolkiah—the most visionary leader. The country is economically rich with main industry of petroleum and petrochemical based with total GDP of 11,96 billion USD in 2016 with per capita GDP of $76,700 in 2017. The unemployment rate remained 6.9% in 2017 (http://www.theodora.com/wfbcurrent/brunei/brunei_economy.html). The government has been encouraging economic diversification mainly into business service, financial service, hospitality and tourism, transport and logistics, and manufacturing primary resources. The diversification is aimed to provide business opportunities for SMEs. Brunei is made up of microenterprises, small and medium enterprises at the percentage of 52, 44, and 3%, respectively, of the registered business. Majority of SMEs are in wholesale and trading businesses with the inclusion of service-based SMEs. The primary resources sector, Islamic financial market, and halal market have been identified as key growth area for local SMEs. The government provides various forms of assistance such as financing entrepreneurial development, investment incentive, technology transfer, infrastructure, and various other facilities. The SMEs development plans are in accordance with the national long-term plan at the Principles of Asia-Pacific Economic Council (APEC). APEC identified five major priority accesses for the development of SMEs: human resource development, information access, technology and technology sharing, and financing and market access.

In Brunei, only 8% of total private sector business establishments fall in the category of large businesses including foreign banks, shipping and insurance companies and Brunei Shell Petroleum, and its various subsidiaries. The remaining 92% covers the SMEs that also fulfill the 74% of nation's employment needs

---

[1] All the statistical data about Brunei was extracted from http://www.heritage.org/index/country/brunei

(www.bsmenet.com). The Bruneian SMEs are facing the same problems of not doing their business strategically in order to get the competitive advantage [20].

Because of the relative importance of the SMEs within the context of Bruneian business, it is very important to agree on the definition of SMEs, as contribution of SMEs may be estimated only on the basis of what definition for SMEs is accepted in a country. For simplicity, we stick to the definition of Yap et al. [13] for this study. Accordingly, they defined small organizations having 50 or less employees and medium-sized organizations having employees size from 51 to 250.

1.1.2 Strategic planning process among SMEs

While discussing the strategic planning among SMEs, we should consider both dimensions of strategic planning such as (1) strategic planning on the performance of SMEs and SISP among SMEs. However, both are interrelated; if the SMEs deploy strategic planning process at the outset then, there is a strong possibility that these SMEs will use the SISP. The strategic planning on the performance of SMEs has been extensively discussed in the theory and prior literature [13–16]. Strategic planning is concerned with the establishment of long-term organizational objectives and the development and implementation of plan to achieve them in order to improve the performance of an organization and to set up the directions by developing policy measures [15]. In other words, SMEs must have long-term plans as well operational plans to evaluate both external and internal factors [18, 19]. Since the focus of this study is to highlight the SISP in SMEs so that we can find an answer by doing this, how capacity building of these firms in the competitive environments can further be achieved?

Within the context of SMEs, we need to discuss the different views for the strategy; it can be acknowledged that it is difficult to come up with one single definition for the strategy concept. There are various definitions such as Seth and Thomas [21] who defined strategy as a plan that aligns the enterprise aims, process, and policies toward achieving better allocation for organizational resources. Andrews [22] provided another definition: "Strategy is a plan for the control and utilization of organizational resources to achieve desired corporate goals (e.g. gain market share, image) and gain advantage over competitors." Similarly, Gibcus and Kemp [23] defined strategy as a "coordinated plan that gives the outlines for decisions and activities of a firm and is focused on the application of the resources that a company has, and the disposal of these resources thus enabling the firm to achieve its own goals." For this research, the term strategy is defined as follows: a plan that is intended to provide the organization with better resources' control and utilization and competitive advantage. Finally, the terms IT and IS are two separate terms but are often used interchangeably. For the purpose of this study, we use the term "IT" to represent both IT and IS and IT strategy as "a plan for controlling, using, and utilizing IT/IS resources to gain competitive advantage over rivals."

IT can help organizations in leveraging competence and increasing the competitive advantage. It assists organizations in achieving their strategic and operational goals [24], and thus IT/IS is considered to be a significant factor for SMEs' success. However, IT/IS needs to be managed effectively to achieve these benefits. According to Earl [25], IT strategy provides organizations with the most important systems that contribute to competitive advantage. These systems could be internal systems which aim to improve efficiency and effectiveness of business operations or external systems. Earl [25] summarizes the objectives and importance of IT strategy in these benefits: facilitating alignment of IT investments with organization objectives, managing IT resources in an efficient and effective way, and establishing IT architectures and policies in the organization. Blili and Raymond [6] point out that those SMEs have to look for long-term advantage from information systems and they should recognize the significance of the right investment decisions. They link the strategic planning for information systems with an organization's survival. They also consider the rapid change in technology as a motivator for having effective strategic planning for IT.

Some studies [26–28] found that about 75, 76, and 80% organizations engage in strategic IT planning, but strategic IT plans were not implemented extensively. Lederer and Sethi [29] found that only 24% of the projects in the strategic IT plans had been initiated more than 2 years into the implementation stage. Gottschalk [30] in his study of four Norwegian organizations found that 42% of the projects in the formal IT strategy had been implemented after 5 years. Ward and Griffiths [31] found that despite a belief in its importance in the past decade, many organizations have developed perfectly sound IT strategies that had been left to gather dust. Similarly, Falconer and Hodgett [32] in their Australian survey found that proportion claiming to undertake strategic IT planning ranged from 58% in large organizations to 29% in medium-sized organizations and only 19% in small organizations.

Based on the above discussion, it can be shown that SMEs are a significant factor for a country's economy that can be safely be marked as an engine of growth for the nation's economic development. However, SMEs are facing many competitive and environmental problems. One of the creative and effective solutions for these problems is using IT in an appropriate way. However, formulating IT strategy, which is driven by business strategy and objectives, could provide a smart and efficient use of IT resources in SMEs. Recognizing this, it appears that formal approaches to developing IT strategy would benefit SMEs. In the next section, we review the previous literature to establish a link with this study.

2. Review of literature

Literature is full of studies that has not only highlighted the various IT strategies that are applied and used among SMEs [25, 31, 32, 39, 40] but also included studies that highlighted the benefits of having IT strategic methods [7, 25] and studies focusing on the barriers to IT strategy development [7, 51]. At the outset, review of the literature was examined from more general studies focusing on the impact of the strategic IT processes on the organizations to the specific studies that has provided a base for this study.

The past several studies were conducted to find out the strategic role of information systems and the impact it brought to the businesses. Pyburn [33] conducted an exploratory study that involved IS managers and top management. He noted that following factors are very critical in influencing the success or failure of SISP, namely, (1) perceived success of the IS manager, (2) volatility of the business, (3) complexity of the IS environment, (4) IS managers' and top management personality, and (5) physical proximity of the IS manager to the senior managers. Pyburn's work was basically focusing on top management as a determining factor for SISP success, but he ignored several important aspects such as techniques, processes, and implementation issues. Sexton and Van Auken [34] found in their longitudinal analysis that survival rates of SMEs which apply formal strategic planning process are higher. Several other researchers emphasized the success of SISP among SMEs is related to the managers [15, 35]. Some others studies [36, 37] focused solely on managers' characteristics and their impact on strategy development. However, the generalization of these studies is limited to owners/managers' characteristics. Similarly, King and Teo [38] suggested various factors that need to be understood such as management commitment and impact on firm performance, return of investment, and increased market share. Researchers like Peppard et al. [39] and Maharaj and Brown [40] suggested supporting organizations in determining potential opportunities to deploy Information Systems (IS) with great competitiveness. The organizations such as SMEs should deploy IS in certain phase such as strategic awareness, situation analysis, and strategic conception to strategic formularization to strategy implementation leading toward change management action plan to finally evaluating the strategic plan.

The trend in SISP got its first turn with the first version of the Nolan stages that appeared in 1979 [41] and explained the dynamics of increasingly vital production factor called the information technology. His theory provided a widespread framework of development of IT in organization. Jackson [42] studied several strategy concepts to find out the best practice and how companies are best organized for competitive advantages through IT. In addition to it, several approaches were considered such as suggested Earl's five approaches [43, 44] and Segars's [44] rational adoption of the strategic IS planning process with the SISP success. Earl [43] classified SISP experience with five categories if SISP approaches: (1) business led, (2) method driven, (3) administrative, (4) technological, and (5) organizational. His findings suggest that each of the five distinct approaches have a different likelihood of success with the "organizational" approach being the most effective and "method driven" the least effective approach. Segars [44] conducted an empirical study of over 250 top IS executives to investigate the issue of design dimensions of planning systems and the influence of internal (within system) and external (system and context) coalignment on SISP. The findings suggested that SISP is multidimensional concepts and strategic planning systems that exhibits high level of comprehensiveness, high level of formalization, control focus, top-down planning flow, and high level of participation and consistency that are directly associated with SISP success and termed this approach as rational adoption.

Miller and Cardinal [45] claim that strategic planning provides better results than non-planning. Ward and Peppard [46] stressed on the reconciliation of the IT and business to improve competitive advantage. Bergeron et al. [47] studied two well-known planning methodologies: Porter's [48] value chain and Wiseman's [49] strategic thrust for identifying IT opportunities from a competitive advantage perspective. The result indicated that while there were overall similarities between the two methodologies, however, Wiseman strategic thrust framework is more applicable for organization in unstable environments. Gottschalk [50] stressed on the need for improved implementation of IT, failure to do could lead to lost opportunities, nonfulfillment of the objectives, and problems in future planning. He suggested understanding the link between strategic plan and implementation within the organization. Jantan and Srinivasaraghavan [51] studied the IT deployment process and competitive advantages among 81 Malaysian business organizations and confirmed that strategic deployment of IT does affect the level of competitive advantage among the organization. Factors such as good technology management, innovation culture, and strategic planning and training were found to influence on the organizational competitiveness.

Gordon and Gordon [52] conducted a pilot study of eight Fortune 500 manufacturing companies to find out the interaction between IT and business units as a key to success. Bergeron et al. [53] studied 110 small enterprises and suggested a contingency model based on the notion of "fit" between the organization's management of IT, its environment, strategy, and structure that has brought a significant difference. Allen and Helms [54] suggested linking strategic practices and organizational performance to Porter's [55] generic strategy. He provided a list of critical strategic practices that are significantly associated with the organizational performance for each of Porter's generic strategies: differentiation, focus differentiation, cost leadership, and focus cost. In addition, a number of other studies like Ghobadian and O′ Regan [35] and Gunther and Menzel [37] focused on specific industry sectors. They concluded that SISP practices are influenced by the industry types.

Whereas some studies like Sharma [56] and Adendorff et al. [57] are limited to a single-case study. There is no surprise that several studies in strategic planning were conducted in developed world like UK-based study of Ghobadian and O′ Regan [35] and Pemberton and Stonehouse [58]. Gunther and Menzel [37] studied in Germany and Polatoglu [59] studied in Turkey. However, the results of these studies are not related to the developing countries because of various economics, social, and cultural differences. Majama et al. [60] conducted a study among Botswana's SMEs and found that strategic planning efforts do exists within SMEs, but most of these firms engage in strategic planning activities to a limited extent. The study focused on barriers of not doing the SISP in form of owners/managers' limited knowledge of strategic planning. Results show that some of these SMEs do not plan because of the size of the business. Some of these SMEs admitted of not having any final business decision-making process leading toward poor or no planning at all.

We now examine the specific studies that have provided a framework for this study. Earl [25] provided a classification for IT strategy models which he called "framework of frameworks." It includes three main categories of frameworks: (1) Awareness frameworks which include three subsets of frameworks: refocusing frameworks, impact models, and scoping models (2) Opportunity frameworks which include four subsets of frameworks: systems analysis frameworks, application search methods, technology fit frameworks, and business strategy frameworks (3) Positioning frameworks which include three subsets of frameworks: scaling frameworks, spatial frameworks, and temporal frameworks Earl [25] provided examples for each subset. These examples were investigated by Levy et al. [61] in the UK context to find out their applicability to SMEs. The results of that study are as follows: The awareness frameworks are of value for SMEs because they enable them to understand their environment. This will help SMEs to set their business goals effectively and to decide the changes required to achieve these goals. Examples for this category are the strategic opportunities framework, Porter's generic strategies, and information intensity matrix. In the opportunity frameworks, the systems analysis frameworks and business strategy frameworks are very useful for SMEs. On the other hand, application search methods and technology fit frameworks are less useful for SMEs because they depend on extracting information from business strategy which may not always exist. The example given of a business strategy framework is Porter's five competitive forces model; the example of a systems analysis framework is Porter's value chain; and the example of application search methods is customer resource life cycle. The positioning frameworks are the least applicable frameworks for SMEs, except scaling frameworks which help to identify the role of information systems in SMEs. The examples given for scaling frameworks are the Strategic Information Systems Grid, sector information management grid, and stages of growth models.

In addition to these studies, Blili and Raymond [6] proposed two main approaches for the IT strategic planning: top-down and bottom-up. They stated that the first approach is more suitable for SMEs because it reflects the importance of IT in the view of top management. They developed information systems strategy (ISS) model for IT strategy, and this model consists of various IT basic methods. In their proposed model, they suggested that Critical Success Factors (CSFs) method to be used to analyze the priority and significance of the business activities which lead SMEs to the high performance. They recommended that CSFs should be combined with Porter's value chain and transaction cost method.

Similarly, Levy and Powell [62] built on the ISS model of Blili and Raymond [6] in SMEs. The new model consists of three stages: business context, business process, and strategic content. Each stage includes objectives to be achieved through some basic methods. The business context analysis helps a business to define three main aspects: the business strategy and objectives, the business environment, and the competitive environment. These three analyses can be performed by some basic methods such as CSFs, PESTEL, balanced scorecard, and information intensity matrix. The business process analysis is concerned with three aspects: determining the processes that add value for the business, reviewing if the organization is using the appropriate IT to perform the core processes, and finally, analyzing the organization's current IT tools and functions. These analyses are to be accomplished through some basic methods such as value chain method, Strategic Information Systems Grid, and soft systems methodology (SSM). The strategic content analysis aims to provide recognition for the required IT that can satisfy the organization's objectives. They suggested such techniques as MIT'90 and the 3D model of information systems success for this purpose.

Salas et al. [63] within the Australian context provided an approach to IT strategy development that was based on the Blili and Raymond's [6] work. The model consists of two complementary views: top-down which is done by top management to identify the business objectives and environment and bottom-up which is done by operational managers to analyze the major processes. Both views are targeted to specify the required IT to fulfill the business objectives. They adapted the Strategic Options Development and Analysis (SODA) model to perform the top-down view and business process analysis and modeling to perform the bottom-up tasks. **Table 1** list IT strategy basic development methods that have been used to form the models discussed.

Azyabi [7] conducted a study of 34 SMEs in the Victorian State of Australia that used IT strategic development methods, perceived benefits, and encountered barriers, as pointed out in the previous section and motivated to conduct this study

No.	Basic IT strategy methods	Literature sources
1	Strategic opportunities framework	Levy et al. [61], Benjamin et al. [63]
2	Porter's generic strategies	Levy et al. [61]
3	Information intensity matrix	Levy et al. [61], Levy and Powell [62]
4	Porter's value chain	Blili and Raymond [6], Levy et al. [61], Levy and Powell [62]
5	Customer resource life cycle	Levy et al. [61]
6	Porter's five competitive forces model	Levy et al. [61]
7	Sector information management grid	Levy et al. [61]
8	Strategic information systems grid	Levy et al. [61], Levy and Powell [62]
9	stages of growth models	Levy et al. [61]
10	Balanced scorecard	Levy and Powell [62]
11	Transaction cost	Blili and Raymond [6]
12	PESTEL	Levy and Powell [62]
13	Strategic Options Development and Analysis (SODA)	Salas et al. [63]
14	Soft systems methodology	Levy and Powell [62]
15	3D model of IS success	Levy and Powell [62]
16	Critical success factors (2000)	Blili and Raymond [6], Levy and Powell [62]
17	MIT'90	Levy and Powell [62]

Table 1.
IT strategy basic development methods.

in Brunei, and found that only three methods are found to have indirect influence on IT strategy development: critical success factors, transaction cost, and balanced scorecard. The major benefits include achievement of organizational efficiency, facilitating alignment between business and IT strategies, and improving organizational performance. The most significant barriers to develop IT strategy are financial and human resources limitation and lack of time and focus on day-to-day operations. The results further reveal that small-sized enterprises are less familiar with critical success factors and transaction cost than the medium-sized enterprises. However, there is no difference among manufacturing and service organizations in facilitating alignment between business and IT and obtaining competitive advantages. Small-sized enterprises experience bottleneck and barriers through lack of relevant IT experience and lack of time and focus on day-to-day operation than medium-sized organizations.

Azyabi [7] research has some weaknesses in the form of small sample size and generalizability; however, it is unique in the Asia-Pacific region and has further provided a source of motivation to conduct a similar study within the context of Southeast Asia. In fact from the review of the literature, it was found that researchers have conducted the studies from various dimensions, and no consistent pattern could therefore be applied leading toward a big research gap in the literature. As mentioned, most of these studies were conducted in the Western worlds, and the findings might or might not be applicable to this part of the globe. Up to our knowledge, no such study has focused on the multidimensional aspect of the strategic IT development process, benefits of using, and barriers of not using the strategic development process within Southeast Asian perspective. There is another gap that exists within Southeast Asian perspective, and the present study could fill in the research gap. Although the business environment and business volume among Bruneian SMEs are very different than their Australian counterparts, however by conducting this study, we would be able to find empirical evidence as how one of the Southeast Asian economies and strategic business development approach is different. The findings may further be utilized to generalize among other Southeast Asian context.

3. Methodology

3.1 The instrument

The purpose of this study was purely descriptive in nature. Creswell [64] suggested that descriptive research is to collect data about an existing situation or issue. Yin [65] suggested that survey is an appropriate method for descriptive research. In the light of the above cited discussion, a questionnaire adapted after an Australian study [7] was used for this study. The questionnaire consists of two parts, starting with Section A that collects information on the demographical data about the respondents, organizations, and IT functions. Section B collects information about the IT strategy development methods. Section B is further divided into four parts: collecting information about awareness framework, opportunity frameworks, positioning frameworks, and other frameworks. The data is collected on five-point Likert scale starting with 1 as "fully used," 2 as "partially used," 3 as "familiar and has indirect influence," 4 as "familiar but not used," and finally, 5 as "unfamiliar." So their final mean values of less than 3.00 mean either fully or partially used, and mean values around 3.00 indicate familiar but indirect effect, and finally, mean values of above 4 indicate either not used or unfamiliar with the strategic development.

3.2 Instrument validity and instrument reliability

There are several types of validity measures such as face validity and construct validity. Campbell and Fiske [66] propose two types of validity: convergent and discriminating validity. Convergent validity is measured by average variance extracted for each construct during the reliability analysis that should be 0.5 (50%) or better. **Table 2** shows the reliability values for the various constructs with variance extracted, and all the values are above 50%, thus providing a sufficient evidence of convergent validity. Similarly, Cronbach's α [67] for the constructs ranging from 0.80 to 0.90 further indicate a sufficient level of reliability. In general results show that both validity and reliability requirements are met.

3.3 The sample

A questionnaire was sent to 129 SMEs according to a random sampling plan. The SMEs were selected from a key business directory of Brunei (www.goldpages.com). Out of these 127 organizations, 70 organizations responded, and responses from 67 organizations were retained as they were filled by the top management; three were dropped because of the fact that it was not filled as per instructions. This makes the response rate of 52% sufficient for the survey of SMEs especially in a small market of Brunei Darussalam.

4. Data analysis and results

Data obtained from the survey were analyzed for descriptive, frequency, and student's t-statistics by using SPSS version 19, a well-known statistical package.

4.1 Profile of respondents

The first question in this section asked for some basic demographic information about the respondent's job title, gender, and years of experience with the organization. The summary of the responses are given in **Table 3**. Interestingly, 63% of the respondents with responsibility for IT function were male compared to 37% of the females. Similarly, 43% of the respondents were IT/IS or MIS managers compared to 51% as directors, and only 6% were general managers. As presented, 40% of the respondents have 1–5 years of experience with their organizations, with 37% were having 6–10 years of experience, and roughly around 22% have more than 10 years of experience with their organizations.

Constructs	No of items	Mean	Cronbach alpha (α)	Variance extracted
Awareness frameworks	3	3.63	0.88	0.81
Opportunity frameworks	3	3.53	0.80	0.74
Positioning frameworks	3	3.68	0.87	0.80
Other frameworks	8	3.67	0.84	0.60

Table 2.
Reliability and validity.

Organization characteristics	Frequency	Percentage
Job title		
IT/IS manager	29	43
Director	34	51
General manager	4	6
Gender		
Male	42	63
Female	25	37
Years of experience		
1–5	27	40
6–10	25	37
More than 10	22	22

Table 3.
Profile of respondents.

4.2 Profile of organizations

The second question gathered information about the profile of the respondent's organization such as the years of operation, sector, and the number of employees. This section discusses the survey findings about these aspects and a summary is shown in **Table 4**. Interestingly, 24% of the participating organizations have between 5 and 10 years of operation. Very few (4%) have less than a year of operation. The participating organizations with more than 10 years of operation represent about 44% of the surveyed SMEs. Unfortunately, the share of participating companies from the manufacturing sector was only 12%. Others are mostly from service industry (31.0%). Few are from construction and retail sectors (3 and 6%, respectively). However, the good response rate of 30% was from information and commutation technology (ICT). About 55% of the respondent organizations have between 10 and 50 employees, and 45% of the organizations have between 51 and 250 employees. The SMEs with approximate sales between B$ 100,000 and B$ 250,000 cover the highest response of 28%, and about 22% of the participating organizations did not disclose their sales' figure.

4.3 Profile of the IT function

Question 3 asked the respondents if they have a group of people dedicated to the IT function. The findings, as shown in **Table 5**, reveals that a large majority (82%) of the respondents have people who are dedicated for the IT function, while 18% do not have such people.

4.4 IT strategy basic development methods

The survey questioned the participants about their level of use and familiarity with IT strategy basic development methods. They were asked to respond to this question by encircling a number on a five-point scale where 1 means fully used, 2 means partly used, 3 means familiar and has indirect influence, 4 means familiar but not used, and 5 means unfamiliar. A summary of how the surveyed SMEs are

Organization characteristics	Frequency	Percent
Years of operation		
Less than a year	4	6.0
–5 years	18	27.0
5–10 years	16	24.0
Over 10 years	29	43.7
Industry segment		
Manufacturing	8	12.0
Service	21	31.3
Construction	2	3.0
Retail	4	6.0
ICT	20	30.0
Other	12	18.0
Number of employees		
Less than 10	14	21.0
11–50	23	34.0
51–250	30	45.0
Approximate sales		
< $100,000	9	13.4
$100 K to < $250 K	19	28.3
$250 K to < $500 K	18	12.0
$500 K to < $1 million	7	10.4
More than 1 million	9	13.4
No answer	15	22.0

Table 4.
Profile of organizations.

	Frequency	Percentage
People responsible for IT function		
No	12	18.0
1–5	23	34.0
6–10	18	27.0
More than 10	14	21.0
People responsible for IT decision-making process		
None	32	48.0
1–5	22	33.0
6–10	7	10.0
More than 10	6	9.0

Table 5.
Profile of IT function.

using and are familiar with the IT strategy basic development methods is shown in **Table 6**. From the table data, it is evident that none of the IT strategy basic development methods are fully or partially used by the participating SMEs. Only three IT strategy basic development methods have indirect influence on SMEs: critical success factors (mean score: 3.10), transaction cost (mean score: 3.13), and balanced scorecard (mean score: 3.28). SMEs are generally familiar with many IT strategy basic methods (e.g., customer resource life cycle, strategic opportunities framework, stages of growth models, 3D model of IS success, Porter's value chain, Porter's five competitive forces, soft systems methodology, Porter's generic strategies, Strategic Information Systems Grid, information intensity matrix, and sector information management grid); however, these methods have no effect on their IT strategy development, and finally SMEs are not familiar at all with such methods as Strategic Options Development and Analysis (SODA), MIT'90, and PESTEL. The mean of these development methods is above 4.00 but less than 4.50, which further indicate the marginal familiarization of these methods.

In order to find any difference between basic strategy development methods and organization size, statistical t-test was conducted and the results are presented in **Table 7**. The results further indicate that none of the IT strategy basic development method is used by the Bruneian SMEs either fully or partially even though the SMEs are familiar with these methods. A comparison was also made with the Australian study and results reveal that two of the basic strategy development methods such as critical success method and transaction cost are significant rather than the balanced scorecard.

IT strategy development basic methods	Mean rating	Ranking	Australian study*
Critical success factors	3.10	1	3.00
Transaction cost	3.13	2	3.00
Balanced scorecard	3.28	3	3.39
Customer resource life cycle	3.34	4	3.85
Strategic opportunities framework	3.39	5	3.88
Stages of growth models	3.61	7	3.94
3D model of IS success	3.84	12	4.06
Porter's value chain	3.68	10	4.09
Porter's five competitive forces	3.60	6	4.15
Soft systems methodology	3.79	11	4.15
Porter's generic strategies	3.67	9	4.24
Strategic information systems grid	3.66	8	4.27
Information intensity matrix	3.85	13	4.27
Sector information management grid	3.81	14	4.27
Strategic Options Development and Analysis (SODA)	4.22	15	4.59
MIT'90	4.33	17	4.69
PESTEL	4.25	16	4.72

**Azyabi [7].*

Table 6.
Results of IT strategy development basic methods.

				T-test for equality of means				
IT strategy basic development methods	**Organization size**	**Means**	**F**	**T**	**df**	**Sig. (2 tailed)**	**Remark**	**Australian study**
Transaction cost	50	3.11 3.16	1.862	−.169	65	0.867	Non-sig	Significant
Critical success factors	50	3.14 3.06	0.993	0.242	65	0.809	Non-sig	Significant
Balanced scorecard	50	3.47 3.06	4.65	1.456	65	0.150	Non-sig	Non-sig

Significant at 95% confidence level.

Table 7.
T-test results of the use of the IT strategy basic methods based on organization size.

						T-test for equality of means	
IT strategy basic development methods	**Industry sector**	**Means**	**F**	**T**	**df**	**Sig. (2 tailed)**	**Remark**
Transaction cost	Manuf Non-manuf	3.25 3.23	3.39	−0.197	65	0.845	Non-sig
Critical success factors	Manuf Non-manuf	3.75 3.06	0.603	−1.071	65	0.288	Non-sig
Balanced scorecard	Manuf Non-manuf	3.25 3.75	0.435	−0.833	65	0.408	Non-sig

Significant at 95% confidence level.
Manuf: Manufacturing; Non-manuf: Non-manufacturing.

Table 8.
T-test results of the use of the IT strategy basic methods based on industry sector.

Another comparison was made to explore the differences between industry sectors regarding the same three IT/IS strategy methods. The responding SMEs were divided into two main industry sectors: manufacturing and non-manufacturing. The results (presented in **Table 8**) reveal that there are no significant differences between these two industry sectors regarding the use of three IT/IS strategy basic methods.

5. Discussion

The findings indicate that none of the IT strategy basic development methods are used by the Bruneian SMEs either fully or partially, even though they are familiar with most of these methods. One qualitative question asked respondents to add any further comments about IT strategy development in SMEs. Some of them mentioned that these methods are well recognized in academic field but are not known in the SME context under these terms and names. Furthermore, some respondents reported that these methods could be more applicable for large organizations rather than SMEs. These reasons may help explain to some extent the absence of the use of these methods among the surveyed SMEs. The results support the study of Majama et al. [60] who found that strategic planning efforts among SMEs in Botswana do exist but to a limited extent. The comparison with Australian study was made to find out the difference between the two categories of organization size regarding the three methods which have indirect influence on SMEs' IT strategy development (i.e., critical success factors, transaction cost, and balanced scorecard). The results of student t-test (in **Table 7**) indicate that small organizations (with less than 50 employees) are less influenced by and are less familiar with the transaction cost and critical success factors than medium-sized organizations (with more than 50 employees). On the other hand, no such significant difference can be observed between these two groups of SMEs toward balanced scorecard. The results partially support Blili and Raymond [6], Boynton and Zmud [68], and Levy and Powell [62]. As far as the use of the IT/IS strategy basic development methods are concerned, our results are consistent with the Australian study [7] that further indicated that none of the IT/IS strategy basic development methods are fully or partially used by the participating SMEs. However, on the basis of industry sector and organization size (**Table 8**), our findings are in contrast with the study (ibid) as on these bases IT/IS strategy basic development methods remained insignificant. This might be due to the business dynamics and business practices of the Bruneian business environment which is less competitive, in practice, and/or lack of top management initiative. In addition, Bruneian SMEs are not struggling for their survival solely on IT [69] and are less influenced by the basic strategy development methods compared to Australian counterpart. However, no such difference is significant between Bruneian and Australian SMEs on the basis of industry sector.

6. Lesson learnt

This pioneering study conducted among Bruneian SMEs has met both of its objectives. As mentioned in the introduction, the main objectives of this study were to investigate the extent to which Bruneian SMEs use or are familiar with the basic IT strategy basic development methods. Regarding the first objective on the use of the IT strategy development methods, it was found that none of the provided basic IT strategy development methods is used by these surveyed SMEs either fully or partially; only three methods have indirect influence on IT strategy development in these SMEs: critical success factors, transaction cost, and balanced scorecard. Nevertheless, these surveyed SMEs are not familiar with SODA, MIT'90, and PESTEL, and surveyed SMEs are familiar with other strategy development methods, but these methods had no effect on their IT strategic development. Moreover, no statistical difference was found with the familiarization with the basic IT strategy development methods on the basis of organization size and industry sector that conclude our second objective. In the practice side, this research assists SMEs in recognizing the importance of IT strategy for SMEs, and it therefore provides an insight of IT strategy development in SMEs. The study further found some similarities in the use of basic IT strategy development methods with Australian SMEs on the basis of industry sector; however, on the basis of organization size, the results are in contrast, and it is because of the more developed business practices of Australian SMEs.

The study findings further provide insight in building up an empirical foundation for understanding the organizational use of IT strategy basic methods, among Bruneian SMEs within the Southeast Asian context. The basic question that needs an immediate attention is from the policy planners that are to find out the reasons why these SMEs are not utilizing the basic IT strategy development methods especially when they are aware of the benefits of the strategic process. The plausible reason is that Bruneian business environments do not demand the competitive advantage. This was also supported by one of the studies on e-commerce adoption among Bruneian SMEs and had further concluded that Bruneian businesses need to develop a business culture where competitive advantage could be achieved through e-commerce adoption [19]. To deal with the severity of this problem, the CEO of these SMEs along with the policy makers of Bruneian Small and Medium Business Development Authority (SMBDA), with the help of the Ministry of Industry and Primary Resources (MIPR), should address this issue accordingly. We believe that there are some success stories among small businesses, and the planning agencies could further organize a forum where other small businesses can learn from the best practices. We also believe that until or unless the stated barriers were not curtailed or reduced, these SMEs would not be gaining.

As mentioned, one of the biggest constraints faced by theses SMEs with regard to the SISP emerged from lack of owner's awareness, their reactive behavior, and lack of formal employees' participation in business decisions. This can further be improved by either educating the owners' IT skills and abilities or by employing a formal manager-IT support. This can be possibly implemented by the intervening e-government initiative by e-Government National Centre (EGNC). Once the owners are educated and started developing SISP, these SMEs would increase competitiveness, reduce cost, and share knowledge with the members and stakeholders; the overall business processes would finally be improved to get the business, otherwise outside competitive forces will reshape the local business SMEs.

Like every research this study is not free from its weaknesses and limitations. Properly addressing these limitations in the forthcoming researches could improve the findings. Firstly, the small sample size has been a major impediment especially generalizing the results across the region. Secondly, the small contribution of the manufacturing sector among these surveyed SMEs because of the absence of very large share of this sector in Bruneian business has made the sample size bias in nature which is apparently beyond the control of the researchers. Thirdly, the study needs to include barriers of not doing the SISP to highlight the various reasons that need to be addressed by the relevant authorities Finally, most of the items in the questionnaire are self-reported and would further induce response bias, and we did not do any precautions to address this issue. So caution should be used is generalizing the results. We therefore recommend that future studies would address this issue accordingly.

References

[1] Zubovic A, Pita Z, Khan S. A framework for investigating the impact of information systems capability on strategic information systems planning outcomes. In: Proceedings of 18th Pacific Asia Conference on Information Systems. 2014. pp. 1-12

[2] Kamariotou M, Kitsios F. Strategic information systems planning. In: Khosrow-Pour M, editor. Encyclopedia of Information Science and Technology. 4th ed. USA: IGI, Global Publishers, Idea Group, Inc.; Chapter 78. 2018. pp. 912-922

[3] Kamariotou M, Kitsios F. Innovating with strategic information systems planning: A structured literature review. In: Proceedings of the 2nd International Conference on Applied Innovation. 2015

[4] Ullah A, Lai R. A systematic review of business and information technology alignment. ACM Transactions on Management Information Systems. 2013;**4**(1):1-30

[5] Bhagwat R, Sharma MK. Management of information system in Indian SMEs: An exploratory study. International Journal of Enterprise Network Management. 2006;**1**(1):99-125

[6] Blili S, Raymond L. Information technology: Threats and opportunities for small and medium-sized enterprises. International Journal of Information Management. 1993;**13**(6):439-448

[7] Azyabi N. IT/IS strategy development in victorian SMEs. Unpublished Master thesis. Melbourne, Australia: Monash University; 2009

[8] Rafiqual I, Abdullah R, Maya NMS. Report on Small and Medium Enterprises in Brunei Darussalam. Brunei: ITB, Publication; 2001

[9] Delone W. Determinants for success for computer usage in small business. MIS Quarterly. 1998;**12**(1):51-67

[10] Reynolds W, Savage W, Williams A. Your Own Business: A Practical Guide to Success. 2nd ed. Sydney, Australia: ITP Thomas-Nelson; 1994

[11] MacGregor RC, Bunker DJ, Waugh P. Electronic Commerce and SMEs in Australia: An EDI Pilot Study. Proceedings of 11th international BLED E-Commerce Conference, Bled, Slovenia, 1998, June 8th–10th. pp. 284-294

[12] Delvecchio M. Retooling the staff along with the systems. Bests Review. 1994;**94**(11):82-83

[13] Yap CS, Soh CPP, Raman KS. International systems success factors in small business. OMEGA: International Journal of Management Science. 1992;**5**(6):597-609

[14] Hormozi AM, Sutton GS, McMinn RD, Lucio W. Business plans for new or small businesses: Paving the path to success. Management Decision. 2002;**40**(8):755-763

[15] Kraus S, Harms R, Schwarz EJ. Strategic planning in smaller enterprises-new empirical findings. Management Research News. 2006;**29**(6):334-364

[16] Wang C, Walker EA, Redmond JL. Explaining the lack of strategic planning in SMEs: The importance of owner motivation. International Journal of Organizational Behavior. 2007;**12**(1):1-16

[17] Siddique CM. A comparative study of strategic planning practices of SMEs and large-sized business organizations in emerging economies: The case of UAE. Strategic Change:

Briefings in Entrepreneurial Finance. 2015;**24**:553-567

[18] Stonehouse G, Pemberton J. Strategic planning in SMEs-some empirical findings. Management Decision. 2002;**40**(9):853-861

[19] O' Regan N, Ghobadian A. Formal strategic planning. Business Process Management Journal. 2002;**8**(5):416-429

[20] Seyal AH, Rahman MN. A preliminary investigation of e-commerce adoption in Bruneian small and medium organizations. Journal of Global Information Technology Management. 2003;**6**(2):6-26

[21] Seth A, Thomas H. Theories of the firm: Implications for strategy research. Journal of Management Studies. 1994;**31**(2):165-191

[22] Andrews KR. The Concept of Corporate Strategy. Homewood, IL: Irwin; 1971

[23] Gibcus P, Kemp RG. Strategy and Small Firm Performance. Scientific Analysis of Entrepreneurship and SMEs; 2003. http://www.entrepreneurship-sme.eu/pdf-ez/H200208.pdf

[24] Dong X, Liu Q, Yin D. Business performance, business strategy, and information system strategic alignment: An empirical study on Chinese firms. Tsinghua Science and Technology. 2008;**13**:348-354

[25] Earl MJ. Management Strategies for Information Technology. Englewood Cliffs, NJ: Prentice-Hall; 1989

[26] Galliers RD. Strategic information systems planning, myths, realities and guidelines for successful implementation in. In: Galliers RD, Baker BS, editors. Strategic Information Management. Oxford: Butterworth-Heinemann; 1994. pp. 129-147

[27] Finnegan P, Galliers R, Powell P. Investigating Inter-organizational Information System Planning Practices in Ireland and UK. Proceedings of the 5th European Conference on IS, 1997, June 19th-21st, Cork. 1. pp. 281-294

[28] Kearney AT. Breaking the Barrier-IT Effectiveness in Great Britain and Ireland. Report by AT. Kearney for the Chartered Institute of Management Accountants. London, UK: A. T. Kearney Ltd; 1990

[29] Lederer AL, Sethi V. Key prescription for strategic information systems planning. Journal of Management Information Systems. 1996;**13**(1):35-62

[30] Gottschalk P. Technology Management. Bergen, Norway: Fagbokforlaget; 1995

[31] Ward J, Griffiths P. Strategic Planning for Information System. Chichester: John-Wiley; 1996

[32] Falconer DJ, Hodgett RA. Strategic Information Systems Planning, an Australian Experience. Proceedings of the Americas Conference on IS, 1997, Aug 15th–17th, Indianapolis. pp. 837-839

[33] Pyburn PJ. Linking the MIS plan with corporate strategy: An exploratory study. MIS Quarterly. 1983;**7**(2):1-14

[34] Sexton DK, Van Auken P. A longitudinal study of small business strategic planning. Journal of Small Business Management. 1985;**23**(1):7-15

[35] Ghobadian, O'Regan. Effective strategic planning in small and medium sized firms. Management Decision. 2002;**40**(17):663-671

[36] Burton RM, Hakonsson DD, Lauridsen JT, Obel B. Strategy implementation require the right executive style: Evidence from

Danish SMEs. Long Range Planning. 2012;**45**(2):182-208

[37] Gunther L, Menzel D. Strategizing in SMEs: Between autocratic instructions and autonomous behavior. In: Lange R, Miller E, editors. Proceedings of the International Symposium on Innovation Methods and Innovation Management. Chemnitz; 2012. pp. 56-59

[38] King WR, Teo SHT. Assessing the impact of proactive versus reactive models of strategic information systems planning. Omega. 2000;**28**(6):667-679

[39] Peppard J, Galliers RD, Thorogood A. Information systems strategy as practices: Micro strategy and strategizing for information systems. Journal of Strategic Information Systems. 2014;**23**(1):1-10

[40] Maharaj S, Brown I. The impact of shared domain knowledge on strategic information system planning and alignment: Original research. South African Journal of Information Management. 2015;**17**(1):1-12

[41] Nolan R. Managing the crisis in data processing. Harvard Business Review. 1979;**57**(2):115-126

[42] Jackson C. Building a competitive advantage through information technology. Long Range Planning. 1989;**22**(4):29-39

[43] Earl MJ. Experiences in strategic information systems planning. MIS Quarterly. 1993;**17**(1):1-22

[44] Segars AH. Strategic information system planning: The Co-alignment of planning system design, its relationship with organizational context, and implications for planning system success [unpublished doctoral dissertation]. USA: University of South Carolina; 1994

[45] Miller CC, Cardinal LB. Strategic planning and firm performance: A synthesis of more than two decades of research. The Academy of Management Journal. 1994;**37**:1649-1665

[46] Ward J, Peppard J. Reconciling the IT/business relationship: A troubled marriage in need of guidance. Journal of Strategic Information Systems. 1996;**5**:37-65

[47] Bergeron F, Raymond L, Rivard S. Fit in strategic information technology management research: An empirical comparison of perspectives. OMEGA: International Journal of Management Science. 2001;**29**:125-142

[48] Porter ME. Competitive advantage. New York: Free Press; 1985

[49] Wiseman C. Strategy and Computers: Information System as Competitive Weapon. Ills: DowJones-Irwing; 1985

[50] Gottschalk P. Implementation of formal plans: The case of information technology strategy. Long Range Planning. 1999;**32**(3):362-372

[51] Jantan M, Srinivasaraghavan K. Information technology deployment and competitive advantage of organizations in Penang, Malaysia. In: Proceedings of International Conference on Business Development Strategies in Asia-Pacific, Mar, 21st-22nd. Universiti Brunei Darussalam; 1997

[52] Gordon JR, Gordon SR. Structuring the interaction between IT and business units: Prototyping for service delivery. Information Systems Management. 2000;**17**(1):7-16

[53] Bergeron F, Buteau C, Raymond L. Identification of strategic information system opportunities: Applying and comparing two methodologies. MIS Quarterly. 1991;**15**(1):89-103

[54] Allen RS, Helms MM. Linking strategic practice and organizational performance to Porter's generic strategies. Business Process Management Journal. 2006;**12**(4):433-454

[55] Porter ME. How competitive forces shape strategy. Harvard Business Review. 1979;**57**(2):137-145

[56] Sharma G. Do SMEs need to strategize? Business Strategy Series. 2011;**12**(4):186-196

[57] Adendorff C, Appels G, Botha B. Strategic management: An eastern cape construction SME case study. Acta Structilia. 2011;**18**(2):40-63

[58] Pemberton J, Stonehouse G. Strategic planning in SMEs-some empirical findings. Management Decisions. 2002;**40**(9):853-861

[59] Polatoglu VN. Strategies that work–the case of an e-retailer in an emerging market. International Journal of Emerging Markets. 2007;**2**(4):395-405

[60] Majama NS, Israel T, Magang T. Strategic planning in small and medium enterprises (SMEs): A case study of Botswana SMEs. Journal of Management and Strategy. 2017;**8**(1):74-103

[61] Levy M, Powell P, Galliers R. Assessing information systems strategy development frameworks in SMEs. Information and Management. 1999;**36**:247-261

[62] Levy M, Powell P. Information systems strategy for small and medium sized enterprises: An organizational perspective. The Journal of Strategic Information Systems. 2000;**9**:63-84

[63] Salas KD, Marshall P, Young J. Is strategy formulation in a financial services company: The dual lens approach. Pacific Asia, Conference on Information Systems, Auckland, New Zealand; 2007. Accessed at: http://www.pacis2007.com/

[64] Creswell JW. Research Design: Qualitative and Quantitative Approaches. Thousand Oaks, California: Sage Publications; 1994

[65] Yin R. Case Study Research: Design and Methods. Thousand Oaks, California: Sage Publications; 2003

[66] Campbell DT, Fiske DW. Convergent and discriminant validation by multi-trait, multi-method matrix. Psychological Bulletin. 1955;**56**:82-105

[67] Cronbach LJ. Coefficient alpha and the internal structure of tests. Psychometrica. 1951;**16**:297-324

[68] Boynton AC, Zmud RW. An assessment of critical success factors. Sloan Management Review. 1984;**25**:17-27

[69] Seyal AH, Rahim M. Understanding electronic commerce adoption in Bruneian SMEs: A replication of the application of TAM and perceived strategic value models. Journal of Electronic Commerce in Organizations. 2010;**8**(4):32-50

Chapter 10

Collaborative Behavior and the Sharing Economy: Pan-European Evidence for a New Economic Approach

Abstract

This chapter analyzes the sharing economy and collaborative consumption behaviors. The study addresses two lines of analysis. The first is theoretical, and it examines the background, definitions, and conceptual framework of the topic. The second is empirical and brings new evidence through a pan-European predictive analysis. From the theoretical angle, I conclude that the exchange behavior evolves toward a new paradigm, from initial digital formats into sharing formats. And for a more adequate interpretation of the sharing exchange theory, the economy will have to move forward and develop a formal apparatus that takes into consideration a set of relatively unusual principles. In particular a combination of new assumptions: rational/emotional decision-making, individual/prosocial interest, monetary/nonmonetary compensation, and ownership/use, which economics will have to incorporate into the functions thereof. From the empirical perspective, my research provides new evidence about the motivations of collaborative behavior. Particularly interesting is the result that self-employed or entrepreneurs are more prone to value collaborative platforms that are oriented as an alternative. On the contrary, managers and qualified employees have more practical and monetary motivations. Both results, theoretical and empirical, could open the door to new strategic orientations for the development of platforms.

Keywords: sharing economy, collaborative consumption, platform economy, access-based economy, peer-to-peer (P2P) markets

1. Introduction

In recent years, day-to-day economic practice has given us a host of examples attesting to the changing nature of economic exchange. For most people, *Uber* and *Airbnb* are possibly the most recognizable examples but, simply by taking a look at the variety of digital exchange platforms and networks currently available, it is possible to see that economic transactions are profoundly changing. These platforms, which complement or replace traditional markets such as passenger transport or tourist accommodation, are two clear examples of the fact that some of the foundations of the economy are structurally changing [1–3].

This development has often been noted from the perspective of sharing or of collaboration [4, 5]. With the advent of Web 2.0 and social networks, whose major difference from the first digital wave is that they enable and facilitate interactive digitalization [6], sharing has modified the economic exchange. Collaborative consumption is the new form of mass sharing between and among people, principally through peer-to-peer (P2P) digital platforms [7]. It implies the coordinated acquisition and distribution of goods or services for use, it is always done in expectation of some type of compensation (monetary or otherwise), and it places access or use over ownership [4, 8, 9]. In this sense, the key question for management research is to establish how consumer behavior has changed and, as a consequence thereof, how these transformations modify the business strategy [3, 10].

But, how should sharing or collaboration be interpreted? What is new in such forms of collaborative consumption? Do they create the need for us to approach economic exchange from a new analytical perspective? Do we have evidence of these new forms of consumption? What effects does collaborative consumption have on the economic activity? These are some of the questions that have inspired this chapter.

In order to answer them, a wide range of conceptual and empirical studies has been reviewed. The analysis extends from the core to the periphery of the issue. Firstly, the background, definitions, and conceptual frameworks of the sharing economy and collaborative consumption will be addressed. Secondly, the set of motivations explaining their rise will be studied, which allowed me to postulate the research hypotheses. Thirdly, new pan-European empirical evidence will be provided. Fourth and lastly, the main conceptual and empirical corollaries of the research will be addressed and discussed.

2. Digital sharing as economic behavior

The first digital wave was consolidated in the late twentieth century and generates new markets (digital markets) that significantly alter forms of consumption and production. Information goods and services, that is, all goods and services that can be digitalized, play a leading role in digital markets [11]. These goods have particular economic characteristics, such as nonrivalry (public goods), which are experience goods (whose utility can only be determined once they have been consumed), and they have a particular cost structure, with very high fixed costs (production) and decreasing marginal costs (reproduction) tending toward zero. The combination of these properties means that the price-setting rule revealed by all the information, which is equal to the marginal cost in traditional markets, does not work in digital markets. In establishing the value of information goods and services, the price is different from the marginal cost, and external network economies play an important role [12]. In addition, a decoupling of the traditional relationship between ownership and use is starting to occur through dematerialization, as represented by information goods and digital markets [13]. However, interpretative models of digital exchange are still based on rational and intangible decision-making, and individuals maximize its utility or the utility of its network only by taking into consideration individual or collective interests, which are still not collaborative [5].

In the early twenty-first century, a second wave of digital technology gave new impetus to the transformation of economic exchange behavior, which evolved from initial digital exchange into sharing or collaborative exchange. However, to understand this new trend, it is important first to define what sharing is. Sharing can be interpreted as one of the forms of people's economic behavior. Its existence and relevance as a type of exchange in human communities has been demonstrated since the beginning of the civilization [14]. Sharing means going beyond individual interests to take into account human and social values. Sharing may have functional motivations, such as survival, but it can also be an altruistic act motivated by convenience, courtesy, or kindness toward others. All sharing practices are related to cultural norms, but sharing is much more than an altruistic act that occurs within the family, close social circles, or among friends. Indeed, it can also occur among strangers. In this context, it is possible to define sharing as "the act and process of distributing what is ours to others for their use as well as the act and process of receiving something from others for our use ([14], p. 126)." In an earlier, more socially oriented approach to the issue, sharing has been interpreted as a "nonreciprocal prosocial behavior ([10], p. 331)."

With the emergence of digital forms of sharing behavior through collaborative consumption, the literature has made significant advances [15]. Especially relevant is the differentiation between collective consumption and collaborative consumption. The literature has traditionally taken collective consumption to mean "those events in which one or more persons consume economic goods or services in the process of engaging in joint activities with one or more others ([16], p. 614)." This approach, which includes a wide range of daily consumption practices, such as drinking and eating with friends, or watching a show together, places emphasis on joint participation, though it seems too broad for the purposes of describing the phenomenon of collaborative consumption. For consumption to be collaborative, people need to adopt a specific form of coordination beyond their group behavior: the coordinated acquisition and distribution of the goods or services consumed. In other words, collaborative consumption is "the act and process of distributing what is ours to others for their use ([14], p. 126)."

Similarly, the literature has made advances in terms of clarifying collaborative consumption, particularly in relation to the delimitation of the differences between it and other types of consumption with prosocial intentions, such as gift-giving or economic exchanges. A number of earlier approaches associated collaborative consumption with traditional market behaviors such as "sharing, bartering, lending, trading, renting, gifting, and swapping ([7], p. 15)," but that overly broad approach was further delimited, with collaboration being restricted to the coordinated "acquisition and distribution of a resource for a fee or other compensation ([5], p. 1597)."

It is therefore necessary to insist on the fact that collaborative consumption behavior implies the coordinated acquisition and distribution of products or services for use, some type of compensation (monetary or otherwise), and access, often temporary, over ownership. In this respect, the notion of access-based consumption would adequately encompass the domain of and motivations behind collaborative consumption in the sense that "instead of buying and owning things, consumers want access to goods and prefer to pay for the experience of temporarily accessing them ([8], p. 881)."

3. Collaborative behavior in economic thought

Economic research addresses the sharing economy and collaborative consumption as if it were a conceptual umbrella that integrates diverse phenomena related to new forms of economic exchange and economic behavior. This new, sharing interpretation of exchange and behavior [10, 17] has been given many different names. Among them we find "product-service systems" [18], the idea of a consumption "mesh" or network [19], "collaborative consumption" [4, 7], the idea of "prosumers" [20], "commercial sharing systems" [9], "access-based consumption" [8], and even a new form of "crowd-based capitalism" [21]. All of these new exchange practices have two commonalities: "(1) their use of temporary access nonownership models of utilizing consumer goods and services, and (2) their reliance on the Internet, and especially Web 2.0, to bring this about ([5], p. 1595)."

Conceptually, collaborative consumption behavior has been delimited by two distinct conceptual frameworks (**Table 1**). Consumer theory addresses the phenomenon from the perspective of a cultural and identity-based form of alternative exchange and behavior [22]. It has therefore paid greater attention to the concept of sharing, to types of consumption, and to collaborative markets or to the antiestablishment foundations of sharing [4, 7, 9, 23–26]. In contrast, information systems theory analyses the phenomenon from the perspective of digital P2P platform and network uses and behavior [27, 28]. These two approaches simply place more or less emphasis on the main components of collaborative consumption. While consumer theory has emphasized the analysis of motivations to explain nonownership access and uses, the information systems approach focuses on the study of technology acceptance models (TAMs) and theory of planned behavior (TPB) models that make using collaborative platforms and networks possible. The salient idea behind this second approach is that collaborative consumption operates through technological platforms (Web 2.0 or mobile applications). Within this context, the problem of motivations behind collaborative consumption behavior becomes the problem of motivations explaining the use of online collaborative consumption platforms. Thus, the success of such digital sharing platforms would explain the sharing behaviors of their potential users and resource providers [29]. In other words, participation behavior in collaborative consumption platforms can be formulated as an intent of acceptance and, therefore, can be approached from the perspective of TAMs and/or TPB models [30].

From the information systems approach, we are able to understand collaborative consumption as a "peer-to-peer-based activity of obtaining, giving, or sharing the access to goods and services, coordinated through community-based online services ([17], p. 2047)." In fact, this new type of exchange and behavior is an economic and technological phenomenon driven by new development of information and communication technologies (ICTs), advances in consumer awareness, and the proliferation of collaborative online communities that make commerce more social, sustainable, or fairer [31, 32].

Approach	Authors	Definition
Consumer theory (restrictive)	Belk [4]	The acquisition and distribution of a resource for a fee or other compensation (nonmonetary)
Consumer theory (expanded)	Botsman and Rogers [7]	An economic model based on sharing, swapping, trading, or renting products and services, enabling access over ownership
Theory of the firm (efficiency)	Stephany [3]	Value in taking underutilized assets and making them accessible online to a community, leading to a reduced need for ownership of those assets
Information systems (technology acceptance)	Hamari et al. [17]	P2P-based activity of obtaining, giving, or sharing access to goods and services, coordinated through community-based online services
Functional synthesis	Belk [5] Price and Belk [22]	The use of temporary access nonownership models of utilizing goods and services, and reliance on the Internet, and especially Web 2.0, to bring this about

Table 1.
Sharing economy and collaborative behavior: definitions and conceptual frameworks.

4. Toward new economic approaches

I just showed that, through new forms of collaborative consumption, exchange behavior evolves the economy toward a new interpretative paradigm, from initial digital markets to sharing markets. Sharing exchanges incorporate and reveal a lot

Characteristics	Initial digital exchange	Sharing exchange
Technology	ICTs and Internet 1.0 (noninteractive digitization)	ICTs and Internet 2.0 (interactive digitization) Social networks and social media
Products	Information goods and services (digital ownership)	Digital uses of goods and services (information or knowledge intensives)
Good properties	Nonrivalry (public goods)	Divisibility (rival goods become public)
	Experience goods	Experience uses
	High fixed and low marginal costs	Low fixed and marginal costs
Markets	Digital, noncoincident, and semiregulated	Digital, noncoincident, and unregulated (temporary and diffuse economic activity)
Key market stakeholders	Consumers and businesses engaged in e-commerce	Consumers/producers and businesses/platforms that coordinate electronic exchange
Golden rule of the market	Price differs from marginal cost	Price or fee equal to marginal use
	Price does not reveal all the information	Information is revealed before the price or fee
Efficiency sources	Network economies	Sharing economies
	Cheap inputs of information and knowledge	Cheap inputs of sharing uses of goods, services, information, or knowledge
Basic process and economic activity	Digitization	Sharing
	Intangibles assets	Disintermediation
Production and labor organization	Networked business and labor	Networked individual
	Temporary work	Contingent work (e.g., gigs)
Ownership/use relationship	Semi-identification between ownership and use (dematerialization)	De-identification between ownership and use (repersonification; use without ownership)
Economic interpretation and market structures	Rational and intangible decision-making	Rational and emotional decision-making
	Individual and collective interest	Prosocial interest (ethics, sustainability)
	Information and knowledge exchanges	Access over ownership exchanges
	Monetary compensation	Monetary or nonmonetary price or fee
	Entry and exit costs (e.g., lock-ins)	Free entry and exit
	Network competition	Sharing competition

Table 2.
Exchange in the initial digital economy and the sharing economy.

of information and knowledge, often before the transaction takes place. The basic sharing market stakeholders are consumers/producers and businesses/platforms that coordinate but do not control sharing exchange [33]. The economic properties of sharing exchange are therefore those of shared uses (divisibility, experience uses, and sharing economies). Many of those properties still need to be studied in much greater depth, and that is especially so for the form of the demand function (price or fee equal to marginal use), for its value creation process through sharing networks, and for the structure of P2P markets [10, 34]. Furthermore, the interpretative apparatus that economics will have to develop in order to address a sharing exchange theory must take into consideration a set of relatively unusual principles. Sharing exchange requires interpretative models that consider a combination of emotional and rational decision-making, individual interest-based as well as prosocial motivations, exchange compensation through a monetary or nonmonetary fee, and the set of sharing economies that it may generate. **Table 2** shows and orders some of the main manifestations of new forms of sharing exchange, comparing them to forms of digital exchange.

5. Motivations of collaborative behavior

The set of driving and impeding forces of participation behavior in digital networks for collaborative consumption is clearly multidimensional and encompasses economic, social, environmental, ethical, and motivational elements that need to be addressed in depth [27]. Among these motivations, the literature has identified: (1) economic benefits, time, space and effort savings, and an awareness of exchange costs [8]; (2) cultural changes linked to a new relationship among goods and services, individual ownership, and consumer identity [5, 7]; (3) a rise in the critical view of excessive consumption [35, 36]; (4) growing environmental awareness [19]; and (5) the desire to belong to a community [4]. Critical mass, idle time, belief in the common good, and trust among strangers have also been identified as predictors of the use and provision of content, goods, and services on digital sharing platforms and networks [7].

However, there is still relatively little empirical evidence of the modeling of or results from digital sharing systems based jointly on the behaviors of their users and providers [28]. For example, a priori, some driving forces have an impact on both groups (such as trust), whereas others only have an impact on one of them (i.e., earning money motivates providers and saving money motivates users). Thus, while participation in digital practices of the collaborative consumption depends on the critical mass of its participants (users and providers), it is necessary to look further into the motivations (joint and separate) explaining participation and collaborative behavior [37]. In accordance with this approach, literature has found that participation in a digital collaborative consumption network was motivated by a broad set of factors such as sustainability, enjoyment, and economic benefits [17]. Along similar lines, a multidimensional set of motivations associated with participation behavior (use and provision) in a P2P network for renting goods and services has been identified. That set of motivations included technological, economic, social, ideological, identity, and prosocial factors [27].

One of the main starting points for collaborative consumption was the evolution from business-to-consumer (B2C) electronic commerce (e-commerce) toward the emergence of consumer-to-consumer (C2C) digital markets. On such P2P platforms and networks, people exchange goods and services on a large scale, often under the banner of an alternative form of consumption that is more social, sustainable, varied, convenient, anticapitalist, or without monetary compensation [14, 38]. In fact, many of the motivations explaining this new form of consumption are actually related to their alternative nature, which differs from that of traditional forms of ownership consumption [23, 24, 39]. Latest research expanded the scope and studied the motivations of users and providers of P2P platforms in Europe [40]. These literature studies have concluded that the providers' motivations differed from the users. The ideology (better community and increased sustainability) explained the providers' participation, while practical reasons (satisfaction of needs, increased value, and convenience) explained the users' participation. Along the same lines, literature has identified that sharing attitudes are linked to moral, social, and monetary motivations [41]. Similarly, monetary incentives are identified as a necessary but not sufficient condition at the moment of sharing individual possessions with others. In this context, a first working hypothesis could be that:

Hypothesis 1: Anticonsumer or antimaterialist motivations, captured through the possibility of nonmonetary exchanges, predict the provision of collaborative platforms.

The economic literature has also highlighted a number of economic aspects that might be driving new digital forms of sharing. Such motivations may also be rational, pursuing a behavior of utility maximization. This is the case, for example, when consumers replace exclusive and expensive ownership with low-cost uses through an online collaborative consumption service [42]. Along the same line, literature has obtained results that tended toward practical motivations and utility. Specific costs, utility factors, the perceived risk of product scarcity, and familiarity with sharing were the explanatory factors of the likelihood of sharing [8, 9]. Beyond this initial and partial evidence, the most recent literature has broadened the scope of its objectives in relation to both the motivations and the number of consumers and types of collaborative consumption analyzed [43]. Lower prices were found to be the main motivation in all types of goods and services analyzed. Scarcity, the environment, and access over ownership were also important in some of the types of goods and services studied. In addition, it has also been obtained that the intentions to share are explained based on economic, environmental, and social benefits that would be captured through a mediating effect linked to the perceived utility [30]. At the same time, the enjoyment experienced would be explained through a sentiment of belonging to the community where sharing takes place. Thus, and considering the different motivations of users and providers, I could formulate my second working hypothesis as follows:

Hypothesis 2: Practical economic motivations, like price, novelty, and convenience, predict the use and provision of collaborative platforms.

Other studies have advanced our knowledge of the forms of adoption and repeated use of digital sharing platforms [26]. The motivations linked to perceived benefits could explain user satisfaction and the probability of choosing to use those platforms again. Regarding the motivations and barriers to collaborative consumption in a P2P accommodation platforms, literature has found that sustainability, belonging to a community, and financial benefits were the main motivations, while the lack of trust, of efficiency, and of economic benefits were the main barriers [44]. At the same line, a multidimensional set of motivations that explained participation (use and provision) in a P2P network for renting goods and services has been identified [27]. Those motivations were technological (privacy, process risk, the platform's ubiquitous availability), economic (income, resource scarcity, effort expectancy, thriftiness, product variety), social (knowledge and modern lifestyle), ideological and identity-related (anticapitalism, independence through ownership, prestige of ownership, enjoyment in sharing), and prosocial (sense of belonging, social experience, social influence). Thus, my third working hypothesis is related to the barriers to collaborative behavior:

Hypothesis 3: The lack of a responsible person, the lack of fulfillment of service expectations, the lack of information, the lack of trust in the agents, or the lack of trust in the Internet predict (brake) the use and provision of collaborative platforms.

With the idea of broadening the set of motivations and the diversity of forms and stakeholders of the collaborative behavior, literature has also analyzed the role of sociodemographic characteristics [25]. Women and young people were more likely to share most of the products/objects. Particularly interesting is the result that shared consumption had more to do with personal mind-set or psychological disposition than with some sociodemographic aspects, like income levels. In this sense, I can formulate a working hypothesis about the sociodemographic predictors of collaborative behavior:

Hypothesis 4: Sociodemographic characteristics predict the use and provision of collaborative platforms.

6. Pan-European evidence of collaborative behavior

In order to obtain a representative sample and to compare the situation of collaboration consumption in the countries of the European Union, the European Commission [45] dedicated a *Flash Eurobarometer* (number 438) to a survey of the use of collaborative economy platforms. *Flash Eurobarometers* are ad hoc statistical operations consisting of short—landline and mobile—telephone interviews on a topic of interest. *Flash Barometer* 438 obtained data on the use of collaborative economy platforms from a sample of 14,050 citizens aged 15 years and above in the 28 countries of the European Union (Belgium, Bulgaria, Czech Republic, Denmark, Germany, Estonia, Ireland, Greece, Spain, France, Croatia, Italy, Cyprus, Latvia, Lithuania, Luxembourg, Hungary, Malta, the Netherlands, Austria, Poland, Portugal, Romania, Slovenia, Slovakia, Finland, Sweden, and the United Kingdom) through approximately 500 interviews per country. The universe of the survey consisted of the 412,630,644 European Union citizens aged 15 years and above. The sample design for each country was probabilistic and representative. The margins of error at the 95% confidence level in the case of maximum indetermination ($p = q = 50$) were +0.4% for the entire sample, and around +1.9% for individual country samples. The fieldwork was carried out on March 15 and 16, 2016.

The questionnaire defines a collaborative platform (CP) as "an Internet-based tool that enables transactions between people providing and using a service. They can be used for a wide range of services, from renting accommodation and car sharing to small household jobs ([45], p. 29)." Based on that approach, the survey asked the respondents about their awareness of such platforms and gave them the following options for their answers on use: (1) unaware (UNAWARE) or "You have never heard of these platforms"; (2) aware but does not use (AWNOTUSE) or "You have heard of these platforms but you have never visited them"; (3) initial use (INIUSE) or "You have been on one or more of these platforms and paid for a service once"; (4) occasional use (OCCAUSE) or "You use the services of these platforms occasionally (once every few months)"; and (5) regular use (REGUSE) or "You use the services of these platforms regularly (at least every month)." For all users of such platforms (TOTUSE), which includes initial use, occasional use, and regular use, the survey also gathered data about providing goods and services and gave the respondents the following options for their answers: (1) no provision (NOPROV) or "No, you haven't"; (2) initial provision (INIPROV) or "You have offered a service on one or more of these platforms once"; (3) occasional provision (OCCAPROV) or "You offer services via these platforms occasionally (once every few months)"; and (4) regular provision (REGPROV) or "You offer services via these platforms regularly (every month)." All providers of such platforms (TOTPROV) include initial provision, occasional provision, and regular provision. The various options of those two variables were transformed into individual variables. All of these new individual variables were dichotomous, where 1 = the respondent was aware of and used or provided goods or services via collaborative platforms, and 0 = the respondent answered otherwise.

Having stipulated the levels of use and provision, the survey looked at the driving factors (benefits) and impeding factors (problems) of collaborative platforms compared to the traditional forms of commerce of goods and services. Regarding the driving factors, the survey gave those respondents who were aware of and users of collaborative platforms the following options for their answers: (1) service cost (PRICE) or "It is cheaper or free"; (2) service newness (NEWNESS) or "It offers new or different services"; (3) service convenience (CONVEN) or "The access to services is organized in a more convenient way"; and (4) nonmonetary exchanges (NONMONET) or "The ability to exchange products or services instead of paying with money." Regarding the impeding factors, the survey gave those respondents who were aware of and users of collaborative platforms the following options for their answers: (1) lack of a responsible person when problems arise (LRESPON) or "Not knowing who is responsible in case a problem arises"; (2) lack of fulfillment of service expectations (LFULLSERV) or "Being disappointed because the services and goods do not meet expectations"; (3) lack of information (LINFORM) or "Not having enough information on the service provided"; (4) lack of trust in the agents (LTRUSTAG) or "Not trusting the provider or seller"; and (5) lack of trust in the Internet (LTRUSTINT) or "Not trusting the Internet transactions in general." All of these variables were dichotomous, where 1 = the respondent answered positively about the driving or impeding factors, and 0 = the respondent answered otherwise.

Lastly, the survey gathered sociodemographic data in order to be able to characterize the users and the providers of collaborative platforms. Specifically, data were gathered on age, gender, years of education, number of household members, type of locality (village or rural area, small, midsized, or large town/city), and occupational status: self-employed or business person, employee (director, qualified professional, manual worker, and nonmanual worker), unemployed or nonemployed (stay-at-home parent/carer, student, retiree, or unemployed person).

Table 3 shows the descriptive statistics of the variables relating to the use and provision of collaborative platforms in Europe. Regarding awareness and use of collaborative platforms, the survey found that more than half of European citizens were unaware of these new forms of exchange (53.2%), while a further third was aware of them but had never used them (33.9%). Thus, 12.9% of the European population aged 15 years and above stated that they were users of collaborative platforms, with the following distribution: 3.2% initial use (one transacted exchange), 6.5% occasional use (once every few months), and 3.2% regular use (at least every month). In relation to the provision of goods and services via collaborative platforms, of the users of such platforms (12.9%), almost three quarters had never provided any (72.1%). The remaining 27.9% of users (3.6% of the European population) had provided goods and services, with the following distribution: 7.3% (0.9% of the total) had made an initial provision (provided goods or services once), 15.7% (2.1% of the total) had made an occasional provision (once every few months), and 5.0% (0.6% of the total) had made a regular provision (every month).

For those who were aware of (33.9%) and users of (12.9%) such platforms (46.8%), the survey also gathered data about the driving and impeding factors of their use. Among the driving factors, convenience (39.1%) and price (31.4%) were cited the most, whereas service newness (22.4%) and the possibility of carrying out nonmonetary exchanges (21.8%) came some way behind the two main motivations. Regarding the factors that would limit the use and provision of such platforms, the lack of a responsible person when problems arise in the exchange (36.5%) was the main reason given, followed at some distance by the lack of fulfillment of service expectations

	N	Mean	SD	Minimum	Maximum	Skewness	Kurtosis
Awareness and use							
Unaware (UNAWARE)	13,837	0.532	0.499	0	1	−0.128	−1.984
Aware but not use (AWNOTUSE)	13,837	0.339	0.473	0	1	0.682	−1.535
Initial use (INIUSE)	13,837	0.032	0.177	0	1	5.298	26.068
Occasional use (OCCAUSE)	13,837	0.065	0.247	0	1	3.530	10.465
Regular use (REGUSE)	13,837	0.032	0.177	0	1	5.291	26.998
Total use (TOTUSE)	13,837	0.129	0.336	0	1	2.207	2.872
Provision of goods and services							
No provision (NOPROV)	1778	0.721	0.448	0	1	−0.987	−1.028
Initial provision (INIPROV)	1778	0.073	0.259	0	1	3.298	8.890
Occasional provision (OCCAPROV)	1778	0.157	0.364	0	1	1.888	1.567
Regular provision (REGPROV)	1778	0.050	0.217	0	1	4.158	15.303
Total provision (TOTPROV)	1788	0.279	0.449	0	1	0.987	−1.028
Driving factors							
Price (PRICE)	6477	0.314	0.464	0	1	0.801	−1.359
Newness (NEWNESS)	6477	0.224	0.417	0	1	1.324	−0.247
Convenience (CONVEN)	6477	0.391	0.488	0	1	0.449	−1.779
Nonmonetary (NONMONET)	6477	0.218	0.413	0	1	1.368	−0.127
Impeding factors							
Lack responsible person (LRESPON)	6477	0.365	0.481	0	1	0.560	−1.687
Lack fulfilling expect (LFULLSER)	6477	0.259	0.438	0	1	1.099	−0.792
Lack information (LINFORM)	6477	0.186	0.389	0	1	1.614	0.605
Lack trust in agents (LTRUSTAG)	6477	0.250	0.433	0	1	1.154	−0.668
Lack trust in Internet (LTRUSTINT)	6477	0.272	0.445	0	1	1.027	−0.947

Table 3.
The use and provision of collaborative platforms in Europe.

(25.9%), the lack of trust in the Internet in general (27.2%), and the lack of trust in the agents (buyers and sellers) of the exchange in particular (25.0%). Lastly, the lack of information (18.6%) was the reason that the respondents cited the least.

Regarding sociodemographic characteristics, the mean age was 54 years and the majority of the respondents were women (58.4% women, 41.6% men). Of the individuals in the sample, 43.4% had 20 or more years of formal education. From an occupational perspective, of note was the high presence of retirees (37.3%) and of manual workers (20.3%). Most households comprised two members (44.0%). Finally, regarding the localities of European citizens (rural, small or mid-sized town/city, or large metropolitan town/city), the sample was equally divided (into three-thirds). Furthermore, in relation to countries, the sample skewed toward the European Union's most populous countries in central and Eastern Europe (35.7% of the sample).

The basic aim of my study is to find out if these sociodemographic characterization variables, together with the motivation/barrier variables, can be turned into predictors of use and provision behavior on collaborative platforms. To that end, we performed an odds ratio (OR) analysis. Formally, it is usually defined as the ratio of the odds of a condition occurring in a population group to the odds of it occurring in another group. It is a measure of the statistical association between dichotomous variables, which has been widely used in social research for three main reasons: firstly, because the OR determines a predictor and a confidence interval (95% CI) between binary dichotomous variables, which enables probability relationships to be established; secondly, because it is useful for examining the predictive effect of one variable on another, while the other variables remain constant in a logistic regression model; and thirdly, because OR offers a quick and efficient interpretation in case studies and controls.

The interpretation of an OR analysis is as follows. If the value of the OR is less than 1 and the confidence interval (95% CI) is situated below the unit, the predictive relationship between the two variables analyzed is an inverse relationship. If the value of the OR is greater than 1 and the confidence interval (95% CI) is situated above the unit, the predictive relationship between the two variables analyzed is a direct relationship. Whenever the confidence interval (95% CI) includes the unit, the predictive relationship between two variables cannot be determined [46, 47].

If I begin by taking the use of collaborative platforms (n = 1792), the first thing to highlight is that its driving forces are clearly linked to motivations of an economic and practical nature (**Table 4**). Convenience and price are the two main drivers of collaborative platform use in Europe. In contrast, the driving factor relating to nonmonetary exchange, which could be identified as being ideological in an antiestablishment or anticapitalism sense, clearly disincentives the use of collaborative platforms. Among the impeding forces, it should be noted that the lack of fulfillment of expectations in relation to the service offered via the collaborative platform disincentives the use thereof. In contrast, the lack of trust in the Internet would not act as an impediment to total use.

Among the sociodemographic predictors of the use of collaborative platforms in Europe, the analysis performed provides us with a set of results worth highlighting. Firstly, men are more inclined than women to use such platforms. Secondly, the younger age ranges (54 years and below) are more likely to make a total use than the older age ranges. And thirdly, households with more members have a greater probability of having a user of collaborative platforms among them than households with fewer members.

Regarding human capital and occupational status, the joint use of collaborative economy platforms in Europe is also linked to the fact of being a student or having many years of education and to professional contexts of entrepreneurship, managerial responsibility, or being highly qualified. In fact, students or people with 20 or more years of formal education are much more likely to use collaborative platforms

	Users (n = 1792)		Providers (n = 496)	
	OR	(95% CI)	OR	(95% CI)
Motivations/barriers (driving and impeding factors)				
Price	**1.687**	**(1.505–1.890)**	1.063	(0.860–1.312)
Newness	1.094	(0.962–1.245)	1.077	(0.846–1.372)
Convenience	**2.334**	**(2.089–2.608)**	0.953	(0.775–1.173)
Nonmonetary exchange	**0.668**	**(0.580–0.769)**	**1.384**	**(1.062–1.803)**
Lack of a responsible person	1.089	(0.973–1.218)	**0.747**	**(0.601–0.929)**
Lack of fulfillment service expectation	**1.234**	**(1.093–1.394)**	1.234	(0.986–1.544)
Lack of information	1.055	(0.918–1.212)	0.990	(0.760–1.289)
Lack of trust in the agents	**1.217**	**(1.076–1.377)**	1.043	(0.828–1.314)
Lack of trust in the Internet	**0.878**	**(0.775–0.994)**	0.973	(0.767–1.236)
Sociodemographic predictors				
Age				
15–24 years	**1.262**	**(1.039–1.532)**	0.871	(0.578–1.311)
25–34 years	**2.386**	**(2.077–2.740)**	**1.436**	**(1.106–1.866)**
35–44 years	**2.097**	**(1.858–2.367)**	0.989	(0.775–1.262)
45–54 years	**1.420**	**(1.260–1.601)**	0.878	(0.684–1.595)
55–64 years	**0.755**	**(0.680–0.883)**	1.070	(0.815–1.406)
65 years and above	**0.246**	**(0.212–0.286)**	0.727	(0.514–1.028)
Gender (1 = male, 0 = female)	**1.456**	**(1.318–1.608)**	**1.409**	**(1.144–1.736)**
Human capital (years of education)				
Still studying	**1.536**	**(1.240–1.903)**	0.887	(0.570–1.381)
Up to 15 years	**0.170**	**(0.128–0.226)**	1.224	(0.669–2.237)
16–19 years	**0.616**	**(0.553–0.687)**	0.839	(0.664–1.059)
20 or more years	2.313	(2.088–2.563)	1.170	(0.943–1.453)
Occupational status				
Self-employed/entrepreneurs	**1.828**	**(1.573–2.125)**	**1.843**	**(1.391–2.443)**
Employees—directors	**3.012**	**(2.575–3.522)**	1.006	(0.746–1.356)
Employees—qualified professionals	**2.181**	**(1.832–2.596)**	1.147	(0.820–1.605)
Employees—nonmanagement workers	**1.572**	**(1.403–1.762)**	**0.688**	**(0.539–0.878)**
Employees—manual workers	**0.781**	**(0.626–0.974)**	**1.673**	**(1.087–2.574)**
Nonemployed—parents/ carers	**0.598**	**(0.475–0.754)**	0.822	(0.491–1.376)
Nonemployed—students	**1.373**	**(1.092–1.726)**	0.787	(0.482–1.284)
Non-employed—retirees	**0.271**	**(0.237–0.310)**	**0.718**	**(0.527–0.977)**
Unemployed—job seekers	0.886	(0.680–1.153)	1.330	(0.787–2.247)
Household members				
One	**0.598**	**(0.524–0.681)**	1.200	(0.915–1.574)
Two	**1.137**	**(1.029–1.257)**	0.915	(0.742–1.127)

	Users (n = 1792)		Providers (n = 496)	
	OR	**(95% CI)**	**OR**	**(95% CI)**
Three	**1.212**	**(1.067–1.377)**	1.067	(0.821–1.386)
Four or more	**1.203**	**(1.053–1.374)**	0.906	(0.685–1.198)
Locality				
Village or rural area	**0.736**	**(0.658–0.823)**	1.042	(0.824–1.318)
Small or mid-sized town/city	0.940	(0.848–1.043)	0.980	(0.789–1.217)
Large town/city or metropolitan area	**1.419**	**(1.280–1.574)**	0.986	(0.795–1.222)
Country groupings				
Continental Europe[1]	**1.249**	**(1.113–1.403)**	1.207	(0.954–1.526)
Mediterranean Europe[2]	**0.735**	**(0.651–0.831)**	1.000	(0.773–1.294)
Northern Europe[3]	1.058	(0.932–1.202)	**0.748**	**(0.566–0.987)**
Central and Eastern Europe[4]	1.029	(0.928–1.141)	1.028	(0.829–1.276)

Notes: OR: odds ratio and 95% CI: confidence intervals at 95%. ORs and 95% CI in bold are significant.
[1]Continental Europe: Belgium, France, Luxembourg, the Netherlands, Austria, and Germany.
[2]Mediterranean Europe: Greece, Spain, Italy, Portugal, Cyprus, Malta, and Croatia.
[3]Northern Europe: Denmark, Finland, Sweden, the United Kingdom, and Ireland.
[4]Central and Eastern Europe: Bulgaria, Czech Republic, Estonia, Hungary, Latvia, Lithuania, Poland, Romania, Slovenia, and Slovakia.

Table 4.
Predictors of P2P platform use and provision in Europe.

than people with fewer years of education. As far as occupational status is concerned, the self-employed and business people, employees who are directors, employees who are qualified professionals, and employees who are nonmanual workers are the most likely to use collaborative platforms. In contrast, employees who are manual workers, stay-at-home parents/carers, the unemployed and, in particular, retirees are much less inclined toward collaborative consumption via platforms.

Finally, the predictors by geographical area also provide relevant information, firstly, because the impetus behind collaborative consumption comes from large towns/cities and metropolitan areas, whereas living in villages and rural areas would disincentive collaborative consumption via platforms. By country, we also observe a greater likelihood to use collaborative platforms in continental Europe—Belgium, France, Luxembourg, Netherlands, Austria, and Germany—whereas in Mediterranean Europe—Greece, Spain, Italy, Portugal, Cyprus, Malta, and Croatia—the situation is the inverse.

The analysis of predictive factors for the provision of goods and services via collaborative platforms (n = 496) in Europe (**Table 4**) reveals a picture that clearly differs from the use of such platforms. Of the motivational predictors of collaborative provision, the first element to highlight is that such provision has a clearly ideological component, in an antiestablishment or anticapitalism sense, because the possibility of doing nonmonetary exchanges becomes a driving factor. Moreover, nonmonetary exchange was the only provision-driving predictor to be identified, because the other economic and convenience factors were not significant. Regarding the impeding forces, the lack of a responsible person would not disincentive the collaborative provision of goods and services.

From the perspective of the sociodemographic predictors, the collaborative provision of goods and services in Europe would be motivated by a much narrower set of factors than the one identified for collaborative uses. Men, the young population aged between 25 and 34 years, the self-employed or entrepreneurs, or manual workers would be the most likely to make collaborative provisions of goods and services. In contrast, nonmanual workers, retirees, or citizens of countries in northern Europe—Denmark, Finland, Sweden, the United Kingdom, and Ireland—would be the least likely to make collaborative provisions.

7. Discussion: new consumer behavior, new economic approaches

Through an analysis of a representative sample of 14,050 citizens aged 15 years and above in the 28 countries of the European Union in 2016, in this study I have characterized the profiles of users (1792) and providers (496) of collaborative platforms and have identified their motivational and sociodemographic predictors. The main strength of this study is that it provides us with results based on a representative sample of the entire European population; this adds value to the literature because samples that are not representative of the population, or that focus on specific collaborative platforms or consumption, have habitually been analyzed thus far [17, 27, 28]. Two main conclusions were drawn from this analysis.

Firstly, through an odds ratio (OR) analysis, the study obtained a set of forces (motivational and sociodemographic) that are capable of predicting the use and provision of collaborative platforms in Europe. Regarding users, the main driving forces identified were of an economic and practical nature (Hypothesis 2: convenience and price), and the impeding forces would also be situated on this line (Hypothesis 3: lack of fulfillment of service expectations and lack of trust in the Internet). Beyond these results, which are consistent with studies confirming the importance of motivations of practicality and utility in the explanation of the use of collaborative consumption platforms [8, 9, 26, 44], emphasis should be placed on the importance of predictors of a sociodemographic nature (Hypothesis 4). Younger people; men; people living in households with more members; people with more years of education; people within entrepreneurship, managerial responsibility, or highly qualified contexts; people living in large towns/cities or metropolitan areas; and people who are citizens of continental Europe are more likely to engage in collaborative consumption via digital platforms. Given that a number of studies have pointed out that lifestyle is more important than level of income [25], this finding is important because certain sociodemographic profiles were identified that, in population contexts (i.e., in representative samples of the entire population), would incentivize collaborative consumption and behavior.

And secondly, the results obtained for the predictors of the provision of goods and services via collaborative platforms in Europe are clearly different from those for the predictors of use. The first thing to note is that, unlike use—and as some studies have already highlighted [27, 40, 41]—provision has a clearly ideological motivational component (Hypothesis 1). The possibility of doing nonmonetary exchanges is the only predictive provision-driving factor. Among the impeding factors, the lack of a responsible person would not disincentive provision via collaborative platforms. As in the case of users, there is a set of sociodemographic predictors for providers, albeit fewer in number: men, the young population aged between 25 and 34 years, the self-employed or entrepreneurs, or manual workers would be the most likely to make provisions of goods and services. In contrast, nonmanual workers, retirees, or citizens of countries in northern Europe would be the least likely to make such provisions.

Particularly interesting is the identification of categories of specific occupational status that would incentivize or be more sensitive to use and provide P2P collaborative platforms. The self-employed or entrepreneurs would be the most likely to make provisions and uses of goods and services, and this is consistent with the dual role that research in consumer theory has identified [48]. This result has important implications regarding the management strategy. It is true that management research has identified a group of strategic recommendations for firms that would like to understand and take advantage of the sharing economy [5, 49–51], but literature has not counted occupational status as a predictor. Based on our results, entrepreneurs and self-employed are more prone to value initiatives that are oriented as an alternative of the usual consumption models. Self-employment or entrepreneurship entails a mindset of aspects that firms may desire to attract or promote for some stakeholders. Broadening the set of motivations allows firms to better understand how their stakeholders are more likely or not to be participating in collaborative consumption. Profiles such as entrepreneurs and self-employed have a dynamism that firms may encourage, and understanding how these profiles are motivated is crucial to attack the right people or to develop marketing using the right strategies.

On the contrary, managers and qualified employees have more practical and monetary motivations, so that they are more sensible to sharing initiatives oriented toward the practical utility of sharing. In this context, knowing the practical and useful motivations of managers and qualified workers is also relevant to the firm strategy, especially for those who choose to develop collaborative platforms more oriented to economic optimization than to alternative exchange and behavior.

However, all this new evidence does not yet address the multidimensional set of factors that would explain the transformations of economic behavior related to the emergence of sharing exchange and P2P markets [34, 38, 52, 53]. In my empirical exercise, we have identified a number of additional sociodemographic motivations, but we still know very little about the effects of collaborative consumption and behavior. For example, what form does the collaborative consumption function take? Does it complement or replace the noncollaborative consumption function? What proportion of total consumption does collaborative consumption represent? How does this new form of consumption affect other aggregates of the economy? What is its multiplier? The search for answers to these questions will undoubtedly set the course of future research.

In the meantime, a connection between the conceptual frameworks of the sharing economy should be noted. The salient idea behind this connection is that, through new forms of collaborative consumption and behavior, exchange evolves toward a new interpretative paradigm, from initial digital formats into sharing formats. And for a more adequate interpretation of the sharing exchange theory, the economy will have to move forward and develop a formal apparatus that takes into consideration a set of relatively unusual principles, especially interpretative models that consider a combination of emotional and rational decision-making, individual interest-based as well as prosocial motivations, exchange compensation through a monetary or nonmonetary fee, and the set of sharing economies, that it may generate. In the same way, the business strategy should begin to combine the traditional financial approach to the benefits with the concept of profit, that better summarizes the collaborative behavior.

References

[1] Grassmuck VR. The sharing turn: Why we are generally nice and have a good chance to cooperate our way out of the mess we have gotten ourselves into. In: Sützl W, Stalder F, Maier R, Hug T, editors. Cultures and Ethics of Sharing. Vol. 2013. Innsbruck: Innsbruck University Press; 2013. pp. 17-34

[2] Heinrichs H. Sharing economy: A potential new pathway to sustainability. GAIA: Ecological Perspectives for Science & Society. 2013;**22**(4):228-231

[3] Stephany A. The Business of Sharing: Making it in the New Sharing Economy. New York: Palgrave Macmillan; 2015

[4] Belk RW. Sharing. Journal of Consumer Research. 2010;**36**(4):715-734

[5] Belk RW. You are what you can access: Sharing and collaborative consumption online. Journal of Business Research. 2014;**67**(8):1595-1600

[6] Carroll E, Romano J. Your Digital Afterlife: When Facebook, Flickr and Twitter are Your Estate, What's Your Legacy? Berkeley, CA: New Riders; 2011

[7] Botsman R, Rogers R. What's Mine Is Yours: How Collaborative Consumption Is Changing the Way we Life. London: Collins; 2011

[8] Bardhi F, Eckhardt GM. Access-based consumption: The case of car sharing. Journal of Consumer Research. 2012;**39**(4):881-898

[9] Lamberton CP, Rose RR. When is ours better than mine? A framework for understanding and altering participation in commercial sharing systems. Journal of Marketing. 2012;**76**(4):109-125

[10] Benkler Y. Sharing nicely: On shareable goods and the emergence of sharing as a modality of economic production. Yale Law Journal. 2004;**114**:273-358

[11] Shapiro C, Varian HR. Information Rules. A Strategic Guide to the Network Economy. Boston, MA: Harvard Business School Press; 1999

[12] Torrent-Sellens J. Knowledge products and network externalities. Implications for the business strategy. Journal of the Knowledge Economy. 2015;**6**(1):138-156

[13] Varian HR. Intermediate Microeconomics: A Modern Approach. Ninth International Student Edition. London: WW Norton & Company; 2014

[14] Belk RW. Why not share rather than own? The Annals of the American Academy of Political and Social Science. 2007;**611**(1):126-140

[15] Belk RW. Extended self in a digital world. Journal of Consumer Research. 2013;**40**(3):477-500

[16] Felson M, Speath JL. Community structure and collaborative consumption. American Behavioral Scientist. 1978;**21**(4):614-624

[17] Hamari J, Sjöklint M, Ukkonen A. The sharing economy: Why people participate in collaborative consumption. Journal of the Association for Information Science and Technology. 2016;**67**(9):2047-2059

[18] Mont O. Clarifying the concept of product-service system. Journal of Cleaner Production. 2002;**10**(3):237-245

[19] Gansky L. The Mesh: Why the Future of Business Is Sharing. New York: Penguin Press; 2010

[20] Ritzer G, Jurgenson N. Production, consumption, prosumption: The nature of capitalism in the age of the digital

prosumer. Journal of Consumer Culture. 2010;**10**(1):13-36

[21] Sundararajan A. The Sharing Economy. The End of Employment and the Rise of Crowd-Based Capitalism. Cambridge, MA: MIT Press; 2016

[22] Price LL, Belk RW. Consumer ownership and sharing: Introduction to the special issue. Journal of the Association for Consumer Research. 2016;**1**(2):193-197

[23] Ozanne LK, Ballantine PW. Sharing as a form of anti-consumption? An examination of toy library users. Journal of Consumer Behaviour. 2010;**9**(6):485-498

[24] Albinsson PA, Perera BY. Alternative marketplaces in the 21st century: Building community through sharing events. Journal of Consumer Behaviour. 2012;**11**(4):303-315

[25] Hellwig K, Morhart F, Girardin F, Hauser M. Exploring different types of sharing: A proposed segmentation of the market for "sharing" businesses. Psychology & Marketing. 2015;**32**(9):891-906

[26] Möhlmann M. Collaborative consumption: Determinants of satisfaction and the likelihood of using a sharing economy option again. Journal of Consumer Behaviour. 2015;**14**(3):193-207

[27] Hawlitschek F, Teubner T, Gimpel H. Understanding the sharing economy. Drivers and impediments for participation in peer-to-peer rental. In: Proceedings of the 49th Hawaii International Conference on System Sciences. Honolulu: IEEE; 2016. pp. 4782-4789

[28] Matzner M, Chasin F, Todenhöfer L. To share or not to share. Towards understanding the antecedents of participation in IT-enabled sharing services. In: Proceedings of the 23th European Conference on Information Systems. Münster: ECIS; 2015. pp. 1-13

[29] John NA. The social logics of sharing. The Communication Review. 2013;**16**(3):113-131

[30] Barnes SJ, Mattsson J. Understanding collaborative consumption: Test of a theoretical model. Technological Forecasting and Social Change. 2017;**118**:281-292

[31] Kaplan AM, Haenlien M. Users of the world, unite! The challenges and opportunities of social media. Business Horizons. 2010;**53**(1):59-68

[32] Wang C, Zhang P. The evolution of social commerce: The people, management, technology, and information dimensions. Communications of the Association of Information Systems. 2012;**31**(1):105-127

[33] Wiertz C, de Ruyter K. Beyond the call of duty: Why customers contribute to firm-hosted commercial online communities. Organization Studies. 2007;**28**(3):347-376

[34] Einav L, Farronato C, Levin J. Peer-To-Peer Markets. Discussion Paper: 15-029. Stanford Institute for Economic & Policy Research (SPIER). Stanford, CA: Stanford University; 2015

[35] Coyle D. The Economics of Enough: How to Run the Economy as if the Future Matters. Princeton, NJ: Princeton University Press; 2011

[36] Leismann K, Schmitt M, Rohn H, Baedeker C. Collaborative consumption: Towards a resource-saving consumption culture. Resources. 2013;**2**(3):184-203

[37] Shaheen SA, Cohen AP. Car sharing and personal vehicle services: Worldwide market developments and emerging trends. International

Journal of Sustainable Transportation. 2013;7(1):5-34

[38] Plouffe CR. Examining "peer-to-peer" (P2P) systems as a consumer-to-consumer (C2C) exchange. European Journal of Marketing. 2008;**42**(11/12):1179-1202

[39] Brodie RJ, Ilic A, Juric B, Hollebeek L. Consumer engagement in a virtual brand community: An exploratory analysis. Journal of Business Research. 2013;**66**(1):105-114

[40] Belloti V, Ambard A, Turner D, Gossmann C, Demkova K, Carroll JM. A muddle of models of motivation for using peer-to-peer economy systems. In: Proceedings of the 33rd Annual ACM Conference on Human Factors in Computing Systems. Seoul: ACM; 2015. pp. 1085-1094

[41] Bucher E, Fieseler C, Lutz C. What's mine is yours (for a nominal fee)—Exploring the spectrum of utilitarian to altruistic motives for Internet-mediated sharing. Computers in Human Behavior. 2016;**62**:316-326

[42] Buczynski B. Sharing Is Good: How to Save Money, Time and Resources through Collaborative Consumption. Gabriola Island: New Society Publishers; 2013

[43] Balck B, Cracau D. Empirical analysis of customer motives in the share economy: A cross-sectoral comparison. Working paper: 02/2015. Magdeburg: Universität Magdeburg; 2015

[44] Tussyadiah IP. An exploratory study on drivers and deterrents of collaborative consumption in travel. In: Tussyadiah IP, Inversini A, editors. Information and Communication Technologies in TourismChamp: Springer; 2015. pp. 817-830

[45] European Commission. The use of collaborative platforms. Flash Eurobarometer 438 Report. Brussels: European Commission; 2016

[46] Greene WH. Econometric Analysis. 7th ed. New York: Person; 2012

[47] Hensher DA, Rose JM, Greene WH. Applied Choice Analysis. Cambridge, MA: Cambridge University Press; 2015

[48] Ertz M, Lecompte A, Durif F. Dual roles of consumers: Towards an insight into collaborative consumption motives. International Journal of Market Research. 2017;**59**:725-748

[49] Matzler K, Veider V, Kathan W. Adapting to the sharing economy. MIT Sloan Management Review. 2015;**56**(2):71-77

[50] Kathan W, Matzler K, Veider V. The sharing economy: Your business model's friend or foe? Business Horizons. 2016;**59**(6):663-672

[51] Habibi MR, Davidson A, Laroche M. What managers should know about the sharing economy. Business Horizons. 2017;**60**:113-121

[52] Rodrigues R, Druschel P. Peer-to-peer systems. Communications of the ACM. 2010;**53**(10):72-82

[53] Galbreth M, Ghosh B, Shor M. Social sharing of information goods: Implications for pricing and profits. Marketing Science. 2012;**31**(4):603-620

Chapter 11

The Transformation of Business Models in Technology-Enabled M&A: A Case Study of Amazon

Abstract

Little is known about how a configuration of dynamic capabilities (DC) contributes to the transformation of the business models (BM) of ICT acquirers. The chapter addresses this limitation by taking a strategy-as-practice theory perspective. The inductive (illustrative) case study Amazon.com acquisition of Whole Foods (2017) demonstrate how acquires sense new customer group and new key activity; seize new resources and key partnerships and transform organization by mean of new promotional channels and new customer relationship, therefore change cost structure, create new revenue streams, and develop new customer value proposition. The chapter develops a practice-driven model as a practical guide for scholars who have been studying DCs and BMs, as well as for those who are new to the field.

Keywords: dynamic capabilities, business model, merger and acquisition

1. Introduction

A focal firm's growth strategies and performance are greatly influenced by the integrative type of strategies, collaborative (alliances, networks, joint ventures) or consolidative (mergers, acquisitions), to foster the innovation and to deliver new customer value propositions. In recent years, collaborative and consolidation strategies have received great attention in strategic management literature. Researchers in strategic management argue that the performance outcome of a specific growth strategy is usually affected by the dynamic capabilities and business models [1–3]. What is the research gap in the existing literature on dynamic capabilities and business models? First, dynamic capabilities in merger and acquisition are complex events in the process of sustain completive advantage of merging business for which we have an incomplete understanding, in part because researchers have tended to consider an only explanation of them. What is more, there are very few research papers that applied the dynamic capabilities' framework as a tool of the business analysis of a reinvention of a business model of an acquirer company in M&A processes. Second, the reinvention of business models of acquirers is still an open area for research due to the following reasons. Johnson et al. [4] gave brilliant ideas on a reinvention of business models and their building blocks for focal companies, but still, a question remains, what capabilities are needed in a reinvention of business models in the process of M&A? Pursuing scientific rigor and helping practitioners to reinvent of their business model, Amit and Zott [5] integrated dynamic capabilities with business model design process, but what about reinvention of operationalized components of the model or building blocks of business models in M&A process? To reinvent building blocks of business models, Kim and Mauborgne [6] recommended to apply "four steps framework: eliminate, reduce, increase and create," namely, to eliminate and to reduce elements of business model thereby to eliminate and to reduce expenses as well as increase and/or create as new some elements of business model thereby to increase a revenue stream and to create a new customer value proposition [2]. However, it is silent about what dynamic capabilities are needed for that.

Capturing valuable insights from the dynamic capabilities' framework [4] and business model canvas [2], this chapter aims to integrate two theoretical perspectives in the cohesive conceptual model. Why is it important to combine the dynamic capabilities and business model literature? Adoption of seminal Teece's framework [7] of dynamic capabilities and operationalized components (building blocks) of business models [2], in online and offline grocery businesses, allowed the construction of the conceptual model for practitioners and scholars, which consequently can be tested by methods of statistical analysis in future research.

The motivation for the research is as follows: the author wanted to know how acquisition-based dynamic capabilities support a reinvention of building blocks of business models. The chapter discusses how a focal firm makes strategic decisions under uncertainty and deals with the commercialization of innovation by means of dynamic capabilities to sense a new demand, capture new resources and partnerships, transform channels and customers' relationship, and deliver a new customer value proposition, particularly, by means of acquiring new technologies, advanced engineering team, and new users' base. That is what Amazon did with Whole Foods in 2017. This case study of Whole Foods acquisition by Amazon was selected due to the following reasons. Firstly, this empirical literature is still at an early stage, and opportunities abound to dig deeper into the linkages between dynamic capabilities (DC), a reinvention of business models, and long-run firm performance. "The research paradigm of dynamic capabilities is still relatively new. Accordingly, illuminating case studies are likely to yield powerful insights" ([8], p. 1400). Secondly, the chapter digs deeper into the acquisition-based DC in M&A to develop an integrated practical example of how dynamic capabilities and building blocks of business models are interrelated in successful M&A process in the ICT industry. The main contribution of the chapter is an emerging conceptual model of research that integrates acquisition-based dynamic capabilities' frameworks [7] and business model canvas [2] together and, thereby, illustrates how acquisition-based dynamic capabilities underpinning a reinvention of business models in M&A process. This conceptual practice-driven model can be a practical guide for scholars who have been studying DCs and BMs, as well as for those who are new to the field. What is more, the chapter has contributed to the interest of the strategy practice group of the Strategic Management Society by answering questions which the group attempt to answer: what are the capabilities required to perform strategy work, and what are the microfoundations of the activities involved in the doing of strategy?

2. Literature review

The recent scientific discussion in the field of strategic management broadly favors the idea of dynamic capabilities in order to overcome potential rigidities of organizational capability building [9]. "The theoretical and practical importance of developing and applying dynamic capabilities to sustain a firm's competitive advantage in complex and volatile external environments has catapulted this issue to the forefront of the research agendas of many scholars" ([10], p. 917). This is especially true for strategic behavior in the digital economy, as shown in this chapter. This chapter examined DC in the online grocery business industry in which the external environment shifted to some extent from a click (online grocery) to a brick (offline grocery). DC can usefully be thought of as belonging to three clusters of activities and adjustments: (1) identification and assessment of an opportunity (sensing); (2) mobilization of resources to address an opportunity and to capture value from doing so (seizing); and (3) continued renewal of core competencies (transforming) [7]. Sensing implies that the organization must constantly scan, recognize, and appraise opportunities and threats across various markets and technologies. Investigating customer needs is a typical sensing activity. Once an opportunity has been sensed in order to bring the new services, processes, and activities, the organization should seize the opportunity. To seize an opportunity may require renewal and reconfiguration of organizational capabilities and investment in technologies, equipment, and markets. Thus, transforming is how to organize new and old resources for organization's value maximization. One key implication of the DC concept is that firms are not only competing on their ability to exploit their existing resources and organizational capabilities but also on their ability to explore, renew, and develop their organizational capabilities [11]. During the past two decades, research in DC has promised to unlock the understanding of how competitive advantage arises in dynamic markets. However, to date, empirical work has, by and large, focused on what DC is. There has been little work demonstrating how they actually operate and contribute to competitive advantage other than at the conceptual level [12]. Stefano et al. argue that despite the exceptional rise in interest and influence of dynamic capabilities, criticisms of the dynamic capabilities' perspective continue to mount [13]. Common concerns are related to a lack of consensus on basic theoretical elements and limited empirical progress [13]. Specific capabilities that have been identified and studied involve research and development [14], product innovation [15], ambidextrous organizational structures [16], network responsiveness [17], and human capital management [18]. However, there are only a few pieces of research on specific dynamic capabilities that have been identified and studied involving merger and acquisition. Teece argues that it might be "because assets are bundled together often tightly linked inside incumbent firms, it may be difficult to obtain assets in the desired configurations through asset purchase or sale in mergers and acquisitions" [7]. However, by Eisenhardt and Martin [11], practice with homogeneous acquisitions (i.e., those in the related markets) was positively associated with the accumulation of tacit and explicit knowledge about how to execute acquisitions and achieve superior acquisition performance. Making strategically important investment choice on M&A, dynamically capable management team needs such managerial capabilities as sensing and shaping, seizing and reconfigurations (transforming), as well as reinvention and implementation of new business model [7].

Value creation through M&A requires the simultaneous identification of target with similar dynamic capabilities on certain dimensions and different dynamic capabilities on other dimensions. "While similarity is seen as an indicator for efficiency-based synergies (scale and scope), complementarity provides firms with both efficiency synergies and value created from those differences that are mutually supportive. Studies give clear empirical evidence that complementarities are a significant factor for M&A success" ([19], p. 272). Through the interaction of complementary characteristics, value creation does not only derive from cost savings, but the value is also created by a growing turnover and market share [20]. Complementarity has been studied in terms of top management team complementarity [20], technological complementarity [21], strategic and market complementarity [22], or product complementarity [23]. However, the study in terms of complementarity of dynamic capabilities in M&A is still waiting for researchers.

Proposition 1. The success of consolidative strategies (merger or acquisition) is provided by the degree of similarities and complementarity between the dynamic capabilities of two merging businesses.

In recent year, the business models have received increasing attention of strategy researchers. Business models characterize the focal firm's plan for its value creation and capture [24]. From the point of view of Johnson et al. [4], a business model consists of four main elements, the synthesis of which delivers value, customer value proposition, profit formula, key resources, and key processes. Osterwalder and Pigneur [2] with real 470 business practitioners from 45 countries extended a number of elements and developed Business Model Canvas with nine building blocks: customer segment, value proposition, channels, customer relationship, revenue stream, key resources, key activities, key partners, and cost structure. Slightly adapted Johnson et al. [4] and Osterwalder and Pigneur [2], Teece proposed three main components of the business model: "Cost Model: Core Assets and Capabilities; Core Activities; Partner Network. Revenue Model: Pricing Logic; Channels; Customer Interaction. Value proposition: Product and Service; Customer Needs; Geography" ([25], p. 41). With respect to brilliant contributors to dynamic capabilities and business models' frameworks, there is still a gap in understanding what and how dynamic capabilities lead to new cost structure and revenue streams and how dynamic capabilities foster new value proposition of acquirer's company in M&A process. We must understand how acquisition-based dynamic capabilities transform and reinvent components of a business model acquirer's company.

What exactly is meant by the reinvention of building blocks of business models? The reinvention of building blocks of business meant the process of the transformation of the most important activities, capabilities, and resources of the company to reduce cost, to increase revenue stream, to deliver new customer value proposition, and thereby to sustain competitive advantages. How acquisition-based dynamic capabilities support a reinvention of building blocks of business models? There are three sets of acquisition-based dynamic capabilities which should be developed to transform and reinvent a business model of an acquirer to achieve competitive advantage. The first set of acquisition-based dynamic capabilities (sensing and shaping) is contributing to select new key activities and new customer segments, thereby contributing to an acquirer to shape emerging market demand and new technologies needed. The second set of acquisition-based dynamic capabilities (identifying and seizing) is supporting an acquirer's company to obtain new key idiosyncratic (VRIN) resources and to extend a partnership's networks. The third set of acquisition-based dynamic capabilities (transforming and reconfiguring) is contributing an acquirer's company to transform new customer relationships and promotion channels and, thus, to deliver the new customer value proposition. Thereby, an acquiring company would result in a new cost structure by eliminating and reducing capital expenditure and operating expenses, due to an economy of scope, and would generate new revenue streams by increasing and creating new key activities. A result of those transformation processes, acquirer's company can newly sustain competitive advantage. The theoretical framework of the research is presented in **Table 1**.

Proposition 2. Business model's elements of both acquirer's and the target's companies can successfully fold into the new business model by means of acquisition-based dynamic capabilities and contribute to reduce

Acquisition based dynamic capabilities of the acquirer	Sensing and shaping	Identifying and seizing	Transforming and reconfiguring	Resulting and sustaining
Designing new building blocks (operationalized components) of the business model of acquiring organization:	Sensing new key activities Shaping new customers' segments	Identifying and seizing new key resources Identifying and seizing new key partners	Transforming channels Transforming customers' relationship Reconfiguring new customers value proposition	Result in new revenue streams Result in new cost structure Sustaining new competitive advantages

Table 1.
The theoretical model of research: bridging together acquisition-based dynamic capabilities and reinvention of a business model.

cost, to create a new revenue stream, to deliver a new value proposition, and therefore to sustain competitive advantage.

3. Research design and methodology

"Building theory from case studies is a research strategy that involves using one or more cases to create theoretical constructs, propositions and/or midrange theory from case-based, empirical evidence" ([26], p. 25). Yin defines the case study research method as "an empirical inquiry that investigates a contemporary phenomenon within its real-life context; when the boundaries between phenomenon and context are not clearly evident; and in which multiple sources of evidence are used" ([27], p. 23). Some critics suggest case study research is useful only as an exploratory tool or for establishing a hypothesis, and some would claim it is unscientific [28]. When it comes to the validity of qualitative case study research, the validity refers to the extent to which the qualitative research results accurately represent the collected data (internal validity) can be generalized or transferred to other contexts or settings (external validity) [28]. Ultimately, each case can be viewed as a discrete experiment that could be repeated [29].

This chapter seeks to explore how acquisition-based dynamic capabilities underpinning a reinvention of business models in the M&A process. As objects of research, the author selected the company that is especially active and successful in online shopping and particularly in the online and offline grocery business. The unit of analysis is dynamic capabilities. In this research, two stages of research work will be involved. Firstly, to justify propositions, the author did the contextual content analysis which relied on an archival search that included financial statements, annual reports, internal documents, industry publications, and CEO statements to get at a microlevel understanding that really boosts data and the better understanding of the microfoundations of DC and building blocks of business models of acquirers and targets.

Even though a strategy-as-practice or process-based approaches in empirical qualitative research usually have an element of ethnographic or discursive analysis using primary data (sometimes in addition to secondary data, sometimes alone), the current chapter relied on an extensive search of secondary data. The key to secondary data analysis is to apply theoretical knowledge and conceptual skills to utilize existing data to address the research propositions. The major advantages associated with secondary analysis are the cost-effectiveness and convenience it provides [30]. A major disadvantage of using secondary data is that the secondary researcher did not participate in the data collection process and does not know exactly how it was conducted. However, the obvious benefits of using secondary data can be overshadowed by its limitations [31]. Original survey research rarely uses all of the data collected, and this unused data can provide answers or different perspectives to other questions or issues [30]. In a time where vast amounts of data are being collected and archived by researchers all over the world, the practicality of utilizing existing data for research is becoming more prevalent [30, 32].

The aim of the content analysis of illustrative case study of Amazon's acquisition of Whole Foods at 2017 is to explicate the relationship between acquisitions-based dynamic capability and reinvention of acquirer business model and, thus, sustained competitive advantage. Content analysis is a qualitative research method that uses a set of procedures to classify or otherwise categorize communications [33]. Typically relying on archival data to extract criteria of interest to strategic management scholars, content analysis has aided in analyzing corporate strategies [34], organizational boundaries [35], new product development [36], organizational resources [37], strategic groups [38], and joint ventures [39]. Any source of communication such as shareholder letters, interview narratives, video records, speeches, or transcripts from recorded meetings of executives could be used by a strategy researcher as an effective data source for content analysis. It provides a good match theoretically between the information being assessed (how information is being content analyzed) and the context from which it is drawn (does the type of text being used as a source of content analysis data fit the propositions?).

Generally, three broad types of content methodologies exist [40, 41]: human-scored schema, individual word count systems, and computerized systems using artificial intelligence. Human-scored systems involve training of coders to classify text according to specific classification categories. In this system, the first step is a determination of what aspect of text will serve as the unit of analysis (word, phrase, sentence, paragraph, full text). Then, categories are developed for classification, and coding rules are developed for each category. In contrast to human-scored schemas, individual work count systems classify text into several semantically equivalent categories and then use frequency of an occurrence to determine the relative importance of each category in a text [33]. Finally, artificial intelligence systems incorporate features that consider the syntax and lexicon of words [41]. Thus, there is a mechanism to resolve words with more than a single meaning. For this study, the author has chosen human-scored systems and individual work count systems. Dynamic capabilities served as a unit of analysis.

To justify the first proposition, the author has chosen human-scored systems and classified text into three specific classification categories, namely, sensing, seizing, and transforming dynamic capabilities. When it comes to the format of the presentation, the author has adopted a conceptual frame developed by Teece [42]. The conceptual frame helped to unravel data in the text that the author has collected in search of similarities and complementarity of the micro-foundations of the dynamic capabilities of both companies. To justify the second proposition, the author applied an individual work count system, the text has been allocated within nine building blocks of the business model of both companies (as semantically equivalent categories), and identified compatibilities and complementarity of companies' business models. Then, the author has allocated operationalized components of the business model into each cluster of dynamic capabilities (sensing, seizing, and transforming) to demonstrate how acquisition-based dynamic capabilities underpinning the transformation of the business model. The second stage of research involves a demonstration of the development process of the new conceptual model of research by using illustrative content analysis finding and literature research outcomes. This empirical research helps to fill a gap in the literature which is primarily 75% theoretical and only 25% empirical—focusing on proving the existence of dynamic capability [43]. The chapter discusses and interprets the results of the qualitative and explorative research in the next subchapters.

4. Data analysis and interpretation

Teece argues that individual corporate histories and illuminative case studies yield powerful insights to dynamic capabilities research. [5]. In a move that surprised the 2017 year, Amazon, the largest online retailer, announced its intention to purchase Whole Foods for $13.7B in cash. Amazon had been dabbling with traditional brick-and-mortar activities for a few years already—from owning a few physical stores to running experiments like "Amazon Fresh" and later "Amazon Go." However, its competitors including Walmart were far ahead than Amazon with revenues of $ 486 billion as compared to Amazon's $136 billion [44]. Some have interpreted Amazon's move as a signal that the online giant is finally giving in and investing big in brick-and-mortar retail. How is this particular acquisition different from any other acquisition where the target firm is attractive because of its business channels and market reach? Most acquisitions are carried out to acquire these target firm's capabilities; how is the Amazon acquisition of Whole Foods different? The answer is this acquisition is carried out to acquire big data of more affluent customers with an interest in eating healthy and sustainable foods spending extra money to purchase. Digging deeper, though, it is clear that Amazon's real interest is in two things: first, the treasure trove of consumer data that comes with this acquisition; and second, Whole Foods private brand product [44]. The big data from Whole Foods customers are literally "rich." What exactly is in the Whole Foods data that Amazon would want? The answer is grocery buying habits and patterns. Preferences and correlations between purchases of different products and even different categories [44]. Jeremy Stanley, vice president of data science for Instacart, one of Amazon's competitors in the grocery space, recently told CNBC: "One of the wonderful things about groceries is that compared to other e-commerce purchases, groceries are habitual and frequent. People need groceries every week" [44]. Amazon can also use its process and technology expertise to take enormous costs out of the supply chain and store operations of Whole Foods while improving the in-store experience. Amazon has mastered the "test and learn" approach to large-scale innovation that most companies aspire to. Whole Foods provides Amazon with an incredible platform for the transformation of industry [45].

Justification of proposition 1. The success of consolidative strategies (merger or acquisition) is provided by the degree of similarities and complementarity between the dynamic capabilities of two merging businesses.

The persistence of existing dynamic capabilities depends on the impetus for change (sensing), the strength of the perceived need to change (seizing), and the managerial capacity to integrate and recombine resources (transforming) as desired [46, 10, 7]. Zahra et al. [10] argue that the lack of success to solve a problem with current capabilities triggers the development and use of new dynamic capabilities.

The research has explored the selected dynamic capabilities of the target's company and acquirer's company. The justification of the first proposition is given in **Tables 2** and **3**. The research has identified several similarities in the dynamic capabilities of two companies. Both companies were successful to sense emerging market demands, to seize opportunities by developing products and platforms, keeping leading positions. Thereby, the dynamic capabilities of sensing and seizing of two companies are quite similar.

However, companies were not always successful in transformation or reshaping resources: Amazon's low grocery's margins, difficulties to deliver food considering their perishability nature, as well as Amazon Go store's technology faced problems. Regarding Whole Foods, there is a massive cost disadvantage compared to their traditional grocery competitors. There are also several complementarities of the dynamic capabilities of an acquirer and a target. One of Amazon's weaknesses is the huge cost of losses due to food items becoming bad, a problem which the company had never faced with toys and books. Even though the grocery business was approximately $ 800 billion per the year 2016 in the USA alone [47], Amazon has limited knowledge and experience in the offline retail environment. That is why, for Amazon Fresh to be successful, the company needed to acquire more expertise in perishable grocery procurement. In contrast, Whole Foods becomes an organic

Products	Sensing	Seizing	Transforming	Result in
Online and offline food stores	Amazon sensed the need for having its footprint in the physical stores combined with online stores. Amazon saw a grocery business as an emerging business opportunity	Amazon set up a subsidiary Amazon Fresh, a grocery delivery service. Later Amazon decided to enter into food and consumable goods manufacturing through Amazon Elements, by establishing a partnership with TreeHouse Food Inc.	In March 2017, Amazon announced Amazon Fresh Pickup, a drive-in-type grocery store for Amazon Prime subscribers. In January 2018, Amazon started up offline retailing Amazon Go, first brick-and-mortar convenience food store on Amazon	Grocery's *margins were low*, and its goods were *difficult to deliver* considering their perishability nature. Amazon Go store's *technology faced problem* in tracking over 20 people

Source: Developed by author.

Table 2.
Dynamic capabilities of Amazon before the acquisition of Whole Foods.

Product	Sensing	Seizing	Transforming	Result in
Whole Foods	Whole Foods found that "where food comes from and how it is grown matter" (case)	Whole Foods becomes an organic supermarket which distinguishes itself by offering "highest quality natural and organic products"	Whole Foods attempted to expand to 1000 stores, it could either build stores more closely together or build lower-cost stores in areas that had more price-conscious consumers [32]	Whole Foods has *a massive cost disadvantage* compared to its traditional grocery competitors [32]

Source: *Developed by author.*

Table 3.
Dynamic capabilities of Whole Foods before the acquisition.

supermarket which distinguishes itself by offering "highest quality natural and organic products." However, Whole Foods recent poor performance stems from a major strategic mistake they made about 4 years ago. Whole Foods in its current incarnation is a niche business that can only profitably sell "food for the 1%" but is trying to sell to everyone [45]. Therefore, Amazon can provide resources for future Whole Foods development, and at the same time, Amazon can develop their own offline grocery business.

Justification of proposition 2. Business model's elements of both acquirer's and the target's companies can successfully fold into the new business model by means of acquisition-based dynamic capabilities and contribute to reduce cost, to create a new revenue stream, to deliver a new value proposition, and therefore to sustain competitive advantage.

Having analyzed both Amazon and Whole Foods building blocks of business models, the research justified the second proposition, as shown in **Tables 4** and 5. The acquisition-based dynamic capabilities helped Amazon to reinvent of building blocks of the business model as follows. Amazon sensed new key activities and new customers' segments for their business: Whole Foods customer has over $1000 per month disposable income. Amazon has a better understanding of the customer than any other retailer. The Motley Fool estimates that over 80 million people are Amazon Prime members. With this big data, it is capable of building analytic models which can predict what these consumers will want, how much they will want, and when they will want it.

Amazon seized new key (idiosyncratic) resources by acquiring Whole Foods logistic system, customer's base, and a key partners' network.

To be successful in the offline retail food segment and in own-brand grocery stores, Amazon needs to have knowledge of traditional retailing and effective supply chain management in both factories and retail stores. Amazon has limited knowledge and experience in the offline retail environment. The company learned about food market through Amazon Fresh but now can learn about food stores or grocery manufacturing. Amazon has good supply chain management in a warehouse for online retail order, but now Amazon is certain whether this experience is transferable to an offline retail store. Hence, Amazon reconfigured new *customers' relationship and channels.*

While Amazon's purchase of Whole Foods enables them to add a tremendous amount of data to their coffers, the true differentiator lies in the company's mastery of using data to better understand their customer's needs, predict shopping behaviour and generate longevity with its loyal customer base [47]. Therefore, Amazon transformed its *customer value proposition,* delivering new value to the clients of both companies and capturing new value for shareholders. "This partnership presents an opportunity to maximize value for Whole Foods Market's shareholders, while at the same time extending our mission and bringing the highest quality, experience, convenience, and innovation to our customers," John Mackey, Whole Foods CEO, said in a statement [49]. Given the jump in Amazon's stock price after the announcement, shareholder approval of the deal has virtually paid its total cost. When people suggest that Amazon has overpaid for Whole Foods, they completely miss this point [45]. Amazon also can help Whole Foods buy high-quality products more cost-effectively and thus improve gross margins while keeping customers satisfied. As results, Amazon can change *cost structure* as well as potentially increase *revenue streams* for mobile professional users and can result in a new competitive advantage. Adding Whole Foods selection of items to its Amazon Fresh grocery delivery service could give the company a competitive advantage against Peapod, FreshDirect, and Google, whose express delivery service now reaches almost 90% of the USA [50].

Building blocks of the business model	**Amazon business model**	**Dynamic capability of Amazon**	**Whole Food business model**
Customer segments (Scope)	• Millennials • Global consumer market (North America, Europe, Asia)	*Sensing*	• The more affluent customer with an interest in eating healthy and sustainable foods spending extra money to purchase
Key activities (Scope)	• Customer focused product development • Well-developed supply chain	*Sensing*	• Natural and organic foods supermarket chain operations • Production of packaged goods, prepared foods, body care, pet foods, and household goods
Key partners (Resources)	• The business alliances and collaborations with logistic partners • Partnership with third-party sellers	*Seizing*	• Supplier and procurement partners • Agriculture and sustainability partners • Whole trade certifier partners
Key resources (Resources)	• Amazon Web Services • Big data analytics • Productive employees • Physical warehouses	*Seizing*	• Distribution & procurement centres • The network of 412 stores across 42 US states, as well as ten stores in Canada, and nine stores in the UK
Channels (Organization)	• Amazon.com • Country-specific online portals • API (for AWS)	*Transforming*	• The network of physical retail outlets • Retail infrastructure, procurement, production, and distribution network
Customer relationship (Organization)	• Fuse data, technology, and content to engage a loyalty program (their best customers) with geo-location reminders to incentivize store visits	*Transforming*	• A full range of products to its customers on a self-service basis through its online sales channel, which enables customers to browse products, place orders, and arranges deliveries
Customer value propositions	• Eliminating the checkout line • Real-time offers via mobile push notifications when customers are in store	*Transforming*	• The diverse catalog of premium products • The commitment to organic and sustainable sourcing • Offering online shopping services on desktop and mobile platforms
Cost structure	• Investing profit back into the technology and the infrastructure	*Result in*	• The procurement of products and supplies

Building blocks of the business model	Amazon business model	Dynamic capability of Amazon	Whole Food business model
	• Research & Development • Low-cost structure		• The operation and development of the online sales channel • The maintenance of IT and communications infrastructure
Revenue streams	• Revenues from product and service sales • Utility computing fees (for AWS) • Economy of scale	*Result in*	• The sale of various organic and fair-trade products

Source: *Developed by author*

Table 4.
Acquisition based dynamic capabilities of Amazon.com in the reinvention of their business model by acquiring Whole Food.

The reinvention of the business model of Amazon.com	Microfoundations of acquisition-based dynamic capabilities of Amazon.com
Selection, sensing, and shaping *new activities* and *new customer's segments*	Amazon is discovering the power of virtual and physical channels that interact seamlessly in support of the customer. Amazon has begun to test that logic with its venture into physical bookstores. Amazon is sensing more affluent customer with an interest in eating healthy and sustainable foods spending extra money to purchase. The proposed acquisition of Whole Foods catapults those efforts and provides extraordinary opportunities for experimentation in and execution of integrated retailing [45]
Identification and seizing *new resources* and *a new partnership*	Amazon did not just buy Whole Foods grocery stores. It bought 431 upper-income, prime-location distribution nodes for everything it does [44]. Amazon has mastered the "test and learn" approach to large-scale innovation that most companies aspire to. Therefore, Whole Foods provides Amazon with an incredible platform for the transformation of an industry
Reconfiguration and transforming *new customer relationship, new channels, and new customer value proposition*. Result in *new cost structure and new revenue stream*	This acquisition gives Amazon to reinvent and reengineer the process of buying, moving, and selling goods of Whole Foods. With 460 locations and a history of highly localized habits and preferences, Amazon will benefit from a trove of data that it can mine to write the future [52]. The brand Whole Foods is a good compliment to Amazon Fresh and Go and allow them to more aggressively target fresh food delivery to the at-home market. Amazon will ultimately be able to tailor the grocery shopping experience to the individual to better understand their needs, predict shopping behavior, and generate longevity with loyal customers

Source: Developed by author.

Table 5.
Bridging perspectives together: the reinvention of the business model and micro-foundations of acquisition-based dynamic capabilities.

5. Findings and discussion

"The literature on dynamic capabilities has addressed the fundamental question of how companies develop the skills and competencies that allow them to compete and gain an enduring competitive advantage... However, the literature does not tell much about the antecedents of new firms' dynamic capabilities" ([33], pp. 919–920). This chapter addresses the latter issue in great depth. The author used contextual content analysis [32] to justify two propositions. The contextual analysis provided a comprehensive solution to the challenge of identifying and categorizing key textual data [51]. Content analysis transformed unstructured data into organized information to give you a competitive edge [51].

When the chapter explored acquisition-based dynamic capabilities and business models of Amazon and Whole Foods, the research found the acquisition enabled a series of strategic innovations to integrate Whole Foods products with Amazon functionality and vice versa. Bridging two perspectives together, **Table 5** demonstrates what and why Amazon did with Whole Foods at the end of 2016 and how acquisition-based dynamic capabilities support a reinvention of building blocks of business models.

Amazon has high dynamic capabilities in *online technology but not in food distribution*. When some dynamic capabilities are missing, a company has the option to develop them internally or purchase them from outside. Amazon needed to acquire more knowledge of the retail market, improve management of its supply chain for the offline retail store, and continue investing in R&D for the grocery retail business. Dynamic capabilities of Amazon and Whole Foods are aligning and allowing them to improve existing products by *sharing' experience, advanced technologies, and broad users' base*. With Whole Foods acquisition, Amazon would benefit as it would get access *to tons of consumers and lifestyle data packed into consumer's buying habits* [44]. Whole Foods is an attractive platform for Amazon for the transformation of an industry. Therefore, two propositions have been justified empirically. Does click successfully meet brick? The integration of Amazon and Whole Foods is not fully finished. Amazon is trying to become Walmart—not just an online megalith but also a physical powerhouse with dynamic pricing and stocking strategy—faster than Walmart can become Amazon [44].

With Whole Foods acquisition, Amazon would benefit as it would get access to tons of consumers and lifestyle data packed into consumer's buying habits [44]. Morgan Stanley analysts think that the new Whole Foods has the ability to close the pricing gap between it and its competitors [53]. Zahra et al. [10] argue that entrepreneurs and other key organizational decision-makers failing with current applications spur attempts to change. However, key dynamic capabilities, such as transforming resource and developing new competencies, might be challenging for Amazon. Should Amazon manufacture its own products to make a higher margin? Could Amazon's offline retail marketing concept be developed globally [54]? To become one of the biggest offline retail players, Amazon needs to educate customers and make a lot of investment. According to Tom Caporaso, the chief executive officer of Clarus Commerce, the Amazon Go business model relied on several recent technological innovations that required more time for testing [55].

Don Stuart, a managing partner at Cadent Consulting Group, concurred that even for the biggest online retailer like Amazon, to make the platform was a huge challenge [55]. What novel have I learned that goes beyond these existing frameworks of dynamic capabilities and business models? How do we need to change these frameworks based on insights from the case? The current research gave

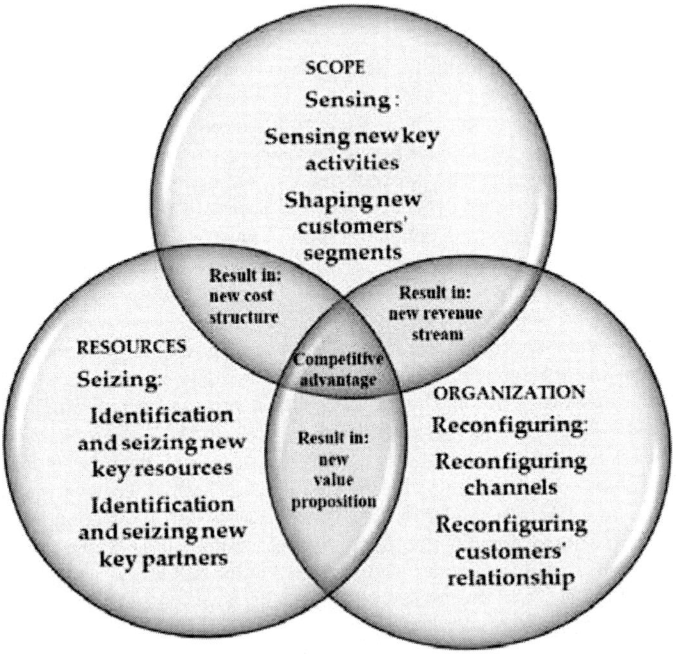

Figure 1.
The conceptual model of future research: bridging together acquisition-based dynamic capabilities and a process of the transformation of a business model.

substantially more insights into the role that dynamic capabilities can play in acquisitions and how dynamic capabilities relate to business model transformation. Besides contributing to dynamic capabilities view on competitive advantages by adding fresh insights about successful acquisition practice, the research core contribution is in the emergent conceptual model for future research on the reinvention of a business model in merger and acquisition process as shown in **Figure 1**. Collis and Montgomery [56] argue that good corporate strategy requires a continual reassessment of the company's scope, requires continual investment in building and acquiring strategically valuable resources, and develops organization ability to marshal them. Thereby, the conceptual model also integrates a great corporate strategy triangle: strong market positions (scope), high-quality resources, and an efficient organization [56] as shown in **Figure 1**.

The conceptual model makes dynamic capabilities more visible, tangible, and to some extent measurable with the help of business model canvas.

6. Conclusion, limitations, and future works

When some dynamic capabilities are missing, a company has the option to develop them internally or purchase them from outside. Teece argues: "In short, the business model outlines the (industrial) logic by which customers are served and money is made" ([25], p. 41). The current chapter contributes to theory and practice by illustrating how this logic works in the M&A process. The model demonstrates that the intersection of sensing and seizing capabilities can result in a new and more efficient cost structure; the intersection of sensing and transforming capabilities can result in the generation of a new revenue stream. The intersection of seizing and transforming capabilities can result in a new customer value proposition. Thereby, the acquisition-based dynamic capabilities are transforming the acquirer's business model and underpinning the acquirer's competitive advantage. The conceptual model integrates dynamic capabilities and business model perspectives in the new conceptual model for future research that encourages practitioners to grasp an exact relationship between the micro-foundations of each perspective. The conceptual model makes dynamic capabilities more visible, tangible, and to some extent measurable at least on the level of expected results (reduced cost and increased revenue streams). The resulting model is given in **Figure 1** also advances the discourse on DCs and BM.

There are several strong limitations to the research. Due to a limitation of the number of submitted pages, the research has provided only one evidence from M&A practice. Through the small data size and missing validation through a lack of robust analysis, the current chapter serves more as an introduction to the research, then as the results. Thereby, the chapter, being of an exploratory and interpretive in nature, raises several opportunities for future research, both in terms of theory development and findings validation. The conceptual model discussed in **Figure 1** could also be used to generate a number of hypotheses for further empirical testing using a broader sample and quantitative research methods.

What is more, because changing the BM is a central top-management task, there is potentially very fruitful link to top management team (TMT) theory [57]. For example, what dynamic managerial capabilities are more needed in BMI in M&A the process: managerial cognition capabilities, social capital, or human capital [58]? What is more important and what are less important dynamic managerial capabilities for decision-making processes in technology-enabled M&A deals (idea, justification, due diligence, negotiation) and for integration processes in M&A deals (acquisition integration, synergy management) [59]? The study can also be extended in longitudinal and comparative ways.

References

[1] Teece DJ. Business models, business strategy, and innovation. Long Range Planning. 2010;**43**:172-194

[2] Osterwalder A, Pigneur Y. Business model generation, Self-published. Hoboken, NJ, USA: John Wiley and Sons, Inc.; 2010

[3] Christensen CM, Alton R, Rising C, Waldeck A. The big idea: The new M&A playbook. Harvard Business Review. 2011;**89**:1-17

[4] Johnson MW, Christensen CM, Kagermann H. Reinventing your business model. Harvard: Harvard Business Review. 2008;**86**:57-68

[5] Amit R, Zott C. Business model design: A dynamic capability perspective. In: Teece DJ, Leigh S, editors. In the Oxford Handbook of Dynamic Capabilities. Oxford, UK: Oxford Handbooks; 2016

[6] Kim C, Mauborgne R. Blue Ocean Strategy, from theory to practice. California Management Review. 2005; **43**(3):105-121

[7] Teece DJ. Explicating dynamic capabilities: The nature and micro-foundations of (sustainable) enterprise performance. Strategic Management Journal, John Wiley & Sons Ltd. 2007; **28**(13):1319-1350

[8] Teece DJ. Dynamic capabilities: Routines versus entrepreneurial action. Journal of Management Studies. December 2012;**49**(8):1396-1401

[9] Schreyogg G, Kliesch-Eberl M. How dynamic can organizational capabilities be? Towards a dual-process model of capability dynamization. Strategic Management Journal. 2007;**28**:913-933

[10] Zahra SA, Sapienza HJ, Davidsson P. Entrepreneurship, and dynamic capabilities: A review, model and research agenda. Journal of Management Studies, June 2006;**43**(4): 917-955

[11] Eisenhardt KM, Martin JA. Dynamic capabilities: What are they? Strategic Management Journal. 2000;**21**(10-11): 1105-1121

[12] Armstrong KBA, Macintosh R, Maclean D. Unblocking the conceptual log jam: Using a rules perspective to make sense of dynamic capabilities. In: Paper Presented at Strategic Management Society (SMS) 32 Annual Conference "Strategy in Transition". Prague, Chez Republic. October 6-9, 2012. 67 p. Available from: http://prague.strategicmanagement.net/pdf/Prague_Program_WEB.pdf. [Accessed 2018-17-01]

[13] Stefano GD, Peteraf M, Verona G. The organizational drive train: A road to integration of dynamic capabilities researches. The Academy of Management Perspectives. 2014;**28**(4): 307-327

[14] Helfat CE. Know-how and asset complementarity, and dynamic capability accumulation: The case of R& D. Strategic Management Journal. 1997; **18**(5):339-360

[15] Danneels E. The dynamic of product innovation and firm competence. Strategic Management Journal. 2002;**23**: 1095-1121

[16] O'Reilly C, Tushman M. Organizational ambidexterity: Past, present, future. The Academy of Management Perspectives. 2013;**27**(4): 324-338

[17] Kleinbaum M, Stuart TE. Network responsiveness: The social structural micro-foundations of dynamic capabilities. The Academy of

Management Perspectives. 2014;**28**(4): 353-367

[18] Chatterij A, Patro A. Dynamic capabilities and managing human capital. The Academy of Management Perspectives. 2014;**28**(4):395-408

[19] Bauer F, Matzler K. Antecedents of M&A success: The role of strategic complementarity, cultural fit, and degree and speed of integration. Strategic Management Journal. 2014;**35** (2):269-291

[20] Krishnan HA, Miller A, Judge WQ. Diversification and top management team complementarity: Is performance improved by merging similar or dissimilar teams? Strategic Management Journal. 1997;**18**(5):361-374

[21] Makri M, Hitt MA, Lane PJ. Complementary technologies, knowledge relatedness, and invention outcomes in high technology mergers and acquisitions. Strategic Management Journal. 2010;**31**(6):602-628

[22] Kim JY, Finkelstein S. The effects of strategic and market complementarity on acquisition performance: Evidence from the U.S. commercial banking industry, 1989–2001. Strategic Management Journal. 2009;**30**(6):617-646

[23] Wang L, Zajac EJ. Alliance or acquisition? A dyadic perspective on interfirm resource combinations. Strategic Management Journal. 2007;**28** (13):1291-1317

[24] Adner R. Ecosystem as structure: An actionable construct for strategy. Journal of Management. 2017;**43**:39-58

[25] Teece DJ. Business models and dynamic capabilities. Long Range Planning. 2018;**51**:40-49

[26] Eisenhardt KM, Graebner ME. Theory building from cases: Opportunities and challenges. Academy of Management Journal. 2007;**50**(1): 25-32

[27] Yin RK. Case Study Research Design and Methods. 5th ed. Thousand Oaks, CA, USA: Sage publication; 2014. p. 282

[28] Sekaran U, Bougie R. Research Methods for Business: A Skill Building Approach. Chichester, West Sussex: John Wiley & Sons. 2016. p. 448

[29] Yin RK. Case Study Research: Design and Methods. 4th ed. Applied Social Research Series: Sage Publications; 2009;**5**

[30] Smith E. Using Secondary Data in Educational and Social Research. New York, NY, USA: McGraw-Hill Education; 2008

[31] Johnston MP. Secondary data analysis: A method of which the time has come. Qualitative and Quantitative Methods in Libraries. 2014;**3**:619-626

[32] Andrews L, Higgins A, Andrews MW, Lalor JG. Classic grounded theory to analyze secondary data: Reality and reflections. The Grounded Theory. 2012;**11**(1):12-26

[33] Weber RP. Basic Content Analysis. Newbury Park, CA: Sage; 1990

[34] Bowman EH. Strategy, annual reports, and alchemy. California Management Review. 1978;**20**:64-71

[35] Fiol CM. A semiotic analysis of corporate language: Organizational boundaries and joint venturing. Administrative Science Quarterly. 1989; **34**:277-303

[36] Simon M, Houghton SM. The relationship between overconfidence and the introduction of risky products: Evidence from a field study. Academy of Management Journal. 2003;**46**: 139-149

[37] Mishina Y, Pollock TG, Porac JF. Are more resources always better for growth? Resource stickiness in market and product expansion. Strategic Management Journal. 2004;**25**:1179-1197

[38] Osborne JD, Stubbart CI, Ramaprasad A. Strategic groups and competitive enactment: A study of dynamic relationships between mental models and performance. Strategic Management Journal. 2001;**22**:435-454

[39] Merchant H. Revisiting shareholder value creation via international joint ventures: Examining interactions among firm- and context-specific variables. Canadian Journal of Administrative Sciences. 2004;**21**:129-145

[40] Morris RA. Computerized content analysis in management research: A demonstration of advantages & limitations. Journal of Management. 1994;**20**:903-931

[41] Rosenberg SD, Schnurr PP, Oxman TE. Content analysis: A comparison of manual and computerized systems. Journal of Personality Assessment. 1990; **54**:298-310

[42] Teece DJ. Dynamic Capabilities: A guide for managers. Ivey Business Journal, 2011. Available from: http://iveybusinessjournal.com/publication/dynamic-capabilities-a-guide-for-managers/[Accessed: 2016-06-30]

[43] Barreto I. Dynamic capabilities: A review of past research and an agenda for the future. Journal of Management. 2010;**36**(1):256-280

[44] Kumari S, Shah R. Amazon's Whole Foods Acquisition. Banglore: AMITY Research Centers Headquarter. 2017; **317-0289-1**:1-12

[45] HBS Working Knowledge. Amazon, Whole Foods Deals Is a Big Win for Consumers. 2017. Available from: https://www.forbes.com/sites/hbsworkingknowledge/2017/06/17/amazon-whole-foods-deal-is-a-big-win-for-consumers/#706c71347232 [Accessed 2018-17-01]

[46] Penrose E. The Theory of the Growth of the Firm. Oxford: Oxford University Press; 1959. p. 245

[47] Soper S, Zaleski O. Inside Amazon's Battle to Break Into the $800 Billion Grocery Market. Bloomberg. 2017. Available from: https://www.bloomberg.com/news/features/2017-03-20/inside-amazon-s-battle-to-break-into-the-800-billion-grocery-market [Accessed 2018-01-17]

[48] Petro G. Amazon's Acquisition of Whole Foods Is About Two Things: Data and Product. 2017. Available from: https://www.forbes.com/sites/gregpetro/2017/08/02/amazons-acquisition-of-whole-foods-is-about-two-things-data-and-product/#67a70160a808 [Accessed 2018-01-18]

[49] Whitten S. Whole Foods Stock Rockets 28% on $13.7 billion Amazon Takeover Deal. 2017. Available from: https://www.cnbc.com/2017/06/16/amazon-is-buying-whole-foods-in-a-deal-valued-at-13-point-7-billion.html [Accessed 2018-02-17]

[50] Eadicicco L. Why Amazon Bought Whole Foods. 2017. Available from: http://time.com/4828082/why-amazon-bought-whole-foods/ [Accessed 2018-02-17]

[51] SAS® Contextual Analysis. Available from: https://www.sas.com/en_us/software/contextual-analysis.html [Accessed 2018-07-22]

[52] Aziza B. Amazon Buys Whole Foods. Now What? The Story Behind The Story. 2017. Available from: https://www.forbes.com/sites/ciocentral/2017/06/23/amazon-buys-whole-foods-now-what-the-story-behind-the-story/#588dc754e898 [Accessed 2018-01-17]

[53] Fidelity Investment. Amazon's Transformation of Whole Foods Puts the Entire Grocery Industry on Notice. 2017. Available from: https://www.youtube.com/watch?v=ICkoTUbor-U [Accessed 2018-02-18]

[54] Kittilaksanawong W, Karp A. Amazon Go, Venturing into Traditional Retail. Richard Ivey School of Business Foundation. 2017;(8B17M09):21-27

[55] Boyle A. Report Point to Caution Signals for Amazon Go Checkout-free Store. Available from://www.geekwire.com/2017/caution-amazon-go-checkout-free/ [Accessed 2018-01-17]

[56] Collis DJ, Montgomery CA. Competing on resources. Harvard Business Review. 2008;1-13

[57] Foss NJ, Saebi T. Business models and business model innovation: Between wicked and paradigmatic problems. Long Range Planning. 2018; **51**:9-21

[58] Helfat CE, Peteraf MA. Managerial cognition capabilities and the micro-foundations of dynamic capabilities. Strategic Management Journal. 2015;**36**: 831-850

[59] Haspeslagh PC, Jemison DB. Managing Acquisitions: Creating Value Through Corporate Renewal. New York: Free Press. 1991. p. 42

Index